BLOOD AGAINST THE SNOWS

BLOOD AGAINST THE SNOWS

The Tragic Story of Nepal's Royal Dynasty

Jonathan Gregson

FOURTH ESTATE • *London*

First published in Great Britain in 2002 by
Fourth Estate
A Division of HarperCollins*Publishers*
77–85 Fulham Palace Road
London W6 8JB
www.4thestate.com

10 9 8 7 6 5 4 3 2 1

A catalogue record for this book is available from
the British Library

ISBN 1-84115-784-8

Typeset by Rowland Phototypesetting Ltd,
Bury St Edmunds, Suffolk
Printed in Great Britain by
Clays Ltd, St Ives plc

Contents

Acknowledgements

My thanks to Jim Edwards for his warm hospitality, to Lisa Choegyal and all the others at Tiger Mountain for making my most recent stay in Kathmandu go so smoothly, and to the staff of the Hotel Manaslu for looking after me so well.

I must also thank HM The King's Principal Press Secretary, Mohan Bahadur Panday; and, for guiding me around the old Hanuman Dhoka Royal Palace, Tej Ratna Tamrakar. On the history of Nepal I am indebted to the late Dilli Raman Regmi and to Rishikesh Shaha. Rajendra S. Khadka was of great help in translating the full Nepali text of the official report on the massacre.

I received invaluable assistance from royal relations, palace officials, generals, courtiers, diplomats, politicians, newspaper editors and correspondents, doctors, civil servants, shop-keepers and ordinary villagers. Many of those who spoke most frankly requested I guard their anonymity; the others are mentioned in the text. They know who they are and will, I hope, recognize their nameless contributions and accept my gratitude.

I wish to thank my agent, Bill Hamilton of A.M. Heath, for his enthusiasm, and my editor Clive Priddle for understanding and help in shaping the narrative. Finally, Pat Mellor and my wife, Sarah, for being such cheerful travelling companions.

—So shall you hear
Of carnal, bloody and unnatural acts,
Of accidental judgements, casual slaughters,
Of deaths put on by cunning and forced cause,
And, in this upshot, purposes mistook
Fall'n on the inventors' heads.

                                    Hamlet, Act V, Scene 2

PROLOGUE

Shooting Cats

The sound of nearby gunfire was clearly audible inside the British Embassy in Kathmandu on that Friday evening. It started at around nine o'clock. Nobody paid much attention. The firing came from the direction of the Royal Palace, just 500 yards away across a busy road intersection, and did not last long. If it had come from another direction there would have been greater cause for concern: an attack by Maoist insurgents, possibly, or a firefight between extortionists or some criminal gang and the armed police.

The noise of guns going off was forever coming out of the palace. Usually it was the Crown Prince practising on one of the firing ranges, or blasting off at cats, bats, rats, crows or just about anything else that moved among the dense bamboo which overhangs Narayanhiti Royal Palace's northern and eastern walls.

An external attack on the palace would have involved much heavier exchanges. Inside the eighteen-acre Narayanhiti complex is a sizeable army barracks. Two battalions of elite royal guards are permanently stationed there. A complex security system had been installed, using American know-how, shortly after President Kennedy's assassination in 1963, since when it had been repeatedly upgraded. Key security personnel are sent on specialised courses in Britain, the United States and Israel.

The plain brick wall around most of the palace perimeter is deceptive. There are no metal spikes or shards of glass or razor wire, as can be found around most royal or presidential residences. But behind the walls, Nepal's royal family were guarded by a supposedly 'foolproof' four-layer screen. Armed police outside the perimeter and at the main gates; the regular army with fixed heavy weapons covering all possible approaches; in reserve, a rapid deployment commando-style Fighting Force; and, as a last line of defence, the ADCs, or aides-de-camp.

The ADCs represented the cream of the Royal Nepal Army's officer corps. Trained in close-quarter combat and key body protection, the ADCs attached to each member of the royal family accompanied them everywhere. Most came from 'good families'; from their dutiful and constant shadowing of their royal charges they built up close personal relationships. But their essential purpose was to be bodyguards.

Any attack on Narayanhiti would have mobilised all four levels of defence. The noise would have been tremendous – not just gunfire from within the palace grounds, but the wail of sirens as reinforcements and emergency services rushed to the scene. Nothing like that happened around nine o'clock on 1 June. Just a few short bursts of automatic fire. To outsiders it suggested nothing abnormal.

Even those far closer to the epicentre came to the same conclusion – initially, at least. The Queen Mother was talking to her sister-in-law, Princess Helen. A stout wooden door was all that separated them from the noise. On first hearing the shots, they too assumed 'it was the youngsters playing'. The Queen Mother thought immediately of the Crown Prince – and that in all probability he was shooting rats or cats again.

The Crown Prince's habit of discharging automatic weapons inside the palace grounds had become an accepted part of life within Narayanhiti Royal Palace. Everyone knew that Crown Prince Dipendra had a private collection of guns and liked a little target practice at odd times of the day and night. The night-time stillness was regularly punctuated with the clattering fire of some new weapon. That, on 1 June, was the conclusion that most people within earshot came to to explain the three-minute burst of gunfire. But on this occasion they had deceived themselves. During those three minutes there had in fact occurred a slaughter of unimaginable savagery.

Practically the entire royal family had been massacred. The soft-spoken King Birendra was the first to be shot. His wife, Queen Aishwarya, was killed outright, as was his younger son, Prince Nirajan. Birendra's only daughter, Princess Shruti, died of internal bleeding. The King's younger brother and all three of his sisters went down in the hail of bullets, as did six other royal relations. A lucky few survived the onslaught. But by the time assistance arrived, ten members of Nepal's royal family lay dead or dying.

Among them was the man subsequently blamed for the killings, Crown Prince Dipendra. He had then, apparently, turned his gun on himself. The single shot to his head left him virtually brain dead, but his vital functions did not cease for another two days. As a result, during those two days, as was customary, the man who had committed parricide, matricide, fratricide and then bungled his own suicide, was briefly declared King Dipendra of Nepal. Nobody, not even the most morbid of Jacobean playwrights or Greek tragedians, could have invented a plot with so much self-inflicted damage, nor such a bizarre twist at the end.

It was the bloodiest, the most complete massacre of any royal family ever recorded. Imagine it happening in Britain: Prince Charles would have had to shoot dead Queen Elizabeth and Prince Philip, his brothers Edward and Andrew, Princess Anne, his own sons William and Harry and, to end it all, himself, leaving only (at that time) his aunt, Princess Margaret, to assume the throne. And the motive? If the parallels are carried through, it would be because the rest of the House of Windsor were united against his plans to marry Camilla Parker Bowles.

One consequence of the Kathmandu massacre was that the senior line of the royal dynasty – the Shah family – became extinct. The crown passed to the dead King's younger brother, Gyanendra. If Nepal is to remain a kingdom, it is this cadet or junior line of the Shah family that will occupy the throne in future. Tradition requires that a male heir inherit the plumed crown of Nepal, and, apart from King Gyanendra and his son Paras, there are no other princes of the blood left.

Nothing in Nepal's earlier history compared to the massacre in Narayanhiti, but it was certainly not the first time there had been bloodshed within the palace. Internal strife and conspiracies were an all too familiar part of the Shah family's heritage. Indeed, if automatic weapons had existed in the nineteenth century, there were plenty of flashpoints at which bloodletting on a similar scale might well have occurred.

What follows is not an attempt to explain why the massacre of 1 June 2001 occurred. Whatever the motive, it was consumed in the ashes of the dead Crown Prince's funeral pyre. The sequence of events leading up to the massacre throws some light on the matter, but only so far.

However, the way in which kingship is practised in the Himalayas, the role of monarchy and what it means to ordinary people, the very existence of the Kingdom of Nepal in the first place — all these have a direct bearing on what was to happen on that fateful night. To appreciate the profound loss to the Nepalese people, their sense of disbelief and denial, one has to go back in time. For in this mountain refuge of age-old traditions, the King is still revered in ways long forgotten elsewhere. Here the King is held to be a god, the father and protector of all his peoples. The killing of a king is not just regicide; it amounts to deicide as well.

Yet those same traditions of reverence and unquestioning obedience shown to members of the royal family, which for more than two hundred years had helped ensure that an unbroken line of Shah kings occupied the throne of Nepal, certainly contributed to their eventual undoing. Nobody dared to risk incurring royal displeasure by suggesting that some things within the palace were seriously amiss.

At the dawn of the twenty-first century, Nepal's royal family still lived in an unreal world behind Narayanhiti's walls — secluded from public scrutiny, deferred to on all occasions, and yet persuaded that by some quasi-mystical process the institution of monarchy was at one with the wishes of the Nepalese people. To enter the Royal Palace was to find oneself in an Alice-in-Wonderland environment where the principal actors could behave like medieval despots, though in reality their power was gone; where the spirit of feudalism and *noblesse oblige* endured within an artificial vacuum; where unpalatable truths could never be spoken openly, only hinted at.

The old habits of secrecy and intrigue which had served previous generations of Shah kings so well remained; but now they turned in on themselves. Still learning to behave like members of a modern constitutional monarchy, Nepal's royal family struggled to bridge the gulf between their ancient traditions and a more meaningful, contemporary role. Even before the palace massacre, Nepal's monarchy had lost much of its sense of purpose; and with that went family unity. The real tragedy of the Shah dynasty was that, after surviving so many external threats, it should succumb to attack from within. But then that same tendency towards self-destruction had manifested itself many times before.

I

Of Cows and Kings

The Shah dynasty has ruled Nepal since 1769, some seven years before the United States of America came into being. At that time Britain was ruled by a dynasty still known as the Hanoverians, albeit under the strict scrutiny and control of Parliament. In France, the Bourbon kings wielded absolute powers; and the same was true across most of Europe. Monarchy was deemed to be the only legitimate form of government. Not even the most radical of Enlightenment thinkers could foresee the overturning of this stable and time-honoured pattern by the forces unleashed during the French Revolution.

The pace of change was far slower within the Himalayan Kingdom of Nepal. Since 1769 there has been an uninterrupted line of Shah kings, the son or grandson succeeding the father, up until the twenty-first century. That in itself is something of a success story. But the manner in which this first came about, through the single-minded determination of one man, Prithvi Narayan Shah, is quite extraordinary. Rarely has the creation of a new state and its continuance over more than two centuries been so closely entwined with the fortunes of a single family.

The Shah family had for centuries been Rajas of Gorkha, a tiny and impoverished hill state to the west of Kathmandu, just one of twenty-four principalities which divided up the central hill country between them. Further west lay the twenty-two Baisi principalities, each ruled separately by its own raja. So fragmented was the region that no dominant power could emerge in the hills; as soon as one raja threatened, all the others joined together in a defensive alliance against him.

In this perpetual game of diplomatic cat-and-mouse, Gorkha was not even a major player. It was a small and not very well endowed example of the 'one valley kingdom' previously found throughout the Himalayan foothills, from the borders of Afghanistan in the west to eastern Bhutan. The valley's rich red soil may have been well suited for cultivating rice, and the steep encircling hills contributed to its defence. Certainly, the Rajas of Gorkha's decision to build their palace astride a narrow ridge top was determined as much by its defensive advantages as by the site's religious associations or the spectacular views it offers of Manaslu, Ganesh and other ice-bound peaks of the main Himalayan range. But when Prithvi Narayan ascended the throne in 1742 there was no native industry in Gorkha and most of its twelve thousand households lived from subsistence farming and occasional soldiering. In terms of resources, it was scarcely a match for some of the larger hill states, let alone the prosperous kingdoms of the Kathmandu Valley.

This did not prevent the Shahs of Gorkha from claiming illustrious origins. Like many other Hindu kings they were revered by the people they ruled over as living gods, in this case the partial reincarnations of Lord Vishnu. Their human lineage goes back to the Rajputs, warrior princes from the deserts of Rajasthan who were in the forefront of resistance against Muslim invaders. This particular Rajput clan are said to have come from the great citadel of Chittor, from which on more than one occasion the beleaguered Hindu defenders rode forth to certain death while their womenfolk performed *sati*, throwing themselves into the flames of funeral pyres rather than be defiled by the Muslim soldiery. Beyond that, the Shahs claim descent from the earliest Aryan kings, and through them to the sun and the moon.

As with most Hindu royal genealogies, much of this is mythological and was inserted to add lustre to what was otherwise a fairly obscure clan of hill rajas. It is, however, probable that the distant ancestors of the House of Gorkha did flee the Indian plains in the face of Muslim invasion and sought refuge in the foothills of the Himalayas. As exiled princes of Rajput stock, they were either co-opted by local rulers of

less distinguished ancestry or married into their families. By the six-
teenth century there were a dozen small principalities in the central
Himalayan foothills whose rajas were named Shaha or Shah. The
younger son of one of these princely families, Dravya Shah, conquered
the hill state of Gorkha in 1559, and both he and his successors fought
endless border skirmishes to enlarge their domains.

Over the next two centuries the House of Gorkha produced some
notable rulers, celebrated for dispensing justice as well as for their
military successes. But when Prithvi Narayan Shah was born in 1722,
their kingdom was just one of sixty independent hill states which
grudgingly co-existed within the borders of modern Nepal. The hill-top
palace where he grew up commands panoramic vistas of the main
Himalayan range and all the foothills to the south and west.

It was built on a diminutive scale, a dwarf when compared to the
residences of the Malla kings who controlled the Kathmandu Valley
for more than four hundred years. While some of the woodcarvings at
Gorkha Darbar are exquisite, they reveal the skills of Newar craftsmen
imported from around Kathmandu rather than local workmanship. The
Kingdom of Gorkha was not on a trade route and lacked the resources
to employ such skills except on an occasional basis. It was not a rich
inheritance.

Despite the weakness of this power base, Prithvi Narayan Shah had
a grand vision. According to the collection of his sayings known as the
Dibya Upadesh, he had dreamed of great conquests from the outset.
While standing on a mountain ridge overlooking the Kathmandu Valley,
he asked: 'Which is Nepal?' His companions pointed out Kathmandu
and Patan and Bhaktapur, the capitals of three wealthy and independent
kingdoms then known collectively as 'Nepal'. Upon seeing them, 'the
thought came to my heart that if I might be king of these three cities,
why, let it be so'.

He was right in his assessment of the geopolitical situation. Whoever
controlled the Kathmandu Valley could then dominate the rest of the
Himalayan foothills. But it was a mighty gamble for Gorkha to take on
the far wealthier Malla kings, whose resources could buy in mercenaries

belonging to the warrior castes. Fortunately for Prithvi Narayan Shah, the three valley kingdoms were almost constantly at war with one another. But it still took him twenty-five years of continuous and sometimes desperate warfare to win his prize.

According to a legend which is as old as the Kingdom of Nepal, just as Prithvi Narayan Shah was preparing for the final assault on Kathmandu he came upon a holy man in the guise of a hermit. Always punctilious about his religious duties, he offered a bowl of curd to the holy man, which was duly consumed. But when the hermit vomited it all up and offered back the repulsive mess for the King to drink, Prithvi Narayan Shah disdainfully refused. He hurled the regurgitated curd back at the guru, coating his outstretched hands with vomit. At this, the sage became furious, shouting that if Prithvi Narayan had only swallowed his pride and drunk the curd, his every wish would have been granted. As it was, he would still go on to conquer Nepal; but the guru laid a dreadful curse on the King and his successors. Holding up his curd-splattered hands, he prophesied that there would be kings of Prithvi Narayan Shah's lineage for ten generations – one for each of his ten fingers and thumbs that had been defiled. After those ten generations had passed, the Shah dynasty would be no more.

In Nepal, to be cursed by a holy man is a serious matter. But this being who appeared before Prithvi Narayan was no ordinary mortal. He was in fact Gorakhnath, the powerful and sometimes capricious deity who, according to legend, had helped out the King's ancestors on numerous earlier occasions, especially Dravya Shah who had first captured Gorkha. The fact that their seat of power became known as Gorkha is probably due to the Shah dynasty's devotion to Gorakhnath. He became their tutelary deity and his temple still stands beside their ancestral palace, attended by a hashish-smoking priest and scores of monkeys from the surrounding forest which come to take their share of the ritual offerings.

Gorakhnath was deemed to be an historical figure, a Hindu sage who had founded a sect of yogis known as the Kanphata, and an emanation

4

of the all-powerful Lord Shiva, the Hindu god of creation and destruction. He always appeared in human form as a mendicant, usually with a begging bowl, and he lived only on milk, butter and curd, the products of Hinduism's sacred cows. He was a powerful protector, but when angered could be extremely vindictive.

An ancient chronicle tells of how Gorakhnath first visited Nepal some nine hundred years before the Shahs took Gorkha. The local people did not recognise him as a Hindu sage and refused to give him alms. This so enraged him that he resolved to punish the country with a severe famine. He did this by summoning the divine serpents, or *nagas*, which are the dispensers of rain, and making a seat out of their coiled bodies. For twelve years he sat among their coils, performing his devotions; and for twelve years no rain fell.

This caused enormous suffering throughout Nepal, so the King consulted his astrologers and priests on how to end the drought. On their advice he sent messengers to Assam, a distant province in eastern India, to bring back a divine sage called Matsyendranath who was known to be the spiritual adviser, or guru, to the outraged Gorakhnath. Upon learning that his own guru had arrived, Gorakhnath was startled out of his meditation and went to greet him. No sooner had he arisen than the *nagas* began to spread out across the land and rain fell in abundance. The grateful King built two temples dedicated to Matsyendranath and instigated an annual procession in his honour, which is still one of Nepal's largest festivals. The importance of the rain-bringing *nagas* can also be seen, not only in the many temples and water tanks built in their honour, but in the snake-covered throne on which the Kings of Nepal are crowned.

King Prithvi Narayan Shah was careful to fulfil all his religious obligations, including those due to the family's tutelary deity. Why then did Gorakhnath spring a trap for the King and, when he failed the test, call down a curse on his descendants? As with so many Hindu myths, the curse of Gorakhnath works on several different levels. It is about worldly pride, and the awful consequences of failing to submit to religious authority. It is about overcoming physical disgust and recognising the true nature of things beyond the veil of illusion. It is also about ritual purity and, strange to say, the symbiotic relationship between cows and kings.

It was the duty of Hindu kings not only to protect their subjects against intruders but to preserve the purity of the realm. Any defiling act – whether it was committed against temples or Brahmin priests or, indeed, against sacred cows – would dilute that essential purity and, as a consequence, the King's authority.

Among the high-caste Hindus who had sought refuge in the Himalayas, the question of cow-slaughter was particularly worrying. They had chosen exile rather than life under the beef-eating Muslims, but they now found themselves living among all manner of indigenous peoples who did not conform to Hindu caste laws. Some were meat-eaters; practically all consumed copious amounts of home-brewed alcohol; but the worst defilement came from the cow-killers. Many of the hill Brahmins taught that Laxmi, the Hindu goddess of prosperity, was present within every cow; so to slaughter these sacred animals was tantamount to deicide. There was constant pressure from the 'twice-born' priestly and warrior castes to stamp out such practices.

The Shah kings of Gorkha had been more stringent than most hill rajas in condemning cow-slaughter. Another etymological explanation of the name of their royal house is that it may be derived from the ancient Sanskrit word *goraksa*, which means 'cow protector'. Tradition has it that when Dravya Shah was a boy he had to keep watch over the family's herd of cows. When Gorakhnath appeared before him, the young prince offered up a gift of milk. This pleased the deity so much that he foretold the young prince's conquest of Gorkha and much else besides. 'Cow service' had its rewards.

So when some two hundred years later Dravya's descendant, Prithvi Narayan Shah, also encountered Gorakhnath, he behaved properly in offering him a bowl of curd. But by then the conquering general had recruited into his army many warrior tribes – among them Gurungs, Magars and Bhotes from the Tibetan borderlands – who did not follow the strict prescriptions of Hindu caste rules. Some of them were even beef-eaters. The commander of such an army faced far greater problems in enforcing the prohibition of cow-slaughter than if he had remained the raja of a compact hill state. Which is why Prithvi Narayan had to be put to the test. His failure to recognise Gorakhnath and offer unconditional obedience marked him and his clan out for retribution. But it would not come immediately. It could wait another ten generations.

When Prithvi Narayan Shah set out on his road to conquest he had at his disposal only a small army and the slenderest of financial resources. He might have been considered just another clan chieftain turned military adventurer were it not for one thing: he was already a king in his own right. This alone made it possible for him to mobilise the resources of Gorkha for war and to enter into treaties with other hill rajas of equally distinguished lineage. Success in battle may have helped draw other warriors to his standard, but it was his semi-divine status as a Hindu king, the guardian and protector of all his subjects, that made him acceptable as a new ruler in the lands that he conquered.

The concept of divinely ordained kingship has been inseparable from legitimate government throughout the Himalayan foothills since the dawn of history. In fact, the Royal Chronicles known as *Vamshavalis* trace an unbroken line of kings over 4,000 years, far beyond what can properly be called history, to the first mythological Kings of Nepal. These, if they ever really existed, must have flourished during the second millennium BC. Then there were two royal houses: the Gopalas, a dynasty of cow-herders who claimed descent from the moon; and the buffalo-herder dynasty of the Mahisapalas who claimed descent from the sun. Hence, the symbols of the sun and moon still appear on the Nepalese flag. But the genealogies and deeds of these early dynasties, whose very names suggest that they ruled in the period when pastoralism gave way to settled agriculture, belong to myth rather than history.

Eventually, both royal houses were overthrown by the Kiratas, a warlike hill tribe mentioned in the greatest of ancient Hindu epics, the *Mahabharata*. These may well be the ancestors of the Limbus and Rais

7

of eastern Nepal, who are collectively known as the Kirati and nowadays provide many recruits to Gurkha regiments. The Kirata dynasty is said to have ruled for more than 1,500 years and extended its dominion eastwards through the Himalayas as far as what is now the Kingdom of Bhutan.

The Kiratas may well have come under the sway of powerful neighbours to the south, especially the imperial dynasty founded by Chandragupta Maurya around 320 BC. This Mauryan empire was expanding rapidly from its capital Pataliputra (near modern Patna) right across the Gangetic plain around the same time that Alexander the Great made his brief foray into the Indian subcontinent. It is known that the greatest of Mauryan emperors, Ashoka, visited the Buddha's birthplace at Lumbini in 250 BC, and popular legend has it that he also visited the Kathmandu Valley. As with most empires based in the plains of India, the objective was more likely to have been an 'informal ascendancy', to demand tribute rather than direct rule of the hill country.

In much the same way Nepal probably fell within the 'sphere' of the Kushans, who ruled over much of northern India between the first and third centuries AD. Again, when the Gupta empire became the dominant power in the Gangetic plain, Nepal and other hill kingdoms appear to have acknowledged their suzerainty. The Kushans had been great patrons of Buddhism, but by the fifth century the brahmanical revival was under way and it was a Hindu dynasty, the Licchavis, which emerged as uncontested rulers of the Kathmandu Valley.

Nepal entered a period of prosperity and cultural brilliance under its Licchavi kings just as Europe was entering the Dark Ages. The Kathmandu Valley undoubtedly benefited from the unification of Tibet at this time, which encouraged the flow of trade and pilgrims across the Himalayas. A Chinese envoy who visited the court of King Narendradeva in the seventh century described his principal palace in Kathmandu as being of seven storeys and roofed with copper, its interior embellished with semi-precious stones and, in the four corners, golden crocodile heads with water spouting from their jaws. Seated on his throne, the King was 'bedecked with diamonds, pearls and other jewels, wearing earrings of gold and with an amulet of Buddha's likeness on his breast. In the midst of his court, men sprinkle scented water and scatter flowers. On the King's left and right, courtiers are seated on the floor. Behind the throne, countless soldiers stand at arms.' Unfortunately no trace of the Licchavi palaces has survived though stone sculptures of the period, including a remarkable image of Lord Vishnu, attest to a strong influence from India to which the local Newar craftsmen added their own mark.

As a small valley kingdom lying between two potentially great powers, Nepal has always had to maintain a delicate balancing act. At times, the Licchavi kings may have accepted a loose form of Tibetan suzerainty. King Narendradeva is known to have assisted a joint Chinese–Tibetan punitive expedition in 1792 against an Indian prince who had imprisoned and killed visiting Chinese envoys. This campaign shows how far Nepal had progressed from being a remote mountain kingdom to becoming a regional power with trade and diplomatic links stretching across Asia.

Then, in the ninth century AD, the Licchavis were overthrown and Nepal entered its own Dark Age. For more than two hundred years the hill country was the scene of bitter fighting between rival princes. Few records survive from this era of uncertainty and civil strife, which continued until the Malla dynasty rose to power in the Kathmandu Valley during the early thirteenth century.

The Malla kings who ruled over the Kathmandu Valley for more than five hundred years must have had a strong instinct for survival. From the very outset, they had to stave off rival claimants to the throne from the powerful Tripura and Bhonta clans, though more often than not they also fought among themselves. In 1482 the Kingdom of Nepal was divided up between three different lines of Malla kings, each of which ruled from one of three royal cities – Bhaktapur, Patan and Kathmandu. Much of the wonderful architecture of their Durbar squares, the pagoda-roofed temples and palaces entered through golden gates, was commissioned by these later Malla kings, who strove to outdo each other in the splendour of their building as much as in warfare. But their rivalry left them vulnerable to any external ruler who could take them on one at a time.

Looking down from one of the highest points surrounding the Valley, Chandragiri's peak, on to the city kingdoms far below, the youthful King Prithvi Narayan Shah knew that his hopes of conquering Nepal depended as much on the mutual jealousies of those Malla kings as on the fortunes of war. Even if they remained divided, it would be a long, hard, bitterly fought struggle that would stretch the resources of his own tiny kingdom to the limit. But for such a prize, he reckoned, it was worth gambling his inheritance.

The Gorkha armies at first attempted a direct attack on the Kathmandu Valley but were repulsed with heavy losses after failing to take the hill-top town of Kirtipur. This was before the introduction of mountain artillery and muskets into the hills, and it was all but impossible to capture a well-defended town or hillfort by frontal assault. Indeed, the methods of waging war had hardly changed since the Middle Ages; and although Prithvi Narayan Shah purchased a few muskets during a pilgrimage he made to Benares, most of his troops were armed only with curved slashing swords, known as *kukris*, and with bows and arrows.

Mounting an offensive campaign was therefore a long, drawn out process of attrition, a matter of surrounding one outlying fort after another, of cutting the garrison off from reinforcements and supplies until it either surrendered or was forced to do battle in the open. Such tactics meant keeping a large army in the field for extremely long periods – a difficult feat, since many ordinary soldiers needed to return to their homesteads to bring in the harvest. To hold such an army together required exceptional leadership, and Prithvi Narayan Shah was by all accounts a charismatic leader of men. While other hill rajas left their soldiers' pay in arrears, he borrowed heavily through the state treasury in order to keep paying his troops. His concern for their welfare extended to granting pensions to the widows and families of those who died in battle.

Where other rulers kept any lands they conquered to themselves or shared them out among a few favoured generals and ministers, Prithvi Narayan Shah promised his soldiers a share in the spoils of victory. They were offered the right to hold lands as feudal tenants, or *jagirdars*, for as long as they served their king. In doing so, he played upon the hill man's deep-rooted hunger for land and the social prestige that it alone could bring. The promise of holding *jagirs* made his entire army joint beneficiaries in any conquests they made, and so helped keep them in the field. It also encouraged soldiers dissatisfied in the service of other rajas to join his standard, with the result that the more successful he was in battle, the larger his armies became.

From 1744 onwards the Gorkhas gradually encircled their enemies, occupying the high ridges and laying siege to forts which guarded the entrances to the Kathmandu Valley. One of the first to fall was Nuwakot, which controlled one of the trade routes to Tibet. The Gorkhas then switched their attack to the north-east rim of the Valley and captured the forts at Naldum and Madhev Pokhari. With these in his hands, Prithvi Narayan Shah was able to cut off the most important trade artery with Tibet which runs through Kodari, and so deny the Malla kings their accustomed profits from trade. His forces then attacked in the south, effectively isolating the whole Kathmandu Valley from the outside world and imposing an economic blockade on its inhabitants.

In 1767, the Malla kings were finally driven to calling in outside assistance and asked for help from the British East India Company, which dispatched an expeditionary force of 2,400 British and Indian troops. They had to march through the malaria-infested southern plains and up into the hills at the height of the monsoon rains. It was an already enfeebled column which fell into a carefully laid ambush. In this, their first ever encounter with Gorkha warriors, the British were roundly defeated. Only a third of the soldiers who entered Nepal came out alive.

The armies of Gorkha now finally moved down into the Kathmandu Valley in force. But rather than rushing on to besiege the walled cities, they established outposts all around them and prevented the inhabitants from grazing their animals or harvesting their crops. The noose was slowly tightened until the Gorkhas' front lines came right up to the city walls. Only then did Prithvi Narayan Shah order the assault on Kathmandu. This was timed to coincide with the Hindu festival of Indrajatra, when King Jaya Prakash and his subjects were either drunk or engaged in religious celebrations. It is likely that the Malla king was betrayed, for three of the city gates were left unguarded, allowing the Gorkha soldiery to enter. After putting up a brief fight, King Jaya Prakash and two hundred of his followers fled to the nearby city of Patan.

It had taken many years of patient planning, but now Prithvi Narayan Shah had finally realised his youthful dreams of conquest. He entered the city of Kathmandu on horseback and made his way through the streets to the Durbar Square. There he ascended the same throne from which the previous King had only recently presided over the Indrajatra festivities. The living child goddess of Kathmandu, the Kumari, gave her blessing by placing the *tika* on his forehead, smearing on a mixture of vermilion and sandalwood in a ritual that has been repeated by successive Shah kings and Royal Kumaris ever since.

Although Kathmandu was in itself a great prize, Prithvi Narayan still needed to subdue the other two royal cities if he was to rule over a unified Nepal. He moved swiftly against Patan, whose inhabitants were so terrified by rumours about the Gorkhas' ferocity that they put up little resistance. That left Bhaktapur, whence the ex-King Jaya Prakash had fled a second time after leaving Patan and was now organising the city's defence. When Gorkha troops finally broke through its gates at night, some of the defenders set their wooden houses on fire to provide the light their soldiers needed to fight by. The battle raged from street to street for two long days, with the Gorkhas slowly squeezing their opponents into an ever smaller cordon around the Royal Palace. Only when Jaya Prakash was wounded in the leg by a musket ball, forcing him to flee yet again, did Bhaktapur's resistance finally collapse. The last of the Malla kings died in exile, allowing Prithvi Narayan Shah to become the undisputed ruler of Nepal.

*   *   *

King Prithvi Narayan Shah is remembered as a great leader of men and a just ruler. From the very outset, his grand design of unifying Nepal was a battle against overwhelming odds. His ability to mobilise the resources of a relatively small power against far larger neighbours is similar in many respects to his near contemporary, Frederick the Great of Prussia. His concern for the ordinary peasant-soldier won him his troops' undying loyalty and, if they had any complaint, they knew they could present their case directly to the King. This gave rise to the still popular expression: 'If you seek justice, then go to Gorkha.'

If Prithvi Narayan Shah had any weaknesses, they were his strong sense of personal honour and an occasionally vengeful streak. His pride had brought down the curse of Gorakhnath upon his descendants. The citizens of Kirtipur would discover his desire for vengeance to their cost.

Prithvi Naryan was normally magnanimous in victory: when his armies conquered Kathmandu and Patan, he expressly forbade a general massacre or even excessive looting. But when he came to take the hill town of Kirtipur, the site of his first humiliation in battle, which had seen off no less than three Gorkha assaults and did not finally surrender until 1769, a year after Kathmandu's submission, he showed less clemency. He commanded the mutilation of all the male inhabitants, whose noses and lips were to be hacked off. One group alone was spared – those musicians who played wind instruments. The soldiers who carried out this bloody business were Bhotes from the Tibetan borderlands.

When they had finished, the dismembered noses and lips were placed in baskets and found to weigh more than 120 pounds. Perhaps Prithvi Narayan Shah thought that the Bhotes had been overenthusiastic in their nose-slicing, especially in their treatment of higher caste victims. Whatever his reason, he ordered that the perpetrators of this atrocity should be killed.

The conquest of the Kathmandu Valley was in itself a major achievement, but Prithvi Narayan Shah's ambitions did not stop there. His personal prestige was at its peak; thousands of warlike hill men sought to join his armies; and with the riches of the Kathmandu Valley at his disposal he could buy more of the muskets and small cannon that were transforming the ways in which mountain warfare was fought. Historic Nepal was only the springboard to a far broader Himalayan empire. But to achieve this vision of a 'Greater Nepal' he knew he had to act quickly.

By 1769 he was already forty-six years old. Allowing for the average life expectancy of those times, he was a relatively old man. Also, there was at that moment a political vacuum to the south, where the once mighty Mughal empire was rapidly caving in. Certainly they were in no position to intervene against an expansionist raja up in the hill country. That was the least of their priorities.

A new power in the north Indian plains, however, threatened to prove less amenable: the British were rapidly expanding their territories and sought to establish a far broader 'sphere of influence'. They had attempted military intervention in Nepal once before and, despite the disastrous outcome, they might return with far more powerful forces. Prithvi Narayan saw a window of opportunity which he knew might close at any moment.

For all these reasons, the King was a man in a hurry. Most of the remaining six years of his life would be spent in planning campaigns and the diplomacy needed to support them. His attempt to invade the Chaubisi principalities to the west came to nothing because, for once, their normally squabbling rulers formed a united front against the Gorkha menace; but when he turned his armies eastwards there was little to stop them. In a series of swift campaigns he conquered the Kiratis, their poisoned arrows proving no match for modern muskets in the hands of a seasoned and well-disciplined army. All the eastern hill country as far as the Kingdom of Sikkim was overrun, besides which Nepal acquired an adjacent slice of the low-lying Terai that could be used for providing land grants for his soldiers.

By the end of Prithvi Narayan's life, the House of Gorkha held all of what is now central and eastern Nepal. It could scarcely be called a unified state since local laws and customs remained intact even in conquered areas, while rajas who had voluntarily accepted Gorkha overlordship were allowed to continue ruling much as before. The strength of this new Kingdom of Nepal lay in it having the largest and best-disciplined army ever seen in the Himalayas. It was a military machine which needed to make further conquests, for only then could the King and his generals satisfy the land hunger of the rank and file. Territorial expansion was not an option; it became a necessity.

This was the legacy of King Prithvi Narayan the Great. No mightier conqueror had emerged from the Himalayan foothills in more than a thousand years. But broad territories and an unbeatable army were not his only gifts to his successors. During his last years he spent much of his time dictating maxims on correct conduct and wise governance, which were collected in a book known as the *Dibya Upadesh*. He spoke of the state he had founded as a rock, something apart from himself, which should never be sundered; and he dreamed of his Kingdom of Nepal as a garden within which peoples of every tribe and caste could live together in peace and harmony.

Those ideals have informed Nepal's monarchy ever since, though most of the later kings have payed them only lip-service, and the dream of an harmonious multi-ethnic state has yet to be realised. The 'founding monarch' eventually died of a fever at the age of fifty-two, in the palace at Nuwakot, his body covered in blotches. In accordance with the customs of the time, his widow Narendra Laxmi performed *sati* and perished in the flames beside her husband. So, too, did eleven of her maidservants.

2

A Country Called Nepal

King Prithvi Narayan Shah is, quite rightly, considered to be the 'founder of the nation'. Before his conquests there was no such thing as a Kingdom of Nepal. When the term 'Nepal' was used, it signified only the Kathmandu Valley; and even that was not a unified state. He and his immediate successors carved out a completely new kingdom, the likes of which had never been seen before in the Himalayas.

This new country encompassed all of the central Himalayan foothills. To the south lay the plains of India; to the north, the high Tibetan plateau. The hill country in between had always been a border or buffer zone between Asia's two great valley-based civilisations, India and China. 'Like a yam between two boulders' was how Prithvi Narayan Shah described Nepal's position, for it was constantly in danger of being crushed by the far more powerful empires that grew up on either side.

For most of the time, its natural defences of mountains and fever-ridden forests kept potential enemies at bay. There were many ways through these barriers – secret paths known only to local rulers as well as the main trans-Himalayan trade routes – but these were closely guarded, and for centuries it was a capital offence to reveal the 'secrets of the hills' to outsiders.

Deliberate, self-imposed isolation became a cornerstone of Nepalese policy until the latter part of the twentieth century, mainly because it was deemed necessary to protect the country's independence. Precisely because they were so isolated the various peoples of Nepal retained habits and beliefs, about the divinity of kings or local deities who dwelt in the high peaks, long after they had been discarded elsewhere. Which may be the reason why, when the first outsiders arrived in Kathmandu, they thought that they had discovered some forgotten Shangri-la. The reality, at least for most Nepalis, was very different.

On a clear day you can see the Himalayan snow peaks of Kathmandu. The views from the Royal Palace, which stands to the north of the Old City, may not be as good as from further afield, but the proximity of those eternal snows is still felt whenever the winds blow down from the mountains. They are true giants, rising more than 20,000 feet above sea level, the Kingdom of Nepal's single most defining feature. And not only topographically: for, to Hindus and Buddhist alike, those icebound peaks are the abode of the gods, a sacred space hanging between heaven and earth, a place of seclusion into which countless sages and hermits have withdrawn to achieve mystical union with the godhead.

Even Nepalis of a less religious bent are proud that seven of the world's ten tallest mountains either rise entirely within their country or straddle its borders. It is natural that the Himalayas are celebrated so often in verse and song. So too are the forested foothills, the mountain torrents and the steeply terraced rice fields, the simple pleasures of village life such as sitting in the shade of a peepul tree, the heroism of Nepal's great warriors and, of course, the pangs of love.

Some of these gentler aspects of village life are equally praised among other rural communities across the border in India. But the mountains, and the rigours of mountain life, set apart most Nepalis from their fellow Hindus. They are *paharis* – true hill men accustomed to carrying loads hung from straps across their foreheads up the steepest of tracks – as opposed to the soft-living peoples of the plains. Even though many Nepalis now live in subtropical valleys or down in the low-lying Terai, and so rarely have a chance to glimpse the Great Himalaya, those snow-covered mountains are always there in the imagination, an essential part of their being.

There is another characteristic that sets these proudly independent hill men apart from their neighbours in India or Chinese-occupied Tibet. They live within a kingdom that has never been conquered or occupied by a foreign power. Few countries in the world can make such a claim – not even Afghanistan, whose inhospitable terrain, warlike traditions and geopolitical importance as a buffer zone between the Indian subcontinent and the rest of Asia are not that dissimilar from Nepal's. Impoverished they might be, and constrained by ancient and discriminatory customs, but the Nepalese people have at least never been subjected to colonial rule.

That this is so is largely due to Nepal's uncompromising terrain. The entire country is a natural fortress, defended to the north by the ice curtain of the Himalayas and the empty wastes of the Tibetan plateau beyond. As for any potential invader from the south, they would first have to cross the jungles of the Terai which, because they harbour a particularly virulent strain of malaria, have often proved an even better defence than the icebound Himalayan passes. An already enfeebled army would then have to struggle over two ranges of steep and densely forested foothills before they could stare down on their prize, the fertile uplands known as the Pahad, with the Kathmandu Valley in their centre.

Despite these difficulties some foreign armies have succeeded in penetrating as far as the Kathmandu Valley and looting its rich palaces and temples, though none of them stayed for long. During the thirteenth and fourteenth centuries the Valley was subjected to repeated attacks by the powerful Kingdom of Khasa to the west, while in 1349 the mainly Muslim armies of Shamsud-din Ilyas carried out a devastating raid which left most Hindu and Buddhist temples stripped of their treasures and religious images.

The next foreign invaders were the British, whose forces finally broke through the Gorkhas' stiff defences in 1815. They halted at the edge of Kathmandu's valley rather than attempt to occupy the land; the East India Company wanted to impose a treaty whereby Nepal fell within their 'sphere of influence' rather than commit endless troops and resources in trying to hold down such ferocious hill men in so hostile a terrain.

In doing so, the British followed much the same line as previous imperial powers all the way back to the seventh century Tibetan King Songtsen Gampo, and beyond that to the Emperor Ashoka who erected one of his stone pillars at Lumbini in the mid-third century BC. The consistent aim of all these powerful neighbours was to hold some sway over the hill country, not to rule it directly. The difficulties of communication, the fragmented and warlike clans, the poverty of so much of the country, all served as a powerful disincentive to empire-building.

The British remained down in the plains and, as a result, Nepal was again spared direct colonial rule. The Nepalese people may have suffered long from misgovernment and tyranny, but it has always been at the hands of their own rulers rather than some foreign power. They have not known either the sense of subjugation or the burning resentment that this can engender. At the same time they missed out on whatever benefits colonialism brought in terms of education and medicine, of road-building and improved communications and a general broadening of horizons. Instead, Nepal remained shielded behind its mountainous battlements until well into the second half of the twentieth century, a world apart, where ancient customs survived intact long after they had been eroded elsewhere.

The same physical barriers that dissuaded foreign adventurers also worked against the emergence of a single unified state in the hills. The whole country is so broken up by mountain spurs projecting south from the main Himalayan range and by precipitous river gorges which run between them that, until quite recently, it was easier to travel from east to west by going down into the Indian plains and then climbing back into the hills. A more direct path almost always existed, but this invariably meant scrabbling over high passes, trying one's luck with rickety bamboo suspension bridges, or fording swollen streams. Hence, for much of its history, Nepal has not experienced a single dominant power in the hills, but clan chieftains or petty hill rajas whose authority rarely extended beyond their home valley.

Before Prithvi Narayan Shah imposed a sense of unity, more than sixty squabbling principalities carved up the hill country between them, each with its own army, laws and customs. Because the mountains kept the people in different parts of the country apart, it was not unusual for the inhabitants of one valley to speak a completely separate and mutually indecipherable language from those living just a few miles away, as the crow flies, but on the far side of a 12,000-foot ridge. Very often this was because they belonged not just to a different tribe, but to a quite distinct ethnic and linguistic group, the gradual settlement of the Himalayan foothills over more than two millennia having drawn in many diverse peoples.

Among the earliest settlers in the middle hills were tribes of Mongoloid origin who speak a variety of languages belonging to the Tibeto-Burman family. They probably migrated westwards through the Himalayan foothills, long before written records were kept. With their broad features, stocky build and fiercely martial traditions, these native hill men are very different from the predominantly Indo-Aryan peoples of the plains. It is from among these 'martial tribes' that the world-famous Gurkha regiments are mainly recruited.

The Gurungs, perhaps the most famous of these martial tribes, are known both for their military valour and because their home villages spread around the southern flanks of the Annapurna Massif, an area which in recent years has become the most popular trekking destination in Nepal. Their hill-top hamlets may command extraordinary vistas of the Great Himalaya, but this is tough country to farm. Narrow terraces have to be carved out of hillsides so steep that particularly heavy monsoon rains sometimes wash away entire strips of farmland. Land hunger has been endemic here for centuries, which is why so many young men have left to become mercenaries. Gurungs who live in the high country observe a form of Tibetan Buddhism combined with far older animist beliefs; those who live at lower altitudes and have more regular contact with their Hindu neighbours have adopted some of the religious customs and practices of Hinduism, including a version of the caste system.

Their immediate neighbours to the south and west, the Magars, are equally renowned for their martial prowess. Of the thirteen members of the Brigade of Gurkhas to be decorated with Britain's highest award for gallantry, the Victoria Cross, six have been won by Magars, and long before they were recruited by the British they had formed the backbone of local rulers' armies. Living mostly from farming at lower altitudes they had greater contact with Hindus who had come up from the plains, and adopted many of their practices.

Those other fighting tribes recruited into the Gurkhas, the Limbus and the Rais (collectively, the Kirati), inhabit the extreme east of modern-day Nepal. They probably migrated in prehistoric times from the borderlands of China and are generally of slight build with dark, almond-shaped eyes. They too have long been respected for their fighting skills, and according to legend their distant ancestors established one of the first Himalayan empires around 1000 BC. They retained their own distinctive customs, including the communal ownership of land.

Tribal peoples of equally early origin occupied the low-lying forest and foothills in the south. The Tharus, Danwars, Darais and other indigenous tribes were able to survive in this malarial climate because they developed at least partial immunity to the disease. Although local myth traces their ancestry back to the 'noble' lineage of Rajputs, whose womenfolk fled into the jungles and preferred to marry their own servants rather than fall into Muslim hands, they tend to have strongly Mongoloid features and their languages belong to the Tibeto-Burman family. The cutting down of forests and intensive cultivation of the Terai has left only a few isolated pockets of these indigenous peoples, and they are vastly outnumbered by more recent immigrants from the north Indian plains.

Other lowland tribes such as the Rajbansis, Dhimals and Bodos from the eastern Terai, or the shy, forest-dwelling Chepangs and Kusundas of the central hills, are all remnants of very early settlement. Of all these tribal groups, the Tharus have proved most successful in adapting to modern life while still maintaining their distinctive identity. For others, the process of assimilation into the mainstream probably implies their cultural extinction sooner rather than later.

What is considered 'mainstream' in Nepal — basically Hinduism and the Nepali language — was introduced by successive waves of Indo-Aryan settlers from the south and west. The first to arrive were a people known as the Khas who are mentioned by such classical scholars as Ptolemy and Pliny as being a mountain-dwelling, warlike tribe. They entered what is now far western Nepal around the sixth century AD, and subsequently intermarried with the indigenous tribes. Due to their lax interpretation of caste rules, they were looked down upon by the stricter Hindus of the plains.

When these same members of the orthodox Hindu elite, the Rajput princes and their Brahmin priests, found themselves under pressure from Muslim invaders, many of them fled their ancestral lands in Rajputana for the sanctuary of the hills. Among them were the distant ancestors of the present kings of Nepal. Their princely and semi-divine status, together with the Brahmins' superior learning, usually assured them a warm welcome. The Rajputs often married into the native elite or were otherwise co-opted by their rulers, with the result that by the fifteenth century there were dozens of small principalities governed by Hindu princes. On the whole, this was achieved by infiltration rather than outright conquest.

These relative newcomers brought with them their own hierarchical caste system, which in its primitive form divided society into four castes — priests, warriors, merchants or artisans, and cultivators. Over time these subdivided into a whole host of occupational sub-castes such as goldsmiths, tailors, barbers, domestic servants, blacksmiths and, at the bottom of the pile, the 'untouchables', so called because any physical contact with them is deemed to be polluting. Strictly speaking, inter-marriage between castes is prohibited, but the incoming settlers got around this by conferring on local clan chieftains who converted to

Hinduism the equivalent of the Kshatriya, or warrior caste. The same distinction was granted to the offspring of a Brahmin priest and a hill woman, and in time the descendants of these mixed marriages became the dominant group in western and central Nepal.

In time, Kshatriya, the ancient Sanskrit term for the warrior caste, was corrupted into Chhetri in Nepali to describe this peculiarly Nepali caste. As this diluted form of Hinduism spread among peoples who had previously had nothing to do with caste rules, further accommodations were made. Those who continued to drink alcohol, forbidden to Hindu warriors and priests, for instance, were still allowed to call themselves Chhetris but only as Matwali, or 'liquor consuming', Chhetris. Nepalis who accepted a relatively high-caste status were both honoured and entitled to participate in the service of princes. In such ways were many of the originally non-caste peoples of the hills, the Khas of the western hills and the Newars of the Kathmandu Valley, gradually brought within the caste system.

So, although the original teachings of Buddha reject the divisions of caste laws, the predominantly Buddhist peoples of central Nepal such as the Newars and Tamangs have developed their own parallel caste hierarchies. The influence of such ideas is felt least in the high borderlands between Nepal and Tibet. Most of the peoples who settled in this inhospitable region are of Tibetan stock and they all practise a form of lamaist Buddhism. Best known for their mountaineering expertise, the Sherpas from the slopes around Mount Everest retain a rich oral tradition in which history and myth often cross over; though without a written language of their own this is now being eroded.

Even more isolated are the Lobas of Mustang, who inhabit a high-altitude desert on the far side of the main Himalayan range which can only be reached by ascending the world's deepest gorge. The Kingdom of Mustang is an anomaly, a semi-independent principality within the greater Kingdom of Nepal whose relationship with Kathmandu is based on a treaty of 1789 whereby the local kings accepted the Shah dynasty as their feudal overlords. There is still a King of Mustang, and he and

23

his people still speak a unique Tibetan dialect and follow the Sakya school of Buddhism. Here too, however, a distinct culture is being gradually undermined. In government-run schools, all the teaching is in Nepali.

The same process of cultural erosion is going on among the other border peoples, such as the Lhomis and the yak-herders of Dolpo. Collectively, they are known as 'Bhotes', the generic term used by southerners for those who speak a Tibetan language. Their ancestors may have migrated from the high plateau to the north, and their culture may be very close to that of Tibet; yet for more than two hundred years all these Bhotes have been subjects of the kings of Nepal. Only recently, however, have they been taught to think of themselves first and foremost as Nepalese citizens.

It has been estimated that there are as many different languages and dialects spoken within Nepal as in the whole of Western Europe. Certainly there is as great a difference in terms of climate, topography and culture between the moonlike mountains of Mustang in the north and the steaming jungles down by the Indian border as exists between, say, Norway and Sicily. That a country so broken up by razor-backed ridges and precipitous gorges could ever be unified seemed impossible – until, that is, Prithvi Narayan Shah seized control of the three kingdoms in the Kathmandu Valley.

The Kathmandu Valley has always played a pivotal role in the central Himalayan region. Whereas most other valleys have been gouged out by swift-flowing rivers, and are therefore narrow and steep-sided, the Kathmandu Valley resembles a huge rice bowl encircled by mountains. According to both Buddhist and Hindu myths, this bowl once contained a lake which was drained by either Lord Vishnu or his Buddhist counterpart Manjushri carving out the gorge through which the sacred Bagmati River flows down towards the plains. Part of that legend has been confirmed by geologists who have found that the Valley did once form the bottom of a lake; being geologists, they suggest that seismic activity rather than divine intervention caused the lake to drain away. Apart from the Vale of Kashmir, centred around Dal Lake, there is no broader upland valley in the Himalayas.

The Valley enjoys many natural advantages. Sitting above 4,000 feet, it does not suffer the terrible summer heat of the north Indian plains. Its lake-bottom soil is rich and the arrival of the monsoon and winter rains more certain than elsewhere, allowing for the cultivation of two crops a year. The valley floor is crisscrossed with streams that carve deep ravines in places, but which also feed an intricate irrigation system. Just to the north are two relatively easy passes through the High Himalaya. These have been used for centuries by merchants and pilgrims travelling between India and Tibet or the lands of Central Asia and China that lie beyond.

Sitting astride this trade route, surrounded by easily defended mountain ridges, the Kathmandu Valley was well placed for the early development of urban civilisation. The rich soil was good for making the bright red bricks that are still the hallmark of its buildings, while the abundant supply of hardwoods provided the raw material for skilled Newar craftsmen to fashion into the most exquisite carvings. Above all, its wealth and large population, compared to other hill states, distinguished this area.

The Newars, the original inhabitants of this thrice-blessed valley, have always proved themselves adept as traders and craftsmen. Traditionally, the staples of trade were salt and raw wool brought down from Tibet which were exchanged for rice and other foodstuffs that could not be grown at higher altitudes. Higher value goods such as Chinese silks were traded for spices, ivory and coral. Newari metalwork was also much in demand. Trans-Himalayan caravans could number thousands of yaks and pack ponies, and as long as Kathmandu stood at the crossroads of the principal trade routes its merchant community prospered.

Much of this surplus wealth was lavished on building temples and palaces whose richly carved doorways and windows display the skills of Newar craftsmen. The erotic woodcarvings of deities and adepts in tantric embrace which adorn the great Durbar squares – not just in

Kathmandu itself, but equally in the other royal capitals of Patan and Bhaktapur – are almost entirely the work of Newars. So too are the gilt-bronze statues of ancient kings on their stone pedestals, the fine wall paintings and scroll pictures within their palaces, the wheeled chariots and ceremonial masks brought out at religious festivals.

Most of the older temples are built in the distinctive pagoda style, which may have developed from the simple thatch awnings that can still be found protecting village shrines along the southern slopes of the Himalayas or, up in the Tibetan borderlands, Buddhist stupas (bell-shaped relic chambers) or chortens (shrines) made of beaten earth. The movement of Newar craftsmen along the trade routes to Tibet and China, where their skills were much sought after, may have introduced this rudimentary style to East Asia. Later on it was further elaborated into the multi-tiered pagoda – the finest examples being the five-tiered Nyatapola Temple in Bhaktapur and the Taleju Mandir next to the Old Royal Palace in Kathmandu.

The Newars' skills as metalworkers extended to minting coins not only for their own kings but for Tibet and other neighbouring states. The Tibetans had plentiful reserves of gold dust and silver bullion but no mint of their own, so they exchanged precious metal for finished coinage. Since the authorities in Kathmandu repeatedly lowered the gold and silver content, this became a highly lucrative business and one of the mainstays of government finances. But whereas the Newars excel in the peaceful pursuits of trading, farming and a whole range of artisanal activities, they do not have a tradition of soldiering. This may be because so many of them have been city-dwellers for so long, but the main reason is that, until the latter part of the twentieth century, the great majority of Newars have followed Buddhism, that most pacifist of religions.

Buddhism probably entered the Kathmandu Valley in the sixth century BC. The Buddha Gautama was himself a prince of the Sakya line, and even if these Sakyas were little more than clan chieftains they ruled over an area of what is now the Nepalese Terai as early as that date.

Not long after, the new religion spread from its heartland in Bihar up through the neighbouring hills and into the Kathmandu Valley. In a land where family lineage remains all important, there are still Newars of the priestly Sakya clan who trace their ancestry back to the same family as the Buddha.

That Buddhism had a profound impact on the Newar population can still be seen in the thousands of temples, the domed stupas and smaller wayside shrines dotted around the Valley. The oldest and most important for the Newars is the hill-top stupa of Swayambhunath, its whitewashed dome surmounted with a golden spire, surrounded by lesser temples, monasteries and shrines. In legend, the mound on which it stands was formed when a previous manifestation of the Buddha threw a lotus seed into the lake which then filled the Kathmandu Valley, though inscriptions suggest the first stupa was probably built here in the early centuries of the Christian era. The even larger Bodhnath stupa, with its fluttering prayer flags and emblematic eyes looking out in the four cardinal directions, is of more recent construction and has become the focus of Tibetan as opposed to Newar Buddhism. There is a tradition among the Newars, however, that Bodhnath was originally founded by a local king during the fifth century to atone for his having killed his own father.

The Buddhism of the Newars is very different from that found anywhere else. It may have been the religion of the majority in the Valley for nearly two millennia, but throughout that time it has co-existed with Hinduism. The King, the high priests and the warrior castes were usually Hindus, and their concepts of social hierarchy and ritual purity had a profound impact on their Buddhist subjects.

The Newars developed their own system of caste, with its untouchability and prohibitions of inter-caste marriages. The Buddhist monkhood came to resemble the Hindu Brahmins in that their status and priestly duties were defined by their family and caste rather than monastic observance or other forms of merit. Newar monks are allowed to marry and lead normal family lives, and their religious duties are mainly to act as family priests for their hereditary parishioners. As

Buddhists they are permitted to eat meat, including buffalo and pig, and their pantheon of deities, their family rituals and religious festivals are quite distinct. But so far has the exchange of customs gone that nominally Buddhist Newars may have a Brahmin as their family priest, while Hindus often turn to Buddhist or tantric healers. They attend each others' shrines and festivals, each worshipping in their own manner. Even at the holiest of Hindu shrines, the temple of Shiva at Pashupatinath, where there is a blanket prohibition against non-Hindus entering the inner sanctum, the presence of Newar Buddhists is accepted because they are seen as co-religionists.

This intermingling of Hindu and Buddhist traditions is most striking in the role of the Kumari during the yearly Hindu festivals of Indrajatra and Dasain. The Kumari is a living goddess, an incarnation of the primordial mother goddess who is at once wrathful and, as the city's protector, custodial. She is revered as such from the day she is chosen, usually at between two and four years old, until her first menstruation when she has to make way for a new Kumari. During Indrajatra she is pulled in a chariot through the different quarters of Old Kathmandu before giving the *tika*, or ritual blessing, to the King, who is himself a partial incarnation of the Hindu god Vishnu. After the mass sacrifices of buffaloes and black he-goats at Dasain, she must walk fearlessly into the Taleju Temple past long lines to the severed heads of the beasts. Although the Kumari features so prominently in Hindu religious festivals, she is always chosen from the Buddhist Sakyas. The crossover between different religious traditions is encapsulated in the Kumari's closeted and ritualised existence in the house assigned to her just opposite Hanuman Dhoka Palace.

The worship of mother goddesses who must be propitiated by blood sacrifice goes back to before the arrival of either Buddhism or brahmanical Hinduism in the hills. It was part of the old religion, and stone circles at crossroads or on hill tops testify to the antiquity of these cults. There are thousands of these 'power places' all over the Kathmandu Valley, and many of them are still subject to ritual offerings of food. Sometimes these offerings are made to propitiate demons or evil spirits whose thirst for human blood is well known, and who are deemed to cause all manner of ailments. It is possible for both evil and benign spirits to come of their own accord, and one of the reasons that the windows of Newar houses have such densely carved wooden screens is to prevent their entry.

More often, it is believed that these spirits are sent by witches. Throughout the hill country, among both Hindus and Buddhists, popular beliefs about the ability of witches to do harm through casting the 'evil eye' on their enemies, or through the reciting of spells or black mantras, are so widely held that there are still occasional witch-hunts. These usually culminate in the unfortunate suspect being held down and force-fed human faeces through a jute bag, an action which is believed to deprive such witches of their power.

However, most people who suspect they have been bewitched seek out a tantric healer or shaman to take counter-measures. The preference, particularly among Newars, for tantric healers can be traced back to the importance of esoteric tantric cults in the Kathmandu Valley from the early medieval period onwards. Tantrism became embedded in both Buddhist and Hindu rituals, and if its practice gradually moved away from its original search for self-liberation towards an admixture of high magic and formalised initiation ceremonies, it was and still is deemed to be power-enhancing. So it is to tantric adepts that many Nepalese still turn when faced with an illness that a more formal medical approach cannot cure.

Many of the former Kings of Nepal are believed to have undergone tantric initiations. Both the esoteric nature of tantrism and its power-enhancing possibilities must have appealed to those whose very purpose was to be the embodiment of power. These Hindu kings may have been the incarnation of a deity, but they also sought out other means to increase their prowess. So besides their Brahmin priests and orthodox ayurvedic physicians, they turned to astrologers for knowledge of their future and to tantric initiates for enhancing their sexual and physical powers. Most of these experts were Newars, and certain Newar families can claim generations of loyal service to the royal household.

3

The Regency Syndrome

When he knew that his death was approaching, Prithvi Narayan Shah summoned his family and specifically forbade them from carving up the lands he had so painstakingly united. He was all too familiar with the ways in which rival heirs could fight over their inheritance, particularly the families of hill rajas, for it had been one of his favourite strategems to play upon such internal jealousies among neighbouring states in order to weaken them before he attacked them. To prevent this from happening to his own family, he ordained that the Kingdom of Nepal in its entirety was to go to the eldest son, and that in future the principle of primogeniture should always be observed.

The succession went smoothly enough. Prithvi Narayan Shah's eldest son, the twenty-three-year-old Pratap Singh, was proclaimed King of Nepal in 1775. To be on the safe side, he had one of his uncles and his younger brother, Bahadur Shah, arrested and thrown into prison – fearful lest they had ideas of creating kingdoms for themselves. Their sentences were later commuted to exile in India.

Over time the strict rules of succession laid down by Prithvi Narayan became embedded in the Royal Constitution. Although there were frequent disputes over who should wield power, the Kingdom itself remained intact; and, with one notable exception, the crown of Nepal passed from father to eldest son or grandson through ten generations.

The kings of the Shah dynasty were a mixed bunch. Some were wantonly cruel. Others gave themselves over to alcohol, drugs and concubines. But none of that mattered so long as the dynasty survived. Provided they were not actually deposed by rivals or the very institution of monarchy thrown on to the scrap heap of history, there could be good kings and bad kings. The whole country might suffer if the King was vicious or ineffectual, as was often the case. But for the dynasty to survive, the only thing that really mattered was that the King produced an heir – male, legitimate and of pure lineage.

The man who inherited the Kingdom of Nepal in January 1775 was all of these things. King Pratap Singh may have been more inclined to poetry than fighting campaigns, but his lawfully married wife, Queen Rajendra Laxmi, was already pregnant and within four months bore him a healthy son. The royal succession was secure.

Unfortunately, Pratap Singh did not stop there. Before long he had taken another wife, Maiju Rani, unlawfully this time, the daughter of a Newar family and therefore of the wrong caste. Abandoning affairs of state to his ministers, he spent most of his time with his new wife participating in secret tantric rituals that usually involved harnessing sexual energy and the use of powerful narcotics. This naturally displeased Queen Rajendra Laxmi, especially once she learned that her rival was pregnant by the King.

The very possibility of an alternative succession stirred jealousies within the royal court. While the practices of taking multiple wives and concubines might ensure there would be numerous royal offspring, it also provoked bitter rivalries between their mothers – each of whom wanted her own child to be the next King. Such conflicts were endemic in a court culture where the role of the future King's mother was all important. Factions began coalescing around the Senior and Junior Queens. On this occasion, however, the matter was not put to the test, because King Pratap Singh died of smallpox at the age of twenty-five – just before a rival heir was born.

Queen Rajendra Laxmi's sixteen-month-old son, Rana Bahadur Shah, was declared the third King of Nepal unopposed. She was immediately appointed Regent, with extensive powers to govern on her son's behalf, and she quickly took her revenge on her former rival. Maiju Rani's pregnancy was allowed to come to term, for this was, after all, the late King's child she was carrying, but once she had given birth to a son, who was immediately named Sher Bahadur, she was taken away from the Royal Palace and forced to perform *sati*. This, despite the fact that more than a month had passed since the late King's cremation. The new Queen Regent was taking no chances.

Nepal thus had its third King in less than three years. The rules of primogeniture had been strictly observed, but the situation in which Nepal now found itself, with an infant on the throne, was not conducive to strong government. The young King Rana Bahadur would not be able to rule by himself for nearly seventeen years, during which time that almost unconditional loyalty offered by most Nepalese to their monarch would have no natural focus. Over such a long minority there is a natural tendency for the very personal powers of kingship to be gradually eroded. It is one of the in-built weaknesses of any hereditary monarchy.

It did not help that there was a power struggle over who should rule in the boy King's name. Although the Queen Mother Rajendra Laxmi, had been appointed as Regent, her authority was disputed by the late King's younger brother, Bahadur Shah. Both were still in their early twenties; both were headstrong characters who refused to compromise. So when Bahadur Shah argued for a new military campaign, the Queen Mother refused her consent. Infuriated by this, he staged a coup with the support of the Council of Nobles who had been scandalised by some of Rajendra Laxmi's habits, such as affecting masculine ways and dressing her maidservants up as armed men and having them parade around on horses and elephants. Bahadur Shah had her confined to her apartments, where she was forced to wear handcuffs made of silver. But once he had left the capital to join his armies at the front, Rajendra Laxmi adroitly turned the tables on him. She reclaimed the regency and had Bahadur Shah sent into exile.

All this involved considerable political machinations. Mutually hostile factions formed around each of the rival claimants, and the Royal Palace became a whispering gallery as courtiers and generals tried to choose which side to back. It had a corrosive effect on relations between the Crown and the Gorkha nobility. Where Prithvi Narayan Shah had always been able to count on his commanders' loyalty and had rewarded them on their merits, those who now ruled in the King's name had to win over supporters to their cause by offering them military commands, land grants and other favours. Ability was no longer a requirement for holding high office, and Rajendra Laxmi sent some exceptional commanders into exile because she was unsure whether they were completely trustworthy. What she looked for was personal loyalty, especially in men whose extended families and clan connections would help bolster her own power base. Factionalism and intrigue replaced the deep-seated trust that had previously existed between King and nobility; and once factionalism has set in it is very hard to extirpate.

The Queen Mother's party remained in control until she died of tuberculosis at the age of thirty-four, whereupon Bahadur Shah was recalled from exile and himself became Regent. One of his first acts was to purge the court of those factions that had previously been hostile to him. Had it gone on for much longer, such bitter infighting at court might have spelt doom for the Shah dynasty, but against all expectations the new Regent did not try to carve out a personal fiefdom for himself. The Kingdom of Nepal remained intact and, with the resumption of the military campaign against the western hill rajas, rival factions at court put their differences on hold. Nepal's monarchy had survived its first crisis. But the mutual trust which had existed between the King and leading families of Gorkha was gone for ever.

If Prithvi Narayan Shah's victory against overwhelming odds may be compared to the exploits of Frederick the Great, the endless conquests of his younger son Bahadur Shah mark him as the Napoleon of the Himalayas. Under his leadership the armies of Gorkha carried all before them, extending the Kingdom's frontier some four hundred miles to the west. True, he had at his command a formidable military machine, the likes of which had never been seen before in the Himalayas; and he was careful not to get entangled in quarrels with any of the powers down in the plains of India, where the Gorkhas' superiority in hill-fighting counted for nothing against massed cavalry and cannon. But in the specialised art of hill warfare he was, initially at least, unbeatable. So terrifying was his reputation that many hill rajas fled simply on hearing of his approach.

Like his father, Bahadur Shah was a great tactician and leader of men. Yet his successes were not only military. Nearly half of the hill states were won over by diplomacy rather than force of arms. Before the start of his western campaign, for instance, he gained the powerful Raja of Palpa's support by marrying his daughter. Other hill rajas were offered generous terms if they voluntarily acceded to the Kingdom of Nepal. They and their successors could rule over their lands as before, provided they paid a token annual tribute to Kathmandu and allowed Gorkha armies to pass through their territories unhindered.

Bahadur Shah began with a lightning campaign against the Chaubisi kingdoms, to the immediate west of Gorkha, moving his companies so swiftly that he was able to subdue each raja in turn before any allies could come to their assistance. He then moved his campaigning to the western hills, conquering the Kingdom of Jumla and all the other principalities as far as the present-day boundary of Nepal at the Mahakali River. His armies then advanced further west and occupied Kumaon, now part of the north Indian state of Uttar Pradesh. He was planning to invade Garhwal and continue the advance all the way to Kashmir, thereby creating a single empire throughout the foothills of the Himalayas.

Whether such an extended 'Greater Nepal' could have been held together is doubtful, for in the west this Hindu kingdom would have included a sizeable Kashmiri Muslim population. Another weakness, already being felt by Gorkha generals as they moved further west, was the problem of bringing up supplies and reinforcements over extended lines of communication in such rugged country. Very often their troops had to live off the land, requisitioning foodstuffs and transport from the local inhabitants, which might work as a short-term expedient but did little to encourage loyalty among their newly conquered subjects. Bahadur Shah's dreams of yet further conquests had to be abandoned, however, when events closer to home necessitated his return to Kathmandu.

In 1792, a large and well-equipped Chinese–Tibetan army made an incursion into Nepal and advanced on the capital. This punitive expedition was in response to several Gorkha incursions into Tibet, culminating in an attack on Shigatse during which the fabulous riches of the Tashilunpo Monastery were plundered and carried back to Kathmandu. Bahadur Shah had to sue for peace, the terms of which included returning all the looted treasures and sending a tribute mission to Peking every five years – a clause which later Chinese rulers have claimed establishes their suzerainty over Nepal. Even Communist China, which fully recognises Nepal's sovereign status, has occasionally used language reminiscent of the Manchu and Ming emperors by referring to Nepal, along with Sikkim and Bhutan, as the 'gates' which guard its southern borders.

After the peace treaty Bahadur Shah no longer looked unbeatable, and for this failure he was to pay a heavy price. So long as reports of more victories arrived in Kathmandu – and with them the promise of more land grants and military commands for the noble families – his position as Regent had been secure. But despite the enormous expansion of Nepalese territory there were still not enough spoils to go round. The army had to be satisfied first, and the numbers under arms had grown threefold since Prithvi Narayan Shah's time. Most of the newly conquered lands were assigned as temporary *jagirs* to soldiers, though there was a growing tendency for especially valued officers to be granted *birta* lands, which meant that they remained with their families in perpetuity. So although in theory the King held all lands within Nepal, the Crown was actually worse off than before.

The same was true of tax revenues. Keeping the army well armed, paid and fed through these long wars was an extremely expensive business. In fact it consumed practically all the royal government's tax revenues. The Kingdom may have doubled in size, but that did not mean more money flowed into the royal coffers. There were dozens of hill states which had voluntarily joined Nepal, and these sent only token contributions. Instead, the main burden fell on the same Nepali hill farmers who already had to hand over half of their crops to the government, not to mention providing porters for carrying army supplies free of charge. This burden became even heavier when, to maximise his short-term receipts, Bahadur Shah contracted out revenue collection to private tax farmers who were given virtual control of an area in return for sending an agreed lump sum to Kathmandu. The tax farmers leaned heavily on the peasantry; and since they had greater powers within their area than royal officials, there was no longer any means of redress for those who felt they had been dealt with unjustly.

An ad hoc system grew up to satisfy the needs of the military elite. Although imposed in the King's name, there was no real advantage to the royal treasury which tottered from one financial shortfall to another. New demands for cash arose continually, not least from the increasingly restive King Rana Bahadur. For years he had been kept on a tight leash by his Regent uncle; but as a teenager his tastes grew ever more extravagant. He demanded that new additions be made to the Royal Palace at Hanuman Dhoka and that religious festivals be celebrated with more pomp and ceremony. He thought the temples and priests should receive truly royal munificence. All of this may have been a further drain on the treasury, but as the young King approached the day when he would rule in person it became impossible to refuse his requests.

King Rana Bahadur clearly had no affection for his uncle and by one of his first edicts when he assumed full powers the Regent was placed under house arrest. It did not matter that he had served his country well and won countless battles in the west. People at court chose to remember what they perceived to be the more recent humiliation of the Tibet War. Nepal's greatest commander was left to languish in obscurity for a couple of years before being incarcerated for life. His imprisonment lasted only six months: he died in jail under mysterious circumstances, probably from poisoning. For a warrior prince, it was an ignominious end.

The prospects for the House of Gorkha, on the other hand, looked extremely promising. It had survived a long minority and all the perils that went with it. Now there was an adult King on the throne again, and to begin with he showed a vigorous interest in governing the country himself. As for the royal succession, that too looked secure. Rana Bahadur had been married at fourteen, first to his Senior Queen, who bore him a daughter, and then to his Junior Queen who in due course produced two sons. There was every hope that the King would live long enough for his heirs to grow up and attain their majority.

After what looked like a promising start, however, it soon emerged that Rana Bahadur did not relish the high duties he was born to. During his youth he had been deliberately encouraged by his uncle to lead a life of debauchery – mostly to prevent him from exercising his rightful authority. Unfortunately, these habits persisted. As King, he showed no interest in military campaigning and increasingly ignored the business of government. Although he already had two wives through arranged marriages, he now fell hopelessly in love with Kantavati Devi, a young widow of a Brahmin family who had come to worship at the Pashupatinath Temple.

So captivated was he by Kantavati that he had her brought to him at the Royal Palace and demanded she marry him immediately. She put him off for six months, arguing that it was too soon after her first husband's death, for whose soul she had come to pray at Pashupatinath. She also insisted that if they married and had a son together, then this child and not one of his half-brothers should become the next King of Nepal.

The King agreed to her terms, even though to promise so much threw aside the established rules of succession. Additionally, the marriage itself was contrary to Hindu custom on two counts. Widows were deemed unsuitable to marry; and a wife from the Brahmin caste was inappropriate for a king of undiluted Rajput blood. But none of this mattered to Rana Bahadur Shah. They were married and, to the intense displeasure of his two other wives, he made Kantavati Devi his Queen with the full title of *rani*. Within the year she gave birth to a healthy boy, who was named Girvan Yuddha. By then however,

Kantavati had already contracted smallpox, and the King was driven half-mad with the thought of losing her.

Since she herself thought she was dying, Kantavati reminded the King of his promise to her about their son succeeding to the throne. She also pointed out that Rana Bahadur's own horoscope foretold he would die young. This would leave the infant Girvan Yuddha an orphan. She anticipated that, since her son was neither the first-born nor of unmixed Rajput blood, there would be opposition to his succeeding to the throne and argued that it would be far better to have the boy crowned while they were both alive and able to influence the outcome. In other words, she asked the King to abdicate in favour of his son.

To agree to this would not only be a dereliction of the King's duty, it would place the entire Kingdom of Nepal in jeopardy. The inevitable consequence of such a decision would be another long minority, pre-cisely what Nepal did not need at the time. But Rana Bahadur, whose mental state was almost certainly unstable, was won over to the scheme. He was in the habit of putting his personal wishes – or rather those of his beloved – before any reasons of state. So he first declared his eldest and rightful heir illegitimate, and then renounced the crown in favour of Girvan Yuddha, retiring completely from public life to devote himself to caring for his ailing Queen.

Lavish offerings were made to the most revered Brahmins and temples in Kathmandu, and these seemed to have worked because Kantavati Devi did make a partial recovery. But upon seeing her small-pox-ravaged face in the mirror, she committed suicide rather than let anyone look at her. Her death drove the former King over the edge: mad with grief, he ordered his troops to desecrate the temples where offerings had been made. He had the Brahmin priests killed or forced them to commit defiling acts by which they would lose their caste. Any of his soldiers who refused to carry out such sacrilegious acts had boiling oil poured over them.

As Rana Bahadur lay holed up with his grief, a group of leading courtiers withdrew to Nuwakot where the infant Girvan Yuddha was being kept safe. From there the Council of Nobles ordered Rana

Bahadur into exile and, with most of the army behind them, they began to march on the capital. Rana Bahadur fled to Benares, where he occupied his time at first with religious devotions. Only later did he begin plotting to regain power in Kathmandu.

King Rana Bahadur's abdication left Nepal in turmoil with an infant on the throne again, not out of necessity but through a deliberate act of will.

In the absence of anyone else the country was now nominally ruled by the ex-King's second wife, Queen Subarnaprabha, who had remained in Kathmandu and now assumed the regency. In fact, it was governed by a group of *kazis*, or strongmen, who in their struggle for supremacy used every means at their disposal, including assassination. The failings of an individual monarch encouraged the leading families of Gorkha – the Pandes, the Thapas, the Basnyats – to look to their own interests. And where once these had been bound up with loyal service to the King, now the noble clans concentrated on building up their own networks of patronage. In effect, they began to behave like alternative royal dynasties. A political culture based on fear and self-interest developed that was to have grave consequences for future kings of Nepal.

Rana Bahadur's role in these events was not over yet. His ill-treated senior wife, Rajarajeshwari Devi, left him in Benares and returned alone to Nepal where she took charge of the boy-King and, after striking a deal with the influential leader of the Council of Nobles, Damodar Pande, took upon herself the powers of Regent. Her husband had to remain in the 'honourable custody' of the British while they tried to complete a trade treaty with Kathmandu. But when these negotiations failed, they decided to free him and he immediately set out for Nepal with his loyal followers, including his chief bodyguard and adviser Bhim Sen Thapa, intending to seize back his throne.

Queen Rajarajeshwari was rightly alarmed by this and dispatched Damodar Pande south to intercept her husband's party. But the ex-King won over the Nepali troops to his side and re-entered Kathmandu in triumph, where he had Queen Rajarajeshwari banished from court and himself assumed the regency. Damodar Pande and four others were executed. Otherwise Rana Bahadur acted with the restraint needed to gain the support of the nobility.

It helped that his return coincided with a renewal of military campaigning. Gorkha armies stormed westward, taking the Kingdom of Garhwal and the constellation of minor hill principalities known as the Barha and Athara Thakuri. There was no power in the hills that could withstand them. They were poised to continue their advance onwards to Kashmir, with the renewed prospect of a Nepalese empire stretching almost the entire length of the Himalayas. Only the great fort of Kangra stood in their way. But as the Nepali army was besieging Kangra Fort it ran into the armies of another great martial race, the Sikhs, whose wily one-eyed ruler Ranjit Singh sent his own troops into Kangra. The Nepalese were wary of taking on the dominant power in north India and so for a second time their advance towards Kashmir was held in check.

For two years Rana Bahadur held power in Kathmandu, to the accompaniment of constant news of victories and fresh land grants to be distributed. The spoils of war kept his commanders and the noble families happy, at least for the time being. But when in the spring of 1806 the Regent also assumed the powers of *mukhtiyar*, or Chief Minister, there were many at court who feared a renewal of the earlier rule of terror. The corridors of Hanuman Dhoka Palace buzzed with rumours of conspiracies, both real and imagined, while in the great houses of Kathmandu the nobility and military commanders considered their next move.

It was in this atmosphere of mutual suspicion that the Regent summoned his half-brother, Sher Bahadur Shah, to answer charges of purloining state funds and abusing his authority. The session was held late at night, in *darbar*, or open court, with the Regent and members of the Council of Nobles attending. When faced with this most grievous accusation, Sher Bahadur, complaining of a dry throat, asked to be allowed some tea. As Rana Bahadur taunted his half-brother, they began to quarrel violently. Then, when the attention of onlookers was momentarily distracted by a jackal howling nearby, Sher Bahadur seized the moment, drew his sword, and struck the ex-King dead before anyone else could react. One of the *kazis* in attendance then leapt on Sher Bahadur and strangled him with his bare hands.

That *kazi*'s name was Bal Narsingh Konwar and his direct descendants were to assume the princely name of Rana and would rule Nepal for more than a century. Nobody present when their ex-King was cut down could have foretold such an unlikely outcome, for the Konwars were only a minor noble clan at the time. The double deaths within the Shah family did not, however, lead to the collapse of the monarchy or the rules of succession. Throughout all the turmoil, young Girvan Yuddha remained on the throne of Nepal.

During the ensuing chaos, Rana Bahadur's counsellor and bodyguard, Bhim Sen Thapa, alerted the royal guard to Rana Bahadur's death and told them there were more conspirators within the palace. He ordered the guards to surround the hall where the Council of Nobles and courtiers had assembled and instructed them to kill anyone who resisted. The result was a general massacre in which three royal relatives and seventy members of the nobility were executed. But that was not the end of the bloodletting. The purge of every conceivable opposition continued apace, with the banished Queen Rajarajeshwari forced to perform *sati* a week after her murdered husband had been cremated. Fifteen royal mistresses and female servants joined her in the flames.

Already, within two generations of Prithvi Narayan's death, the institution of monarchy had imploded. A royal fratricide had been allowed to take place, and there were enough corpses littering the corridors of Hanuman Dhoka Palace to keep the funeral pyres down by the Bagmati River burning for days on end. The scale of the slaughter was terrible; the damage largely self-inflicted. Not in the goriest of Jacobean tragedies does one encounter so many futile deaths.

Even before the untimely departure of two royal brothers, the very system of government set up by the founding monarch had fallen into ruin. It required a strong King at its head to impose a sense of unity and purpose on the Gorkha clans. Rana Bahadur had signally failed to provide such leadership, preferring to follow his personal preferences by marrying outside his caste, offering up his abdication and then refusing to leave the political stage. The end result was bloody turmoil and the further undermining of royal authority. But all was not lost. If the Shah family were incapable of providing a strong man, there were others ready and able to step into the gap.

In theory, the regency automatically passed to Rana Bahadur's fifth wife, Queen Tripura Sundari. She was just twelve, a member of the Thapa clan who had been married only the previous year. Partly because of her age, but also because of her kinship to Bhim Sen Thapa, the young girl was excused from performing *sati*. Instead she was expected to rule on behalf of the eight-year-old King Girvan Yuddha. However, since she was not much older herself, real authority was concentrated in the hands of Bhim Sen Thapa, who now took on the combined roles of Chief Minister and Commander-in-Chief.

Bhim Sen Thapa took to his new role with relish. Former opponents were arrested and killed on charges of conspiracy against the Crown. No trials were held and no evidence of any real conspiracy produced, but still hundreds of the leading families of Gorkha were purged. Their lands and titles were confiscated and the principal beneficiary was Bhim Sen Thapa and his supporters.

It was a bloody start to a regime that would last more than thirty years. Yet it was during the early part of Bhim Sen Thapa's rule that Nepali military expansion reached its fullest extent. By 1806 'Greater Nepal' stretched from the Sutlej River in the west to the Teesta and the borders of Bhutan in the east. The Gorkhas controlled all of Garhwal and Kumaon, as well as broad tracts of fertile land down in the Terai. At its peak, it was at least a third larger than the present Kingdom of Nepal. Even this was a relatively compact realm compared to the endless plateaux of neighbouring Tibet, but the lands to the south of the Himalayas were much more fertile and densely settled. No greater Himalayan empire had existed before.

Further western expansion, however, was barred by the powerful kingdom of the Sikhs. Any plans to invade the rich valleys of Kashmir had to be abandoned indefinitely, and the Tibet War had shown that any attempt to expand northwards would eventually bring down the wrath of imperial China. And to the south and east, Nepal was hemmed in by the rising power of the British East India Company, whose agents were trying to impose the principle that Nepali control ceased where the hills met the north Indian plains.

This was unacceptable to the Nepalis. Many of the hill rajas they had conquered held lands in the Terai, and these had been transferred to the House of Gorkha and their supporters. Although they rarely visited the Terai except for hunting trips, the royal family and nobility drew much of their revenue from landed estates down in the plains. Since the days of Prithvi Narayan Shah, Gorkhali soldiers had been among those rewarded for their service with *jagirs* in the Terai. The Nepali sphere of influence was encroaching inexorably on villages whose ownership they disputed with the Nawab of Oudh and other client princes of the East India Company. When villagers were carried off by the Nepalis as slaves into the hills, the Company's agents protested that they were British subjects. The southern expansion had set the Kingdom of Nepal on an inevitable collision course with the mightiest empire on earth.

4

A House Divided

The Anglo-Nepalese War lasted from 1814 to 1816 but the outcome was never really in doubt. The British, whose armies on the other side of the world were crushing those of the greatest general Europe had seen in five hundred years, had nevertheless mustered a huge force, vastly superior in both numbers and armaments, and advanced in five separate columns along a seven-hundred-mile front. To begin with the Gorkhas' raw courage and experience of mountain warfare brought some astonishing victories. Four British columns quickly withdrew in disarray, but more troops were thrown into the attack, and sheer weight of numbers, combined with the use of mountain artillery, eventually wore down the Gorkha defences. With British forces poised to march on Kathmandu, Bhim Sen Thapa's government was forced to sue for peace.

The peace treaty signed at Sugauli in 1816 imposed tough terms on the Nepalese. The recently acquired provinces of Kumaon, Garhwal and parts of what are now Himachal Pradesh were annexed by the British, thereby blocking any westward expansion. In the east, a strategic strip of hill country between the Teesta and Mechi rivers was restored to the Kingdom of Sikkim under British guarantee, to prevent further Gorkha forays in that direction. Down in the plains, broad tracts of the Terai were transferred to the British or one of their client states. The Kingdom of Nepal lost roughly a third of its lands and was now surrounded on three sides by British-held territories or protectorates.

In exchange, the British allowed the Nepalese a free hand in their own internal affairs. They did insist, however, that a British Resident be stationed in Kathmandu, and that the *darbar* permit no representative of any other foreign power into the country. They also demanded that in future their Indian army be able to recruit Gorkhas as mercenaries, having been deeply impressed by the fighting qualities of their erstwhile enemy. Otherwise, the Kingdom of Nepal, admittedly much reduced in size, was left to go its own way.

Although defeated in battle, the Nepalese once again escaped direct colonial rule. The British had realised that, as well as the difficulties in imposing order on a hostile population in such difficult terrain, it suited Britain's interests that Nepal remain as an independent buffer state between her own dominions in India and the Chinese and Russian empires in Central Asia. The security of India's northern border would be guarded just as well, and at far less a cost. What went on inside Nepal was, therefore, left largely up to the Nepalis.

The Kingdom of Nepal had survived another crisis. Even its intemperate Prime Minister, Bhim Sen Thapa, who had led his country into war with the British, managed to come through more or less unscathed. He made sure that his own relatives held all the key offices of state and kept the boy-King Girvan Yuddha in strict seclusion. Apart from the occasional ceremony where his presence was required, the King was only allowed to see the Prime Minister and other trusted members of the Thapa clan.

As was the custom, the young King Girvan Yuddha was married in his early teens to two girls even younger than himself. The Junior Queen gave birth to a son when she was probably only fifteen. Although the royal family lived as virtual prisoners within Hanuman Dhoka Palace, at least there was an heir to the throne. As Girvan Yuddha approached the age of majority it was expected that he would shake off his constraints and rule on his own. All might still be well for the Shah dynasty.

Such hopes were dashed when Girvan Yuddha died of smallpox at the age of nineteen, shortly after reaching his majority. The strict rules

45

of succession were observed and yet another infant, his three-year-old son Rajendra Bikram Shah, was placed on the golden throne of Nepal. Once again there would be a long minority; and once again the Prime Minister exercised governing power, showing his true colours by forcing the dead King's second, childless wife to perform *sati*. The question of what to do with the new seventeen-year-old Queen Mother soon resolved itself, too: just two weeks after her husband's death she too succumbed to smallpox. Having lost both his parents, the infant King Rajendra was put in the care of his step-grandmother, Queen Lalit Tripura Sundari. She continued to act as Regent on behalf of the new King, though her kinsman Bhim Sen Thapa remained very much in control.

Bhim Sen Thapa's thirty-one-year rule over the much-reduced Kingdom of Nepal at least provided a period of stability. New buildings and public works were started. A stone bridge connecting Kathmandu and Patan was built over the Bagmati River, and a fountain with an immense golden waterspout, known as the Sundhara, was installed near to where the present day Post Office stands. New courtyards and pavilions were added to Hanuman Dhoka Palace where the Queen Regent, who was herself a lover of poetry and had even translated a portion of the *Mahabharata* into Nepali, presided over a court of some refinement.

Some habits, such as the use of Persian for titles and diplomatic correspondence, were borrowed from the court of the Mughal emperors in Delhi. Others were specifically Nepalese and Hindu. The Queen Regent commissioned several new temples in the Kathmandu Valley, including the remarkable temple dedicated to Shiva at Tripureshwar, all of them built in the traditional pagoda style and embellished with intricate Newari woodcarvings. Her patronage extended to Benares, the most sacred of Hindu cities, where she had constructed a temple and bathing *ghat* for the use of Nepalese pilgrims. Throughout the twenty six years she was Regent she left the governance of the country to Bhim Sen Thapa, which probably explains why she died a natural death at thirty eight, a relatively advanced age for those times.

For most of this period Nepal was at peace with its neighbours. Confined by British India, there was little scope for military expansion, but this caused serious friction within a society where honours and rewards, mainly in the form of land grants, had traditionally been provided by new conquests. Forced to turn inwards, the Nepalese might have found a way forward through trade or by adopting land reforms to improve agricultural productivity, but this did not square with the militaristic and caste-driven values of the Gorkha nobility. Instead, they fought among themselves over the diminishing pool of patronage available. So long as Bhim Sen Thapa remained in control, nobody dared to make a move, but when the young King Rajendra attempted to assert his authority, all the conspirators came out of the woodwork.

Bhim Sen Thapa applied the same approach to Rajendra's upbringing as he had to the two previous kings in his charge. The young monarch was kept completely isolated within Hanuman Dhoka Palace. At the same time, he was steered, just as Rana Bahadur had been before him, towards a life of indulgence and sensual gratification. As the British Resident in Kathmandu noted, King Rajendra was 'hemmed into his palace, beyond which he cannot stir unaccompanied by the Minister, and then only to the extent of a short ride or drive. Even within the walls of his palace the Minister and his brother both reside, the latter in the especial capacity of "dry nurse" to His Highness.' The report concluded that 'the Raja has been purposely trained so as to possess little energy of body and mind'. This was all done to ensure that, when Rajendra did take up his role as King, he would be incapable of exercising real authority without the assistance of Bhim Sen Thapa.

The gradual transfer of power away from the King was made acceptable simply because there had been no real King in Nepal for so long. Nearly half a century had elapsed between Prithvi Narayan Shah's death in 1775 and his great-great-grandson Rajendra Bikram Shah's reaching the age of majority in 1832. During all this time there had been only seven years when a Nepalese monarch could be said to have truly ruled. The rest of the time the country had been governed by a Regent, the Council of Nobles or an all-powerful Prime Minister. The half-century had seen the King become deeply revered but weakened by the long disuse of his powers. The King was still needed, but only to provide legitimacy for those who acted in his name. Indeed it had become so unusual for the monarch to take a hand in government that, whenever an attempt was made to rule in person, it aroused strong opposition from the leading families of Gorkha, who had begun to behave more like rival dynasties than loyal subjects. They formed shifting alliances between each other and with various members of the royal family – half-brothers, cousins and royal bastards – whose position at court was assured but who had nothing to do apart from conspire against one other. The Junior Queens and royal mistresses faced the stark choice of either ensuring their own son became Crown Prince or eventually being forced to perform *sati* when their husband died. There were no half-measures. It is hardly surprising, therefore, that rumours and accusations about young princes being poisoned or deliberately infected with a disease were rife at court. At such times, all that held the royal household together was its thin veneer of ceremony and exquisite manners.

The Queen Regent's death in 1832 undermined the absolute rule of Bhim Sen Thapa. His ancient enemies, the Pandes, knew that the young King was resentful of the constraints imposed on him. Now that Rajendra was approaching the age of majority he might be expected to dismiss his Prime Minister and rule on his own. But before then, there were other deadly rivalries within the royal family to be exploited. Both of Rajendra's wives had borne him sons and each was equally determined that her own offspring be declared Crown Prince. So the Senior Queen, Samarajya Laxmi, allied herself with the Pandes and other Brahmins, while the Junior Queen sought the support of the Prime Minister and the rest of the Thapa clan.

What finally sparked an open confrontation was the unexpected death of the Senior Queen's youngest son. The Royal Physician who had been treating him was interrogated and eventually admitted to nefarious deeds. The Chief Minister and his nephew were immediately arrested on suspicion of poisoning. Their real target, it was alleged, had been the Senior Queen herself, but the plot had misfired. After what amounted to a travesty of a trial, Bhim Sen Thapa was stripped of his office and imprisoned. The Senior Queen's ally, Rung Jan Pande, was appointed Chief Minister in his place. He dared not have Bhim Sen Thapa killed immediately, and instead attempted to confiscate all the lands and properties of the Thapas and their allies. The nobility protested to the King, who was forced to dismiss Rung Jan Pande and release the former Chief Minister from his prison.

King Rajendra wanted to restore the monarchy's authority and rule on his own terms, but his cloistered upbringing had left him lacking either the necessary judgement or self-restraint. He ran through a string of ineffective Chief Ministers, none of whom enjoyed his full confidence, until he found he had to accept Rung Jan Pande once again.

This time, however, the Pandes were determined to destroy Bhim Sen Thapa. After a second show trial he was thrown into an underground dungeon where his guards informed him that his wife had been stripped naked and paraded around Kathmandu. Unable to bear the dishonour, he used a *kukri* smuggled into prison to slit his own throat. His attempted suicide was initially unsuccessful; denied medical attention, he lingered on for another nine days. It was a slow and agonising death. Thus was Rung Jan Pande avenged of his father's murder and all the indignities borne by his clan.

The crisis of King Rajendra's reign was far from over. When his Senior Queen died of malaria on a pilgrimage to Benares, the factions which had supported her rallied around her eldest son, the feeble-minded and uncontrollable Crown Prince Surendra. From an early age he had demonstrated a streak of capricious cruelty which made him deeply unpopular. On a whim he had been known to order his subjects to jump down a well or ride their horses off a cliff, just to see whether or not they died.

Partly to distance himself from such outrages, King Rajendra granted this wayward prince an equal share in the government of the Kingdom. As the King appeared incapable of restraining Surendra, the Council of Nobles demanded the Junior Queen also have a share of power. She immediately recalled the Thapas from exile and there now ensued a purge of the Pandes during which a dozen 'conspirators' were executed. The tables had been turned once again.

The Chief Ministership was then handed to Mathbar Singh Thapa, although with only the Junior Queen's support he was unable to restore order at court. King Rajendra continued to intervene sporadically in the affairs of state, while the Crown Prince remained as uncontrollable as ever. With power divided between three royal personages, nobody actually controlled the Kingdom. As the British Resident in Kathmandu succinctly put it, the country was governed by 'Mr Nepal, Mrs Nepal and Master Nepal'.

An increasingly embattled Mathbar Singh Thapa now decided that the only way to consolidate his power base was to switch allegiance to Crown Prince Surendra, thereby winning over the great majority at court who still stood by the principle of primogeniture – no matter how unsuitable the present heir to the throne. With their support he would persuade the King to abdicate and place the grateful Surendra on the throne, reserving all real authority to the office of Chief Minister.

Before this plan could be put into effect, however, the Junior Queen, Rajya Laxmi Devi, caught wind of it. Like so many Junior Queens before her, she desperately wanted her son to secure the throne and with it her own future. That meant thwarting Surendra. She therefore persuaded her husband that all this talk of abdication was merely a cover for an attempt by Mathbar Singh Thapa to usurp the throne for himself. Faced with this imaginary threat, the King and Queen decided that their Chief Minister had to be assassinated. The man chosen for the job was an ambitious young officer called Jung Bahadur Konwar. Not only was he the son of Bal Narsingh Konwar, the *kazi* who had strangled Sher Bahadur thirty years earlier, he was also the favourite nephew of the man he was now deputed to murder.

Once he had received the royal command, Jung Bahadur had no

choice but to obey: nobody dared resist the Junior Queen's wishes. Mathbar Singh Thapa knew this only too well, and had once explained to Jung Bahadur. 'If the Queen orders it, I will kill you and you will kill me.' Those are the rules when there is absolute authority without any sense of responsibility.

On the appointed day, the Chief Minister was called into the Queen's Chamber on the pretext that she had suffered an injury. There Jung Bahadur shot him in the head; as he fell forward, in the direction of the King and Queen, guards rushed in to slash at the fallen man with their swords. For good measure, King Rajendra himself gave the corpse a good kicking before more retainers arrived to carry it away for cremation.

The murder of yet another Chief Minister only served to plunge the court into deeper crisis. Faction ruled, entire noble families were purged and effective government was sacrificed to maintaining some degree of balance between the King's men and the Queen's men. Among the latter was the minister in charge of civil affairs, Gagan Singh Bhandari, who was secretly the Queen's lover. She also believed she could count on the loyal service of Jung Bahadur Konwar, whose assassination of his uncle was rewarded with command of the army.

But nothing remains a secret for long in Kathmandu, and King Rajendra soon heard about his wife's relationship with the low-born Gagan Singh. He promptly summoned the two sons of his Senior Queen and commanded them to avenge the family's honour. They in turn sought the advice of the new Chief Minister and others loyal to their cause. Their suggestion was that one of Jung Bahadur's brothers do the deed, since he himself was having an affair with one of Gagan Singh's maidservants, who could be persuaded to let him into the house. The true identity of the assassin has never been made clear; the one certainty is that Gagan Singh was shot dead, while at prayer, on the roof of his home.

Queen Rajya Laxmi was known to have a fiery temper, and when she learned that her chief ally and lover had been assassinated she had only one thing on her mind – revenge. At her bidding, all senior officers were summoned to the arsenal and assembly ground known as the Kot, just to the north of Hanuman Dhoka Palace. It was a dark night, and the enclosed courtyard where troops normally mustered was ill lit by flickering torches. Most officers, as well as courtiers, who answered the royal summons probably had no idea what had happened, though they sensed more trouble lay in store for them.

Among the first to arrive was Jung Bahadur Konwar, accompanied by his six brothers, with three loyal regiments in support. The Queen should have been worried by such a show of force, but she counted Jung Bahadur among her supporters, and her immediate concern was to destroy those who had killed Gagan Singh.

The Queen ascended to the upper floor above the main hall of the Kot by means of a wooden ladder and a trapdoor which could be sealed off in an emergency. From the safety of a balcony she demanded that the assembled officers of state name the person responsible for ordering the assassination of Gagan Singh. When nobody spoke up, she pointed the finger of accusation at one man (the wrong one) and ordered that he be executed on the spot. At this point King Rajendra, fearing his own part in the conspiracy might be revealed, slipped away unnoticed, leaving his Chief Minister to argue with the Queen that no one should be executed without a trial. That did not satisfy the Queen; coming down from the safety of the balcony, she rushed towards the accused man with a sword in her hand, its curved blade flickering in the torchlight, apparently determined to kill him herself. She was forcibly restrained and escorted back upstairs by Jung Bahadur and other ministers. Their intervention was timely, for all around the courtyard rival officers and retainers were drawing their own weapons.

At that moment shots rang out from all around the Kot. Jung Bahadur's brothers and loyal followers had already taken up position inside the main hall, covering all the entrances, and on top of nearby roofs. Their gunfire scythed its way through the bodies packed inside the courtyard. No mercy was shown, regardless of rank. Within minutes the flagstones were drenched in blood. Among the dead were counted

more than thirty members of Nepal's aristocracy, including three ministers of state. Nobody bothered to record the number of ordinary
soldiers and retainers also killed that night.

The Kot Massacre of 15 September 1846 was remembered as the
most infamous in Nepal's history, not only because of the numbers
slain, but on account of the base passions it revealed and the dreadful
consequences of that night. Before she had even left the scene of the
massacre, Queen Rajya Laxmi had conferred the dual offices of Chief
Minister and Commander-in-Chief on her apparent saviour, Jung Bahadur Konwar.

Her precipitate action placed immense power in the hands of a
twenty-nine-year-old officer of undistinguished family, but Jung Bahadur had already proved he could be ruthless, and now he moved
swiftly to consolidate his position. He appointed his own relations to
all the key military and political offices in the Kingdom and then carried
out a bloody purge of all possible opponents. Members of the old
nobility who had not been caught up in the Kot Massacre were hunted
down, their lands and titles forfeited. Thousands of their followers
were forced into exile.

If the Queen thought she had elevated a faithful supporter, she was
soon to be disabused. When Jung Bahadur refused her wish to see her
own son become Crown Prince, she decided to have her new minister
assassinated as well. Fortunately for him, the envoy sent to summon
him to Bhandarkhal Palace, where the Queen and her fellow conspirators awaited him, was so frightened that he revealed the plot. Jung
Bahadur's men rode to the palace and caught the conspirators by
surprise. Twenty-three of the Queen's men, including most of the
noble Basnyat clan, were put to death, and the Queen herself kept
under house arrest until she could be put on trial before the Council
of Nobles. The charges, of attempting to murder the Prime Minister
as a prelude to assassinating the Crown Prince and placing her own
son on the throne, were said to 'clearly tend towards the destruction
of the royal family'. Moreover, the Queen's actions had already 'caused
the death of hundreds and brought ruin and misery upon your subjects,

whose misfortunes will not end as long as you remain in the country'. She was exiled to Benares, where she was joined by the King and other members of the royal family, leaving the emotionally unstable Crown Prince Surendra as nominal Regent in Kathmandu and Prime Minister Jung Bahadur fully in charge.

On the banks of the Ganges, meanwhile, the royal exiles plotted their next move: the assassins they eventually sent to rid them of the overbearing Prime Minister were arrested in Kathmandu. Worse still, they were found to be carrying an incriminating letter from the King, evidence which Jung Bahadur used to convince the army that the King should be deposed. On 12 May 1847 a letter was sent to Rajendra in Benares declaring him 'unfit to rule the country over whose destinies Providence has placed you to preside. And hence by the unanimous will of the nobles and people we have set up Prince Surendra Bikram Shah on the throne of Nepal. And be it known unto you that from this day you have ceased to reign.'

Rajendra's response was to attempt an invasion of Nepal, but his pitiful forces were soon dispersed and the ex-King found himself being escorted back to Kathmandu under armed guard. For the remaining thirty-four years of his life he was kept a prisoner in the old palace of the Malla kings at Bhaktapur.

Rarely has a house been so divided against itself as the Shah dynasty during the years between 1837 and 1847 when King Rajendra, his wife, and his demented son and heir all attempted to rule the country. When Nepal most needed a secure, dependable, viable monarchy, it found itself with a family driven by arbitrary and short-sighted urges that led, inevitably, to endless conspiracies and bloodshed.

Only four generations had passed since Prithvi Narayan Shah had seized the throne of Nepal by force of arms, but already it seemed that the curse of Gorakhnath was taking effect. Whether through sheer wilfulness or lack of responsibility, each succeeding king who wielded anything like real power seemed bent on self-destruction. The serpentine logic of palace politics, the life-and-death competition between rival queens, the rivalries of the old Gorkha families, all contributed to this sad state of affairs. But the royal family were themselves largely to blame, and in the end they paid a heavy price.

While the Shah dynasty nominally continued to reign without interruption, henceforth they were prisoners in their own palaces, the succession of kings mere figureheads whose presence at state functions bestowed legitimacy on the men who really ran Nepal. The long years of years of royal captivity had just begun.

5

The Century of Captivity

Even before Jung Bahadur seized absolute power, the Kingdom of Nepal was already moving towards a dual system of government in which the King officially reigned but an all-powerful Chief Minister actually ruled the country. Bhim Sen Thapa had been the first to put this into practice over three long decades, but Jung Bahadur took this process a stage further, by declaring that in future the office of Prime Minister (the title was a new one, reflecting British influence in the subcontinent, and was initially spelt 'Praim Ministar') should become hereditary. Only members of his own family would be permitted to wield absolute power in Nepal.

In doing this, Jung Bahadur deliberately raised a parallel dynasty to the royal family. Appointment to the prime ministership and every other office of any importance, both civil and military, was subject to strict rules of hereditary succession. It was this regime that was to govern the country for the next one hundred and four years, during which time the reigning Shah family were prevented from exercising any real power in the land. Their day-to-day activities were kept under the closest scrutiny by the hereditary Prime Minister and his agents. Only rarely were they allowed to go outside their own palaces.

Although in theory they were still absolute rulers, in practice the Shah kings were restricted to a purely ceremonial role. The monarch's presence was, however, required at certain public functions – to receive foreign emissaries, for instance, or to preside over religious ceremonies or musters of the army – because the King still symbolised the unity of the country, its independence from foreign rule and, above all, the continuity and legitimacy of its government.

The Konwars needed that veneer of legitimacy. For even though Jung Bahadur and his successors arrogated to themselves all powers of decision-making and patronage, their authority was based on the premise that they were acting in the King's name. Notionally, the King remained the source of all authority, the fountain of justice, the dispenser of all honours and lands within his realm. The oath of loyalty taken by every officer and soldier in the army was – and to this day still is – directly to the person of the King, and not to his ministers. This helps to explain how, despite incessant power struggles among its ruling elite, the Kingdom of Nepal managed to avoid any full-scale civil wars over a period of nearly two hundred and fifty years.

By the middle of the nineteenth century, the Shah dynasty had forfeited any meaningful political role, but they at least succeeded in remaining on the throne at a time when many other royal houses were being consigned to oblivion. In Nepal, the royal succession passed uncontested from father to eldest son. The throne could not be left vacant, so the principle of 'The King is dead; long live the King' was adhered to. While the death of a king was an occasion for elaborate mourning, the birth of a son and heir was greeted with widespread public celebrations. The safe delivery of a future king was announced by a nineteen-gun salute from the palace guard firing their rifles in the air, which *feu-de-joie*, was then taken up by the massed regiments on the central parade ground at Tundikhel until the whole of Kathmandu seemed filled with celebratory gunfire. Prisoners were released from jail, three days of holiday declared, and thank-offerings made at the appropriate temples.

As avatars of Lord Vishnu, the god-kings of Nepal were openly worshipped by their subjects. They were the living embodiment of all traditional values associated with Hindu kingship, and their physical presence alone was believed to guarantee the safety of the land and its people. No matter what scandalous behaviour went on within the Royal Palace, nor how capriciously cruel their monarch's commands might sometimes seem, to the ordinary, illiterate and thoroughly superstitious Nepali subject the King was a divine being whose presence should be worshipped and whose peremptory command unhesitatingly obeyed.

Such religious beliefs surrounding Nepal's kings were deliberately encouraged by Jung Bahadur and his successors, precisely because this served to distance further the divine monarch from his subjects. Learned Brahmins supported this policy by declaring that the god-king should not leave the palace precincts for more than twelve hours at a time, and should on no account venture beyond the limits of Kathmandu. In many ways the mystery surrounding the King in his forbidden palace was similar to that of latter-day emperors of China or Japan. It enhanced the mystique of divine kingship, and hence the reverence with which even the most vicious and ineffectual of monarchs was held by his subjects.

Finally, since the King himself was no longer responsible for government, he could not be blamed when things went wrong. By a strange paradox, the absence of responsibility contributed to the popularity of Nepal's monarchy through its century of captivity.

Jung Bahadur's rapid rise to power was in many ways a joint enterprise in which his own extended family were partners. His six brothers had come to his assistance during the Kot Massacre. They had ridden with him to Bhandarkhal Palace where they had killed the conspirators. They had stood by him, with their regiments in support, as he declared King Rajendra and his Queen deposed. So Jung Bahadur was aware that they needed to be rewarded, not just for services rendered but in order to ensure their future loyalty.

What he proposed was a variation on the oriental system whereby the office of grand vizier and other high positions in government remained within the same family. In this case, however, the King had no say in how the all-important office of Prime Minister was automatically transferred on the death or resignation of the holder to the next most senior of his brothers. This brother would already hold the position of Commander-in-Chief of the army, though he also had wide responsibilities for civil government. The next in line was Western Commanding General, the man who really ran the army, with younger brothers holding progressively less important military and civil commands. This meant that before they reached the pinnacle of power they would already have broad experience of governing, while the military nature of the hierarchy would help ensure that the army remained loyal to the Prime Minister at every level. When each surviving brother had held office and either died or resigned, the Roll of Succession passed to the next generation, beginning with Jung Bahadur's eldest son and then working through his nephews in strict order of seniority. By then they too would have worked their way up through the hierarchy and gained much useful experience.

Such a system of hereditary Prime Ministers had numerous advantages for the incumbent. It encouraged loyalty among those who might expect, through the normal progression of events, to inherit immense power and riches. By the same token, it made assassination or other forms of treachery as a rapid path to the top seem much less appealing. For the brother next in line for prime ministerial office had a vested interest in maintaining the order of succession. The very system imposed a strong sense of modern-day Mafia-style family unity among different branches of such an extensive clan. It also avoided the chief weakness of the Shah dynasty's laws of succession, namely the situation when an infant-king inherited the throne. This had required others to govern on the King's behalf, resulting in endless power struggles. Now there would always be an undisputed Rana Prime Minister to rule for him.

The overwhelming ascendancy of a single family needed some further justification, especially since Jung Bahadur's clan, the Konwars, had its origins among only middle-ranking nobles. A more illustrious lineage was required, and the Brahmin priests and genealogists worked overtime to produce one. They discovered that the Konwars' ancestry could be traced back to one of the premier Rajput families, the Ranas of Chittor in Rajasthan. Henceforth, the Konwars were to be known by the princely title of Rana. Their caste status was upgraded to a position above the rest of the nobility, but still beneath that of the royal family.

Thus was the regime commonly known as the Rana oligarchy born.

The royal edict approving this in 1848 expressly forbade the Ranas from marrying into the royal family or their collaterals, but Jung Bahadur simply ignored such stipulations. He himself married a royal cousin, while for his eldest son Jagat Jang he arranged a marriage with King Surendra's six-year-old daughter, a wedding celebrated with great pomp and ceremony. Six dozen richly caparisoned elephants, hundreds of dancing girls waving peacock fans, and an entire regiment of soldiers accompanied the wedding procession from Hanuman Dhoka Royal Palace to the Prime Minister's magnificent residence in Thapathali. The dowry was immense, and naturally entered the new Rana household. But what really mattered to Jung Bahadur and his family was the immense boost to their prestige. Besides, it could be a political bonus to have the royal family as in-laws.

This was the first time that the Shah dynasty had entered into matrimonial relations with their own subjects, but it was to be only the first of many such family alliances. Two of Jung Bahadur's daughters were married to Crown Prince Trailokya, and the practice continued in the next generation when King Prithvi Bir also married two daughters of the ruling Rana Prime Minister. The tradition continues to this day, with Nepal's last three reigning monarchs all marrying into the Juddha branch of the Rana family.

In terms of their genetic background, the modern royal family owes far more to the Ranas than to the House of Gorkha. Their original Rajput bloodline has been diluted in a manner similar to that of the Russian Romanov dynasty, the male members of which were criticised for forever marrying German princesses. The poet Alexander Pushkin vividly illustrated this by mixing two bottles of red and white wine, the red representing Russian Romanov ancestry, the white wine that of foreigners. By the time he had reached his own generation of czars there was only the faintest blush to the wine. Much the same could be said of the Shah dynasty, except that in their case practically all of the white has come from one single family estate – the Ranas.

*　　*　　*

So confident was Jung Bahadur of the efficacy of the family-run autocracy he had established that, in 1850, within four years of the Kot
Massacre, he felt able to delegate his prime ministerial powers to
his brother Bam Bahadur and leave Nepal for an extended visit to
Europe. This was an unprecedented step. No Hindu governor of such
elevated caste had ever ventured outside the Indian subcontinent. To
the orthodox Hindu this was unthinkable: to cross the *kala pani*, the
'black water' of the ocean, would result in the permanent loss of one's
caste.

Jung Bahadur had good reasons for undertaking the journey, however. He hoped that his reception in London by the Prime Minister,
Lord Wellington, and the reigning monarch, Queen Victoria (who was
soon to include among her titles 'Empress of India'), would lead to
fuller recognition of Nepal as an independent kingdom. He also anticipated that, in visiting the distant capital of British India, by far the
most powerful of his immediate neighbours, he would win enormous
prestige in Nepal. As for the problem of losing his caste, he was assured
by the Brahmins that ritual purification ceremonies carried out after
his return would prove effective. To be on the safe side, his entourage
was also equipped with clay jars containing sacred water, and live goats
and flat-tailed sheep, as prescribed for sacrifice, and included cooks
and servants of the correct caste to prepare his meals.

The Nepalese party's arrival caused a great stir in London society.
Their bejewelled helmets and exotic appearance, not to mention their
reputation as both fearsome fighters and oriental despots, ensured they
were lionised by society hostesses. Unsurprisingly, the Nepalis were
puzzled by many English customs. Accustomed to keeping women in
purdah, they found it extraordinary that so many beautiful women
approached them directly and offered their hands. They were invited
to balls and the opera, to the pleasure gardens at Vauxhall and to watch
the horse racing at Epsom. They marvelled at the cleanliness and
orderliness of Victorian London, which had none of the open sewers
or the insecurity of life of Kathmandu. While he was not so impressed
by the democratic nature of Parliament, Jung Bahadur did understand

the importance to Britain's peace and stability of the rule of law. Even the highest persons had to submit to the law of the land, he noted, and when he returned to Nepal Jung Bahadur tried to incorporate this principle into his own country's laws.

Jung Bahadur was also shown Britain's industrial might, its ship-yards and factories turning out weapons of war on an unimaginable scale. Like Peter the Great before him, he was duly impressed. But whereas the Russian Czar sought to emulate Western technology and culture, Jung Bahadur took home a different lesson – simply that a country like Nepal could never challenge such an empire as Britain's and that the best policy was to maintain her friendship by whatever means possible.

Jung Bahadur had an early opportunity to win favour when, in 1857, certain Indian garrisons rebelled against their British rulers. Known to Indians as the First War of Independence, and to the British as the Indian Mutiny, some of the worst of the fighting occurred in areas immediately adjacent to Nepal. The Hindu kingdom had the choice of coming to the aid of its co-religionists, remaining neutral, or assisting the British. Jung Bahadur did not hesitate to take the latter course. He immediately offered Nepalese troops to help put down the mutiny, and himself led a column 9,000 strong down into the plains. For this he won the undying gratitude of the British, who were content to allow him to run the internal affairs of Nepal as he thought best. A belt of land in the western Terai annexed in 1816 by the East India Company was returned to Nepal as a token of gratitude.

Friendship between the two countries was deepened by Jung Bahadur's actions in facilitating the recruitment of Gurkha soldiers into British-officered regiments. This was to become the cornerstone of Anglo-Nepalese relations, with the Gurkhas fighting alongside Britain with great distinction through two world wars. The reward was British recognition of Nepal as a sovereign and independent nation, thereby placing it on a completely different footing from other Indian princely states. In addition, the generally supportive stance of the British Raj served to prop up the conservative Rana regime until the British left

India in 1947. From then on, the Ranas would have to deal with a very different neighbour to the south.

The strategy of currying favour with the imperial power was not the only thing that Jung Bahadur brought back from his journey to Europe. He realised, too, that the only way to understand the British was to learn their language. Although he made little headway himself, he introduced English-speaking Hindus into his household to teach his sons the rudiments of the language.

He was also won over by European architecture and had the new palace he was building on a hill above the Bagmati River finished with neo-classical flourishes. The internal organisation of Thapthali Darbar, with its separate courtyards for his extended family and an enclosed harem for his many wives and concubines, may have been typically oriental, but from now on the Nepalese court would look increasingly to European fashions as opposed to the more traditional influences of the Mughal emperors in Delhi.

These changing tastes expressed themselves in external forms of display – the cut of a general's uniform, for instance, or the use of European-style horse-drawn carriages – rather than on any deeper cultural plane. Even when the Ranas built themselves mock-Palladian mansions, the cooking and eating arrangements within their households remained governed by Hindu caste rules. Their wives and concubines might have adopted the full skirts and crinolines of Victorian fashion, but they still lived according to the local rules of purdah. Beneath their veneer of sophistication, the new Rana elite were entrenched in their conservatism.

The men felt far freer to adopt European styles in everything from their drinking habits through to their taste in furnishings. A tolerance of alcohol is deeply imbedded in Nepalese culture, even among orthodox Hindus, but from the 1850s onwards their tastes switched to imported wines and brandies rather than the distilled rice liquor, known as *rakshi*, and other local brews. Jung Bahadur's sons led the way, and on most evenings there were marathon drinking bouts taking place in some part of Thapthali Darbar. Some of the young inebriates even took to drinking French perfume to cleanse their breath before they greeted their fathers. More than one young Rana died from alcohol poisoning and many more gambled away their inheritances in the wild sessions that accompanied these parties. Some would stake everything they possessed – lands, villages, concubines and slaves – on the throw of a single dice or, in another popular form of gambling, by casting forth sixteen Kaudi shells.

Their style of dress also shifted from the fashions of the Mughal court towards European models, as can be seen in their preference for Napoleonic-style military uniforms which they had specially designed, with the more gold braid the better. Their bejewelled and plumed helmets required not only quantities of diamonds, emeralds and pearls; for the plume to hang correctly, it had to be made from the tail-feathers of a rare variety of the bird of paradise, found only in faraway New Guinea.

All this represented conspicuous consumption in the extreme – especially against the background of the mind-numbing poverty in which 95 per cent of the population lived. But that was considered to be the 'natural state' of the peasantry. Instead of trying to improve the lot of the peasantry, the rulers of Nepal competed with their princely neighbours in India to possess the latest and most luxurious imports: Belgian chandeliers, French porcelain, Chinese vases, Italian glassware, and British-made musical instruments for the household bands which always accompanied them on formal outings. When they did not eat off European crockery they had exact copies made in solid gold or silver. One of Jung Bahadur's brothers had a silver dinner service for one hundred and seventy guests.

As for their domestic arrangements, the Ranas took the Nepalese practice of polygamy to its logical extreme. Jung Bahadur had more than three dozen wives of varying status, not to mention the two hundred or so concubines and maidservants who were watched over by his palace eunuchs. His eldest son, Jagat Jang, had been married to a royal princess but none the less aspired to rival the parental harem, maintaining a hundred dancing girls, a large troupe of musicians and a theatrical group in his own Manohara Darbar residence. To complete the opulence, he built a private zoo in the grounds and filled it with ostriches and other exotic creatures.

The number of wives and concubines to be maintained – not to mention the dozens of offspring who had to be supported – became a measure of just how important an individual was in the Rana hierarchy. Jung Bahadur may have been a compulsive womaniser, but the size of his entourage was not exceptional compared with those of some of his brothers and his successors. One of the reasons he switched bed-chambers and sleeping partners so regularly was for security, so that nobody intent on assassinating him could be sure where he would be on a given night. Hidden beneath his semi-Westernised exterior was the quintessential Nepali strongman, constantly on his guard and trusting no one. At times he seemed to show more affection for his favourite elephants – the ever reliable Jang Prasad and the bolder Bijuli Prasad, who was so adept at fighting wild tuskers – than for any member of his own family.

The orderliness of Western countries continued to impress Jung Bah-adur. He became convinced that Nepal should adopt a new legal system, and on returning to Kathmandu he immediately began codifying and revising the ancient laws of Nepal which were still largely based on the Hindu *shastras* as interpreted by the Royal Priest and other Brahmins.

The result of all this was the *Muluki Ain* of 1854, the first comprehensive legal code in Nepal's history. The *Muluki Ain* was far-reaching. Trial by ordeal was abolished completely. Death sentences or mutilation were restricted to only the gravest of crimes – such as treason, desertion in the face of the enemy, murder and cow-slaughter. The new legal system asserted that for any crime there should be only one punishment, rather than the previous practice of sentencing people according to their caste. Similarly, the discretion of individual judges in sentencing was severely limited, this having been a source of favouritism and unequal justice.

While it was progressive in many ways, the *Muluki Ain* still had to reflect traditional Hindu values. Nearly a third of its content deals with caste rules and offences. It did not abolish *sati*, although it did exclude child brides and women who were pregnant or had young children from performing it. The minimum age at which a girl could be married was left unchanged at five. Slavery and bonded labour remained enforceable by law. Punishments such as branding, castration and other forms of mutilation were restricted but not abolished completely. Since most of these laws were left unchanged until well into the twentieth century, Nepal appeared to many outsiders to be stuck in a more primitive, feudal age where savage punishment made up for the absence of any effective police force.

Shortly after his return from Europe, Jung Bahadur was able to set an example of the new leniency. His brother, Bam Bahadur, warned him of a plot that was being hatched to assassinate both King Surendra and the Prime Minister and put the King's brother, Prince Upendra, on the throne.

The conspirators, including two of Jung Bahadur's brothers, were quickly arrested and brought before the Council of State to be sentenced. Since a member of the royal family was involved, both King Surendra and his deposed father Rajendra were present, though neither took an active role in the proceedings. All those accused were found guilty of treason and the mandatory death sentence was given. To everyone's surprise, however, Jung Bahadur refused to endorse this; nor would he accept the alternative punishments suggested, that their eyes should be put out with hot irons or that they be transported in cages down to the Terai and abandoned to die of malaria. His final decision was that they be locked up in the fortress at Allahabad under British supervision for thirty years.

By the standards of the times this treatment was exceptionally lenient. Moreover, as soon as the conspirators were safely out of the country, Jung Bahadur commuted their sentences from thirty to five years. It has been suggested that this was because the entire plot was a fabrication invented by Jung Bahadur himself in order to remove potential opponents from Nepal until he felt more secure. If so, this would not be the first – nor the last – time that trumped-up charges were used by a Nepalese ruler to consolidate his position.

In finding his brother guilty and then showing leniency, Jung Bahadur provided a forceful reminder to other members of the royal family as to who was really in charge of Nepal. If the innocent could be so easily condemned, what fate lay in store for those who genuinely plotted against the Prime Minister?

Most of King Surendra's thirty-four-year reign was spent as a virtual prisoner in Hanuman Dhoka Palace. His father, ex-King Rajendra, outlived him by a few months; but the old man was placed under even closer guard in the old palace at Bhaktapur. Throughout his confinement, King Surendra meekly agreed to all his Prime Minister's demands: among them the transfer of all royal authority, marriage alliances between their families, and the creation of a new princely title for Jung Bahadur and his successors.

In 1856 the King conferred upon Jung Bahadur the title of Maharaja of Kaski and Lamjung, both of them small hill states inhabited mainly by the warlike Gurung peoples, which he and his male heirs would rule over in perpetuity. The royal warrant, or *lal mohar*, lists the reasons why the King was 'pleased' with Jung Bahadur: he had previously saved Surendra from conspiracies against his life; secured for him the throne of Nepal; treated his father and younger brother leniently, despite their deadly machinations; and promoted friendship with the Queen of England. In return, the King granted Jung Bahadur not only the princely title of Maharaja but absolute power over life and death throughout Nepal. Furthermore, the King accepted that he could be overruled on all matters of importance. It amounted to a complete abdication of royal authority and any responsibility towards his subjects.

Some members of the royal family, however, could not bring themselves to agree with the terms of Surendra's capitulation. His elder son, Crown Prince Trailokya, was determined to reassert the legitimate authority of the Shah dynasty – to the point of vowing never to accept the crown unless the Ranas were first overthrown – this despite being married to two of Jung Bahadur's daughters, one of whom gave birth to his own son and heir, Prince Prithvi Bir, in 1875. His views were well known to his father-in-law, who kept the Crown Prince under constant surveillance and restricted his movements. He could do little while the all-powerful Prime Minister was alive. But when Jung Bahadur died suddenly in February 1877, of cholera contracted during a hunting trip in the Terai, the situation changed completely.

The next oldest Rana brother, Ranaudip Singh, succeeded to the prime ministership as planned. He also decided to appropriate the title of Maharaja of Kaski and Lamjung, arguing that this was attached to the prime ministerial office. In doing so he disinherited Jung Bahadur's sons. The eldest, Jagat Jang, sought out other malcontents in the hope of reversing this injustice. Top of the list was Crown Prince Trailokya, who had his own reasons for wanting to be rid of the new and not very effective Prime Minister.

How far their conspiracy progressed will never be known, for on 30 March 1878 it was announced that the Crown Prince had died. He was only thirty at the time and his death was most unexpected. The official communiqué from the palace declared that the heir to the throne had succumbed to an unfortunate combination of colic and rheumatic fever.

The whispers in the bazaar, however, were very different. Prince Trailokya, it was said, had been poisoned because of his opposition to Rana rule. The chief suspect was Dhir Shamsher Rana, the Prime Minister's younger brother and right-hand man. If, as is quite likely, these rumours were true, then Crown Prince Trailokya became yet another member of the Shah dynasty who was born to be king but who suffered an untimely and unnatural death.

Six generations had now passed since the reign of Prithvi Narayan Shah. The day of reckoning for the ruling dynasty was still far away, if Gorakhnath's prophecy were to prove correct. Although he never ascended the throne, Trailokya was the eldest son and can therefore be included as a direct heir of the founding monarch. His early death meant that the crown passed directly to his son, Prithvi Bir, thus missing out a generation.

All the signs are that, if Trailokya had survived, he would have been a far more forceful king than either his father or his grandfather before him. That might well have placed him in direct conflict with the Rana establishment, whose interests were best served by having a feeble-minded or weak-willed monarch on the throne of Nepal. His very presence at court was seen as a potential threat to the regime. If he became King, a showdown between the Shahs and the Ranas would have occurred sooner rather than later. For this reason, it was plain to every officer and court functionary that Prime Minister Ranaudip Singh and his allies benefited most from Prince Trailokya's sudden departure.

Just how important it was to the Rana elite that they kept a malleable personality on the throne became obvious when the sixty-one-year-old King Surendra fell seriously ill in the spring of 1881. The Prime Minister and his brother, Dhir Shamsher, were so worried that they tried to keep the royal indisposition secret for as long as possible. They also ordered up twenty additional regiments to bolster security around their own palaces.

What they most feared was an anti-Rana coup in which dissatisfied elements of the old Gorkha nobility combined with Jung Bahadur's dispossessed sons – especially as some of these had an intensely loyal following in the army. They were also worried about a smooth succession to the throne. There was already discontent about the royal infant Prithvi Bir being declared Crown Prince. For, while the prospect of a long minority might suit the Ranas, it spelt doom for anything approaching an effective monarchy. Opponents of this line of succession argued that, because the little prince's mother was a Rana, his lineage was impure. Far better to install on the throne Trailokya's younger brother, Prince Narendra Bikram Shah, who was of pure Rajput blood. Traditionalism and political expediency were mixed in equal measure; but the conspirators' plans to blow up the entire Rana leadership as they assembled in the pagoda-shadowed expanse of Nasal Chowk, the principal courtyard in Hanuman Dhoka Palace where coronations and all important gatherings were held, failed to materialise in time.

King Surendra's death was announced on 17 May 1881. His five-year-old grandson, Prithvi Bir, was immediately installed on the throne of Nepal. As an additional security measure, Prime Minister Ranaudip Singh removed the young King from the Old Royal Palace where his uncle and other members of the royal family had easy access to him. Breaking with tradition, Prithvi Bir was brought up in a wing of the Prime Minister's own palace, Narayanhiti Mathillo Darbar, which from then on became the principal residence of the Shah kings of Nepal.

The grandiose new palace that Ranaudip Singh had built in the European style lay well outside the crowded centre of Kathmandu, so the King could be kept at a safe distance from his subjects. Its lofty ceilings, marbled floors and pillared galleries were deemed a more fitting environment for the boy-King to grow up in. There were extensive grounds in which he could ride his ponies. More importantly, it was easier to keep an eye on him there than in Hanuman Dhoka's jumble of courtyards and corridors. Access to the King's person was severely restricted, with even close family members being barred from entering Narayanhiti. A gilded cage was created to keep Nepal's monarchs completely isolated from their subjects. The young Prithvi Bir had little choice but to accept these changed circumstances. He knew no other kind of life.

Such precautions seemed to be justified when, within the year, a plot was 'discovered' to assassinate the Rana leadership and remove the King from the throne. More than a hundred conspirators, including many members of the old Gorkha nobility, were arrested and forced to make confessions. These implicated both the King's uncle, Prince Narendra, and Jagat Jang, who was then on pilgrimage in India. Whether they were actually involved in any plot is doubtful; but it suited the Prime Minister and Dhir Shamsher to have all possible rivals removed. The leniency of their sentences – five years' incarceration under British supervision at a faraway hill station in south India –

suggests they were completely innocent. By contrast, twenty-three less exalted conspirators were beheaded with *kukris* on the banks of the Bagmati. They too pleaded their innocence at the end, but the Rana leadership thought that a stern example needed to be set.

The Prime Minister was still worried about his personal security, however, and built up an extensive network of spies and informers. He also surrounded his residence at Narayanhiti Darbar with hand-picked soldiers of the Guards Regiment who were to prevent anyone entering unless they could give that day's secret password. But even the most comprehensive security arrangements can fail if the person they are supposed to be protecting is too trusting. In the case of Ranaudip Singh, his overreliance on Dhir Shamsher and his sons was to lead to his downfall.

The root cause of the problem was the absence of male heirs. Although Ranaudip Singh had three wives and kept numerous concubines and dancing girls, he had no sons; and as he grew older he became increasingly religious and addicted to hashish. He might be Prime Minister, but he was unable to take decisions.

This was not a matter of urgency so long as his strong-willed brother Dhir Shamsher was alive, because, according to the Roll of Succession, he would eventually become Prime Minister. But when Dhir Shamsher died in late 1884, creating a political vacuum at the top, various Ranas of the next generation started jostling for position. This alarmed Ranaudip Singh so much that he insisted that every senior Rana accompany him on his winter hunting trip to the Terai, so as to prevent any conspiracies being hatched back in Kathmandu. That did not solve the question of who was to succeed him, however.

The main protagonists were the seven sons of Jung Bahadur, who should have taken precedence, and the seventeen sons of the late Dhir Shamsher, whose hopes of promotion had been so suddenly dashed. If either camp managed to seize power, their opponents knew exactly what to expect. Banishment would be the most merciful outcome. So both these rival branches of the Rana family solicited the support of persons of influence. The Queen Mother, Lalit Kumari, and Tara

Kumari and other members of the royal family became deeply involved. Even the Prime Minister's own household was divided, with his senior and junior wives backing opposite sides. Once again, faction ruled in Kathmandu. Sooner or later a showdown was inevitable.

6

The Shamsher Supremacy

All the advantages in a forthcoming showdown seemed to lie with the sons of Jung Bahadur. They were far wealthier than their Shamsher cousins, their allies held more important offices in the government, and they had better contacts into the royal family. Perhaps this gave them a false sense of security. While they played a waiting game, the Shamsher Ranas were secretly organising a daring coup d'état.

Their planning was meticulous. They secured the loyalty of four regiments stationed in the Kathmandu Valley and bribed key advisers to the Prime Minister, his personal secretary and the commandant of his bodyguard, in advance. They also saw fit to consult their family astrologer on what would be an auspicious date for so dangerous an undertaking.

On the evening of 22 November 1885, six of the Shamsher brothers rode over to the Prime Minister's residence in Narayanhiti. They had been informed of the password and were allowed through the main gate. The eldest brother, Bir Shamsher, waited on the ground floor where he was joined by the King's great-uncle, Prince Upendra, who had been summoned to convey royal approval of what was to follow.

Four of the younger brothers, all of them wearing greatcoats, went upstairs in the direction of the Prime Minister's private apartments. There they were met by a senior foreign affairs official who had already been bribed. When challenged by two bodyguards, they claimed to be bringing an urgent communication from the British Resident and indicated the foreign office minister who was accompanying them. While one of the guards rushed to seek orders from the ADC General, the other was browbeaten into allowing them to pass. When the brothers found the door to Ranaudip Singh's room bolted, they simply stressed the urgency of their message. The Prime Minister told a houseboy to open up and the four brothers marched in.

There they found Ranaudip Singh relaxing on a couch, with two maidservants massaging his feet while his private secretary read the newspapers to him. His overbearing senior wife, who had championed the rival claims of Jung Bahadur's sons, was resting on a velvet-covered bed. The assassins pulled their carbines from their greatcoats and took aim. One of them shouted 'This is the fate of those who rule from beneath a petticoat!', then each of them fired in turn, the family drunkard Rana Shamsher apparently missing the target. After checking that their uncle was well and truly dead, the assassins wrapped his blood-stained corpse inside a carpet and threw it down the staircase.

Members of the palace guard finally tried to intervene, but they were soon overpowered by Bir Shamsher's men. Two of the brothers then went to the royal apartments in Narayanhiti and took custody of the boy-King, carrying him out through his bedroom window. Down in the courtyard, the Queen Mother was ready to affix the royal seal of approval on pre-prepared documents appointing Bir Shamsher Rana as Prime Minister and Maharaja. The next step was to win the army's approval, so the ten-year-old King and his mother were made to ride with Bir Shamsher in a state carriage to the Tundikhel parade ground. Those regiments loyal to the Shamshers had been placed on alert and none of the other, mainly unarmed, troops offered resistance. The Queen Mother duly announced that the old Prime Minister had died of natural causes and that Bir Shamsher was appointed in his place. The assembled soldiery presented arms and fired off a nineteen-gun salute in his honour.

There followed the inevitable purge of all opposition. A detachment of troops loyal to the Shamsher brothers was dispatched to Jagat Jang's residence before dawn, and the eldest of Jung Bahadur's sons was shot on sight. Others gained news of the coup before they could be apprehended and most of them – including the King's uncle Prince

Narendra and the Senior Queen Mother – sought sanctuary with the British Resident. One of Jagat Jang's sons foolishly returned to the family palace at Thapthali to gather up whatever jewels and valuables he could find. Although in disguise, he ran into an army patrol and was shot dead in the street.

The whole of Kathmandu was now placed under martial law. Its normally bustling streets and bazaars were deserted except for army patrols guarding the crossroads or raiding private houses to arrest supporters of the previous regime. After lengthy negotiations, the eminent refugees inside the British Residency were granted safe conduct to India and, since they were not allowed to take any property with them, a life of impoverished exile. The immense fortunes amassed by Jung Bahadur and his brothers were confiscated, the Roll of Succession altered so as to exclude all who were not of the Shamsher branch of the family, and the top civil and military commands distributed among the seventeen brothers in strict order of seniority.

Similarly, the palaces and jewellery and private estates of the departed were divided up between the brothers. Bir Shamsher took the lion's share, including the jewelled headdress, the great hoard of coins and precious stones, one hundred state elephants and their equipage, as well as the extensive lands which had belonged to his dead uncle. But he made sure that enough was distributed to retain the loyalty of the entire Shamsher clan. He knew that he needed their support if he was not to suffer the same fate as the last Prime Minister.

The Shamshers' coup d'état had been meticulously planned and boldly executed. Given that they had no legitimate claim to rule Nepal, there was surprisingly little resistance. The mere presence of the boy-King Prithvi Bir at the Tundikhel parade ground was enough to convince the army that the new Prime Minister was acting in his name. Their oath of loyalty was to the King alone, and the habit of unquestioning obedience to whoever was in authority was so deeply ingrained that they were unable to react in a crisis. Quite apart from which, it did not really matter to ordinary soldiers or, for that matter, the great majority of the Nepalese people, which group of Ranas held power. Life went on much the same as before, no matter who was in control.

From exile, attempts were made by the sons of Jung Bahadur to send assassins into Nepal and mount a counter coup, but these conspiracies were all discovered and ruthlessly suppressed. At first the British authorities in India hesitated to recognise a regime that had so blatantly usurped power. However, the view of the British Resident in Kathmandu was that there was not much to choose between Jung Bahadur's family, who were 'equally steeped in blood', and 'the present Minister and his family who are as bad as they can be'. His assessment was that 'unless we mean to change our whole policy towards Nepal, and to abandon strict neutrality for active interference, it seems to me that it does not matter to us which set of cut-throats has the upper hand'.

Such pragmatism would pay immense dividends, for the Shamsher Ranas were to rule Nepal for the next sixty-five years. From the British perspective, they provided stability in a sensitive border area. They also assisted in the continued recruitment of Gurkha soldiers when they were most needed. Around 100,000 Nepalese would serve during the First World War, including the Mesopotamian campaign and on the Western Front, while more than twice that number would fight alongside Britain during the Second World War. The Rana government even sent its own regiments for active service and raised loans to help the war effort. Understandably, the British were not going to undermine so potentially helpful an ally, and no matter what went on inside Nepal they continued to give their tacit support to whoever was its *de facto* ruler.

Britain's recognition of Bir Shamsher's government gave some legitimacy to the new Rana regime, but the entire authority of these hereditary Prime Ministers rested on the fiction that they served the legitimate ruler of Nepal, the King. Such a fiction was easy to maintain while King Prithvi Bir remained a minor, but as he approached adulthood his Prime Minister grew increasingly worried that he might become the figurehead for anti-Rana conspiracies. While the King and his immediate family were kept isolated in Narayanhiti Palace, too many of his half-brothers and cousins were allowed to visit him there.

In particular, there were five male relatives who bore the title of Sahebju, or Count, who lived in various wings of the old Hanuman Dhoka Palace and were at liberty to mix with people in the streets of Kathmandu's Old City. On most afternoons they came to see King Prithvi Bir at Narayanhiti, providing him with much-needed companionship, and very often stayed on for dinner. Bir Shamsher worried that they might be bringing him adverse reports about his government and decided to have them removed. The pretext was a rather sumptuous dinner they had with the King at which partridges and copious amounts of alcohol were consumed. The next day they were summoned by the Prime Minister and accused of inciting the King to drunkenness and debauchery. For this largely imagined 'crime' they were exiled to remote hill districts and had their state pensions greatly reduced.

The loss of his closest companions angered Prithvi Bir so much that he declared he would leave Narayanhiti Palace, complaining about the endless supervision of his life. He had even started packing before, at the Prime Minister's urgent request, the Queen Mother Lalit Rajya Laxmi intervened and persuaded him to calm down and remain in his palace. This tantrum was about as close to independent action as this particular King of Nepal ever came.

By the age of twelve Prithvi Bir was already married to two Indian princesses of Rajput stock. This did not prevent the Prime Minister from cementing his family relationship with the Shah dynasty by arranging for the King to marry two of his own daughters – even though they were only eight and nine years old when the wedding was celebrated. Bir Shamsher was following the matrimonial policy his uncle Jung Bahadur had established a generation earlier. But for the Queen Mother, who had been complaisant to most of his previous requests, it was a step too far. She was, after all, Jung Bahadur's daughter, and the thought of a girl from this junior branch of the Ranas becoming the potential mother of a king was abhorrent to her.

She could not prevent the marriage alliance, but once the Junior Queens arrived in Narayanhiti Palace they fell within her sphere of influence. To begin with she was not too worried, since they were still too young for the marriage to be consummated. But once they reached puberty, the Queen Mother took matters into her own hands. She ensured that pretty and compliant maidservants were constantly being brought into the presence of the King on those days that it was the turn of his two junior wives to sleep with him. Her son was therefore so exhausted by his sexual exploits that no heir apparent could be conceived by these particular daughters-in-law.

Queen Mother Lalit had very practical reasons for promoting such devious stratagems. If a daughter of these Shamsher Ranas became pregnant and her child was declared Crown Prince, the balance of power within the palace would shift decisively against the Queen Mother. The second reason for her taking against these Junior Queens was that their parents had never been formally married: they were little better than the daughters of concubines. In her view, neither girl was suitable material to be the mother of a king – even if their father happened to be Prime Minister and enormously wealthy. Their dowries might, however, be far larger than those of Prithvi Bir's two Senior Queens. The youngest, who was reportedly becoming the King's favourite, had been given an enormous eighty-two carat diamond.

In the end, the Queen Mother got her way. On 30 June 1906 Queen Laxmi Dibyeshwari gave birth to a boy child who was to become King Tribhuvan. His mother was a senior queen of Indian descent and not one of the upstart Shamsher Rana girls.

The Kingdom of Nepal continued to be administered as if it were a large family business, whose only purpose was further to enrich the ruling elite. Such changes as were introduced were mainly in revenue collection and administration. The more efficient these were, the greater the income enjoyed by the hereditary Prime Minister and the senior generals.

A disproportionate share of the nation's wealth was set aside for the army. This was partly to ensure its loyalty, and partly because all the senior positions in the Rana hierarchy below Prime Minister were military commands. To keep such powerful allies required enormous salaries. But apart from a couple of brief and unprofitable border clashes with Tibet, there was not much for the army to do. They marched around the Tundikhel parade ground to make their presence felt in the capital, their only real purpose being to provide a threat of force. This was the mainstay of the Rana autocracy.

The old quasi-feudal system of rewarding the rank and file with temporary land grants, or *jagirs*, was abandoned in favour of cash payments. As a result, a huge area of what were technically Crown lands was freed up, but the Crown did not benefit from this. Neither did the ordinary hill farmers, who continued to scratch a subsistence living from their meagre plots. The main beneficiaries of land transfers were the Rana nobles, who regularly rewarded themselves 'for services rendered' with grants of *birta* land. The cumulative effect was that around a third of all cultivable land in Nepal was reclassified as *birta*, and most of this was owned by a handful of Rana families. They also awarded themselves state-sponsored monopolies and most of the new lands being reclaimed from the Terai's forests. As a result, the Ranas grew exceedingly rich – far richer than the royal family, whose income was strictly controlled by the Prime Minister.

Some Ranas invested their surplus income in trade, though mostly it went on building palaces and on ostentatious living. They soon abandoned the indigenous Newari style of palace architecture, prefer-ring to live in grandiose and usually uncomfortable pseudo-European piles outside Old Kathmandu. Although three dozen of these mock-Palladian palaces survive from the Rana period, they are not much admired these days. This may be because they are florid and overblown: the chaste principles of classical design are constantly subverted by excessive ornamentation. Most Rana buildings, including the original Narayanhiti Royal Palace, owed less to the generally austere colonial architecture of the British themselves than to extremely fanciful variants of the style adopted by Maharajas and Nawabs under British rule. Their high ceilings made them impossible to heat in winter, but practicality was never an important consideration. They were built to impress the visitor. Their sweeping driveways and marble-lined entrance halls were there to declare the importance of their owner in the Rana hierarchy, and not much else.

The appearance of Kathmandu was completely transformed by this spate of building activity. Where once rice fields had advanced to the very walls of the Old City, now the surrounding countryside was dotted with stucco palaces surrounded by walled gardens or open parkland. A broad avenue was created linking Narayanhiti Palace and the Tundikhel parade ground so that the King, accompanied by his Prime Minister and generals, could form a grand procession without having to enter the Old City's narrow streets. This Durbar Marg, or 'Royal Way', became the main axis of the new and far more spacious city growing up beyond Kathmandu's historic limits. As each successive Prime Minister sought to outdo his predecessors, larger and more splendid Rana palaces went up to the north and east of the capital, culminating in the immense Singha Durbar. With its own theatre, a grandiose assembly hall and more than a thousand rooms set around seven grand courtyards, it was reputed to be the largest palace in Asia. Nobody dared surpass Singha Durbar, and it subsequently became the Prime Minister's official residence and seat of his government.

The other symbol of highest rank was the right to engage in big-game hunting, or *shikar*, down in the forests and marshlands of the Terai. Every winter season, the Prime Minister would set off from Kathmandu with an entourage that sometimes numbered several thousand. The King, the Crown Prince, the top generals and other leading Ranas would usually take part in these hunting expeditions. Several hundred trained elephants and thousands of local guides and beaters were employed to corral all the wild animals within a cordoned off area and funnel them into the designated killing grounds. There, the honoured guests would be waiting, either in a hide raised on poles or mounted on elephants, their high-powered hunting rifles at the ready. On one occasion more than three hundred tigers were killed in a single hunt.

The prodigious scale of hunting expeditions in the Nepalese Terai was unusual. But similar tiger shoots went on all over British India, and especially in the quasi-independent Princely States whose rulers — be they Maharajas or Nizams or Nawabs — liked to hide their political impotence behind a façade of refined manners, luxury and ostentation. Much the same could be said of the Shah kings of Nepal during their 'period of captivity'. They were encouraged to be frivolous because this reduced the likelihood of any future King ever trying to reclaim his rightful authority. Again, there was nothing unusual about this — at least not in the milieu of Indian princely courts. An endless round of picnics, polo matches and hunting expeditions were part and parcel of the listless Maharajas' lifestyle.

Nepal's royal family imbibed this culture and adapted it to local conditions in their mountainous kingdom. The aspect of life in which tradition tended to prevail was in culinary arrangements — as caste Hindus it was essential that all their food be prepared by members of the appropriate caste — and in the dress and headgear of ladies of the court. Even then there was a strong compulsion to follow European fashions, though the elaborately curled tresses and pillbox hats worn by queens and ladies-in-waiting were still a feature of the Nepalese court far into the twentieth century.

The Ranas did at least enhance the independent status of Nepal. Full recognition by Britain in 1923 was of great significance, even though it was granted mainly in thanks for the Gurkha regiments' loyal service during the Great War. Among other things, it meant that the King was henceforth addressed by both his own subjects and foreign dignitaries as 'His Majesty', as opposed to merely 'His Highness'.

There was also a fairly smooth transition of government from one hereditary Prime Minister to the next most senior Rana on the Roll of Succession. Not a single Rana Prime Minister was assassinated after the Shamsher brothers' coup of 1885. Although there were plenty of conspiracies, these were confined solely to the ruling elite, and the country remained unified.

There were, however, obvious weaknesses in this hereditary system of government – quite apart from its dubious legitimacy. One was that, when they finally inherited the highest office, each Prime Minister was tempted to do all that he could to enrich himself and advance the prospects of his own family. This was not even considered to be corrupt: there was no distinction between public finances and what the Prime Minister claimed for himself. Moreover, the longer a Prime Minister remained in office, the more comfortable and secure became the position of his immediate family. Some of them clung on to office for decades, and hence those next in line on the Roll of Succession grew progressively older until the regime was ultimately run by a group of deeply reactionary greybeards.

Another temptation was for the Prime Minister to tamper with the Roll of Succession in favour of his own immediate family. Given the Ranas' penchant for taking multiple wives and concubines, there were usually many younger sons and bastards who needed suitable positions in the army or in government service. The danger here was that any adjustment in their favour set back the prospects of other branches of the Rana family, thereby undermining the broad consensus upon which this self-serving regime depended for its survival.

Each time the consensus broke down, the conspiracies began all over again. At least two Rana Prime Ministers were forcibly removed from office. The first to go was Dev Shamsher, whose hold on office lasted just over a hundred days. He was duped into going to his younger brother Chandra Shamsher's house on the pretext of sorting out a private dispute over property. Once inside, the Prime Minister was overpowered and trussed up in his own cummerbund. The coup almost went wrong when soldiers of the Bijuli Garad, the Prime Minister's personal bodyguard, refused to believe their master had been relieved of his office by royal command. But Chandra Shamsher still had an ace up his sleeve. King Prithvi Bir had been brought along in advance, and now he was wheeled out before the restive troops. Somewhat hesitantly, he called the guards to order and pronounced that he had himself appointed a new Prime Minister. As usual, the King's presence was

1. Feeble minded but cruel, King Surendra had his father deposed and handed power to the Ranas.

14. The first coronation of Prince Gyanendra in 1950, during the final days of the Rana regime.

15. Fifty-one years later, Prince Gyanendra is enthroned again after the royal massacre.

enough to overawe the soldiers, and the bloodless coup went ahead. Dev Shamsher was sent into exile, first to eastern Nepal and then into India, where he lived out his days comfortably on a Nepalese government pension.

Chandra Shamsher ruled Nepal for the next twenty-eight years, during which time his branch of the Ranas amassed such wealth that even today his heirs are among the wealthiest in Nepal. It was he who devised a new system of classifying the legitimacy of Rana offspring and their relative position on the Roll of Succession. The children of a husband and wife of equal caste were declared to be 'A' class Ranas, and in future only these could be promoted to the highest offices. The children of marriages between different castes were made 'B' class Ranas, while the illegitimate offspring of lower caste women became 'C' class Ranas. Neither 'B' nor 'C' class Ranas could rise above the military rank of colonel, which effectively excluded them from holding high office. Chandra Shamsher justified these changes as being necessary to achieve an orderly succession, though his real motive was probably to remove rival branches of Ranas from the Roll and so clear the way for his own 'A' class sons.

Almost inevitably, such an exclusive and caste-driven pecking order threw up some astounding anomalies. Two-year-old boys were promoted to general, while hardy veterans had to make do with a colonel's salary. It also created jealousies and divisions beneath the apparent unity of Rana rule. Subsequent prime ministers tinkered with the order to promote their own 'C' class sons, but the triple classification lasted as long as the Ranas remained in power.

The most dramatic overhaul came in 1932 when Prime Minister Juddha Shamsher summoned the entire Rana hierarchy to his residence at Singha Durbar. With machine guns covering the entrance, an armed ADC ensured that everyone was in attendance. Again, the royal presence was used to confer legitimacy on the proceedings. The twenty-five-year-old King Tribhuvan was not even required to speak, but merely entered the room and smoked two cigarettes before departing. The Prime Minister himself then entered with a pistol in each hand

and declared that half the assembled company, including the next in line to become Prime Minister, were struck off the Roll and would immediately be sent into exile. Nobody dared resist, and this variation on the bloodless purge went ahead unhindered.

King Tribhuvan may have helped out on this occasion, but his relations with his Prime Minister were becoming increasingly strained. For, despite his restrictive upbringing within the confines of Narayanhiti Palace, Tribhuvan was both open-minded and more decisive than his forebears. In stark contrast, Juddha Shamsher was an old-style military man whose only response to any calls for change in Nepal was heavy-handed repression. His first instinct was to stand by tradition and defend the status quo.

True, some much-needed changes had been introduced by his predecessors – including the abolition of *sati* in 1920, and the granting of freedom to some 60,000 Nepalese who still lived in slavery in 1924. But in most other respects Nepal remained locked in a feudal age while all around it change was gathering pace. Some aspects of modernity made their way in, to the capital at least. A handful of Nepali language schools were opened, the first newspaper established, a new Post Office and showpiece military hospital constructed. Piped water and electricity was made available to the wealthier residents of Kathmandu. But there was no attempt to bring development to the scattered villages where 90 per cent of Nepalis lived in conditions that had changed little since Prithvi Narayan's time.

Instead, the status quo was to be protected by keeping the Kingdom of Nepal in complete isolation from the changing world outside its borders. Apart from staff at the British Residency and a handful of technical experts, no foreigners were permitted to enter Nepal. It remained a forbidden kingdom. All the early mountaineering expeditions which attempted to climb Everest had to approach it by a very roundabout route through Tibet, the more direct access through Nepalese territory being barred to foreigners.

Plans to build a road link to India were discussed but turned down on the grounds that this would open up the country to foreign invasion. That did not, however, prevent the Rana elite from importing their Rolls-Royces, Hispano-Suizas and Cadillacs, though these had to be carried by teams of porters over two mountain ranges before they reached the capital. Upon their arrival, thousands of labourers were then employed to build a few miles of tarmac road so that the notables could show off their latest acquisitions. Nepal's elite took great pride in these manifestations of 'progress'. One senior Rana boasted to an Indian Maharaja whose collection of limousines was confined to the palace garage because there were no motorable roads within his Princely State: 'At least *we* have the roads to drive them on.'

It was not only foreign luxuries that were coming over the mountains. Even the Ranas' policy of deliberate isolation could not prevent new ideas from creeping in. Gurkha soldiers returning to their villages brought with them a broader perspective of the world, while just across the border Indian nationalists and pro-democracy activists were mounting a growing challenge to the British Raj. For all its mountain ramparts, Nepal could not remain completely immune to these new ideas. Nepalese exiles seeking a fairer and more democratic government in their home country began forming the first political parties. They were joined by some of the wealthy, highly educated and now disinherited 'C' class Ranas, who had their own reasons for opposing the regime in Kathmandu.

Both King Tribhuvan and Crown Prince Mahendra were sympathetic to these liberal ideas. They also wanted to restore the Crown's authority, as is apparent from a conversation they had with the British Representative in Kathmandu. He quotes them as saying: 'We and only we are the descendants of the Sisodia Rajputs and Nepal belongs to us. We, not the descendants of Jung Bahadur nor of Dhir Shamsher, are the hereditary rulers. Under the present system we are kept practically in captivity and have to look to the Prime Minister for our daily bread, the necessities of life and even our private money. Each Prime Minister, while in office, collects all revenue, pays all salaries and amasses all the wealth he can for himself and his immediate family, with the result that there is no progress in Nepal nor prospect of development.' For the first time, the Shah dynasty's right to rule Nepal was being linked with ideas such as 'progress' and 'development'.

Since the royal family were always under the closest surveillance they tended to keep their liberal sympathies to themselves. There were other instances, however, in which King Tribhuvan was better placed to stand up to his domineering Prime Minister. Like so many of his Rana predecessors, Juddha Shamsher sought marriage alliances with the royal family. He succeeded in marrying his granddaughter to Crown Prince Mahendra in 1940, and subsequently arranged for two of his great-granddaughters to marry the younger royal brothers Himalaya and Basundhara. But when he also asked that three royal princesses be given in marriage to three of his sons, the King prevaricated. It was known that the old despot suffered from diabetes and was thinking of retiring from office to devote himself to religion as a 'royal hermit'. King Tribhuvan's waiting game paid off, and Juddha Shamsher resigned the prime ministership before any further weddings could take place.

The new Prime Minister might just have bridged the gulf between Nepal's backward-looking society and the modern world. In his first public address, Padma Shamsher declared himself to be 'the servant of the people', and despite the opposition of conservative Ranas he pressed for a new constitution with a partially elected legislature. But he had neither great wealth nor enough support among the Rana hierarchy to push through his plans. Some of his advisers suggested he stage a coup d'état and have his Commander-in-Chief Mohan Shamsher and other arch-conservatives assassinated, but he could not contemplate so heinous a crime as murdering his own blood relations. Instead, fearful for his own life, he fled to India where he was eventually prevailed upon to tender his resignation in return for a handsome pension.

With that, Mohan Shamsher assumed the titles of hereditary Prime Minister and Maharaja of Kaski and Lamjung. He was the last Rana to be so instated, and the three years that he ruled Nepal were a desperate rearguard action against political activists, bomb plots, incursions by pro-democracy guerrillas, and increasingly strained relations with King Tribhuvan and other members of the royal family. Rather than try to accommodate some of these pressures, Mohan Shamsher ordered waves of mass arrests and relied exclusively on the most reactionary of his Rana relatives. But then another assassination plot was discovered in September 1950, and this time the implications were far more serious. Mohan Shamsher could not be certain, but it looked as if the King himself was involved in the conspiracy.

7

King Tribhuvan & Sons

King Tribhuvan had been a bewildered five-year-old when he ascended the throne of Nepal in 1911. For the next thirty-nine years, like so many of his ancestors he was kept as a prisoner in Narayanhiti Palace. Throughout that period he learned to hide his real thoughts and feelings from a succession of overbearing Prime Ministers. But he was also aware that, in the last resort, their authority depended on the control they had over the King's person. If he could engineer a way to escape that control, then Rana claims to govern on his behalf would be revealed for what they were – a fiction. The legitimacy of the Rana regime would crumble. So he began to plot to free himself and his family from the clutches of his latest Prime Minister, Mohan Shamsher.

It was not easy. The King had to request his Prime Minister's permission even to go outside the palace grounds. On the rare occasions that this was permitted he was always surrounded by secret police. Even within the palace, there were so many spies and informers that Tribhuvan could not confide his plans to anyone outside his own immediate family. So it was to his two younger sons, Himalaya and Basundhara, that he entrusted the most delicate of missions. They were to make contact with officials at the Indian Embassy and sound out whether cooperation would be forthcoming for a daring escape plan.

Although less closely guarded than the King, the young princes' movements were also monitored by the police. On one occasion they were followed to an Indian diplomat's house and had to escape through the back while their host stalled their pursuers in his living room.

India's newly independent and democratic government took a dim view of the Rana regime. The very fact that Jawaharlal Nehru headed the world's largest democracy was the culmination of a long struggle for freedom and representative government. The Ranas had deliberately prevented Nepal from moving down a similar road. If anything, they were moving in the opposite direction.

With Nehru's blessing, the Indian Embassy in Kathmandu was secretly instructed to assist the Nepalese royal family. Mohan Shamsher, meanwhile, had grown ever more suspicious, especially after the King refused to ratify the death sentences passed on some conspirators who had planned his own assassination. The Prime Minister therefore decided to remove Tribhuvan and place the King's eldest son, Mahendra, on the throne. When the Crown Prince declined, the Prime Minister considered banishing the entire royal family to their ancestral palace in Gorkha. Both sides had an inkling of what the other was planning, but no one knew who would move first.

On 4 November 1950, King Tribhuvan drove himself over to Singha Durbar and requested the Prime Minister's permission to go out on a family picnic while the weather remained warm. Mohan Shamsher assumed that this was merely a cover, that the King must have somehow learned about his own secret plans for dealing with recalcitrant royals, and was now trying to provoke him into giving the game away. He therefore readily granted his assent to so innocent a request as a picnic. The date was set for 6 November. The King then returned to Narayanhiti, taking the opportunity to practise his driving technique. There had been few occasions to do so previously.

It was an unusual convoy that pulled out of the palace gates on the morning of 6 November. As usual, a pilot car filled with security guards led the way. Next came the King, at the wheel of his own car, followed by his three sons who were also driving their own vehicles. Also aboard were Tribhuvan's two Queens and his grandson, the five-year-old Prince Birendra. The King had discreetly issued handguns to all adult male members of the family.

The motorcade left Narayanhiti Palace and turned north towards a forested area outside Kathmandu where they were supposed to have their picnic. In fact, their destination was a Rana palace called Sital Niwas which then served as a temporary base for the Indian Embassy. Conveniently, it lay along their route. As the lead vehicle approached its entrance, the Indian Military Attaché swung the gates open. King Tribhuvan took a sharp left into the embassy grounds. He was followed by his three sons. It all happened so quickly that the Nepalese soldiers guarding the gate had no time to respond. Within a matter of seconds, Nepal's ruling family were safely within the embassy compound and claiming political asylum.

The royal family were now barricaded within the Indian Embassy, exiles within their own country, while feverish negotiations went on between the Indian and Nepalese governments. It was a bizarre situation, equivalent today to the entire British royal family seeking asylum inside the American Embassy in Grosvenor Square because they did not approve of the way the country was being run.

When Mohan Shamsher heard of the royal escape he was at a complete loss as to what to do next. He sent his own son to beg an audience and plead with the King to return to his own palace; but Tribhuvan refused, demanding more concrete assurances. Some of the hardline Rana generals wanted to storm the embassy compound and bring out the royal family by force, but that would almost certainly have provoked a massive military response from India. Other expedients had to be found.

The embattled Rana regime formally deposed King Tribhuvan and installed the only male heir left under their control, his younger grandson, Prince Gyanendra, on the throne of Nepal. The three-year-old boy had no idea what was going on as he was taken to Hanuman Dhoka and the bejewelled crown placed on his head for the first time. After a stand-off lasting four days, the rest of the royal family were allowed to board an Indian Air Force plane and were flown to New Delhi. They might have been going into exile, but the royal family were at last freed from the constraints imposed by their Rana prime ministers.

*   *   *

Jawaharlal Nehru, India's first Prime Minister, welcomed the royal refugees from Kathmandu as his personal guests. He had his own plans for Nepal. Firstly, he refused to recognise the boy-King Gyanendra as a legitimate sovereign and persuaded Great Britain and the United States, the only other countries which then had diplomatic relations with Nepal, to follow his lead. As a result, Mohan Shamsher's government was denied international recognition. Instead, it was treated as a pariah regime.

Meanwhile, pro-democracy guerrillas based in India crossed into Nepal and fought several skirmishes with army troops loyal to the Ranas. There followed a series of mass demonstrations around Kathmandu demanding that King Tribhuvan be reinstated as the rightful monarch. Support from within the Rana family was crumbling, with highly placed 'C' class Ranas refusing to cooperate and some of them even leading their troops to mutiny. The internal situation was deteriorating fast, carrying with it the threat of anarchy and civil war on India's sensitive northern border. Nehru certainly did not want that. India's interests, he thought, would best be served by a more limited and peaceful revolution. So he proposed the King Tribhuvan be restored and an interim government set up under him made up of equal numbers of Rana and Nepali Congress ministers. It took time to persuade the various parties, but eventually they all signed up to the so-called 'Delhi Compromise'.

On 15 February 1951, King Tribhuvan flew back to Kathmandu and a rapturous welcome. As he came down the steps of an Indian Air Force DC-3 Dakota, the King was flanked by B. P. Koirala and other pro-democracy leaders whose activists had helped in overthrowing the Rana regime, as if to symbolise that kingship was now inseparably linked with progress and democracy. They were greeted somewhat frostily by Mohan Shamsher, but as the King was driven from the airfield to Narayanhiti Palace thousands of cheering citizens lined the way. On that February day, the King of Nepal reassumed his rightful authority once again after a gap of more than a hundred years.

*   *   *

It was the oddest of revolutions – half-monarchist and half-populist in inspiration, and thoroughly inconclusive in its end results. While it brought an end to Rana rule, the first Prime Minister appointed under the new dispensation was none other than Mohan Shamsher Rana. The inner contradictions of the 'Delhi Compromise' soon made themselves felt. The populist and revolutionary leaders could scarcely sit around the same cabinet table as their Rana colleagues, let alone agree on what should be done. The interim government therefore fell apart, only to be replaced by a succession of equally unworkable and short-lived coalitions. Armed militants briefly took over the Prime Minister's residence at Singha Durbar, there was rioting in the streets, and once again Kathmandu was placed under a curfew. King Tribhuvan may have toppled the Rana autocracy, but he was incapable of putting anything workable in its place. Perhaps the only pleasure he had during the four chaotic years of his rule was to see his old enemy, Mohan Shamsher, dismissed from office and go into permanent exile in India.

He felt betrayed by his own family when his son and heir, Crown Prince Mahendra, insisted on marrying another granddaughter of the old tyrant Juddha Shamsher. The King, his Queens and most of the royal family were against any match with the detested Ranas, but Mahendra was determined to stand up against his parents over the choice of his bride. In doing so he ran up against time-honoured Hindu traditions of filial obedience and unquestioning acceptance of arranged marriages. But Mahendra had his own reasons for sticking to his decision.

While his first wife and the mother of his six children, Princess Indra, lay dying, she begged him to remarry her own sister, and he agreed. The main reason, apparently, was that the younger sister, Ratna, could be trusted to bring up the children as her own and not provide an alternative line of succession. The decision could be seen as statesmanlike: for some of the worst tragedies that had befallen the Shah dynasty arose from the ambition of a junior queen to replace the rightful heir to the throne with her own child.

King Tribhuvan did not see things that way. He objected to the proposed match largely because Ratna was the granddaughter of Juddha Shamsher, the same overweening despot who had tried to marry off his grandsons to three royal princesses. Tribhuvan had scotched those wedding plans. He did not now want to see the Crown Prince marrying another of Juddha's descendants. So when Prince Mahendra insisted on the match, his father threatened either to strip him of his royal titles or, as a last resort, to abdicate and go into exile.

The headstrong prince would not be intimidated and the wedding took place anyway at Nagarjun, outside Kathmandu, in December 1952. Neither King Tribhuvan nor his two Queens attended the marriage ceremony; but in the end he did not exclude the Crown Prince from the royal succession. Within three years of that unrecognised wedding, Tribhuvan was dead, Mahendra was crowned, and his second wife became Queen Ratna Rajya Laxmi.

A precedent had now been set as to how a Crown Prince could defy his parents over marriage plans and still win out. The lesson would not have been lost on Mahendra's grandson, one Crown Prince Dipendra, when at the beginning of the twenty-first century he faced similar parental disapproval over his choice of bride. Especially not as Queen Ratna, by that time Nepal's septuagenarian Queen Mother, was still very much around. She had kept her part of the bargain with her sister and future husband. There had been no children. Instead, Queen Ratna played a pivotal role in bringing up two generations of the Shah dynasty – not just her sister's children, but those of the next generation as well, and especially Prince Dipendra. As Queen Mother, she was used to being respected and listened to on all family matters. For nearly fifty years she was a power behind the scenes in Narayanhiti Palace.

King Tribhuvan's decision to seek asylum in the Indian Embassy may have been dictated as much by fear as by any statesmanlike vision of the future, but in carrying it off he single-handedly changed the shape of Nepalese history. For the next fifty years the Shah kings would be undisputed rulers of their ancestral lands. However, Tribhuvan's promise of bringing Nepal into the modern era did not come good within what was left of his lifetime. His health was already failing him, and in 1955 he died in a Zurich hospital at the age of forty-eight.

It was his son, King Mahendra, who pushed this semi-medieval and backward-looking kingdom halfway into the twentieth century. But his early commitment to democracy, and his decision to hold the first general election in Nepal's history, failed to bring any lasting changes. Within a year the duly elected Congress government was dismissed and all its leaders clapped in jail. With the army's backing, King Mahendra quietly ushered in thirty years of royal dictatorship.

He imposed swingeing measures. All political parties were banned, freedom of the press and of speech seriously curtailed, and the *panchayat* regime, a 'partyless' system of indirectly elected representatives, became the approved method of government. True, there was now a constitution and Parliament; but it was never allowed to debate any matters of importance, its real purpose being simply to rubber-stamp decisions already taken in the Royal Palace. The same is true of the dismal train of 'Prime Ministers and their hand-picked cabinets of yes-men. Nobody dared refuse the King, whose ancient aura of authority was now reinforced by a Kremlin-like Palace Secretariat.

The Royal Palace had at last become the real centre of power. If nothing else, the *panchayat* regime provided strong rule and stability. Apologists for the system have argued that it was more 'indigenous' and in keeping with the traditions of Nepal, or that its principles of 'guided democracy' were more suited to an underdeveloped and largely illiterate society than full-blown multi-party democracy. There may be some truth in this, though in reality the whole apparatus of *panchayat* rule was little more than a fig leaf to disguise Mahendra's very personal, very macho brand of autocracy.

In many respects Mahendra was a larger than life figure — a 'real king' who ruled his country with an iron fist. He pushed for rapid modernisation, opening up this previously isolated country to foreign aid and development programmes. Volunteers from America's Peace Corps poured into the Kingdom and were amazed at what they found:

a country scarcely touched by the twentieth century, where feudalism remained intact and preventable diseases like smallpox and leprosy were commonplace.

In opening up his country to the modern world, Mahendra still remained a fervent nationalist. He was proud of his country's independence and lobbied successfully for its entry into the United Nations. He was particularly adept at playing off the Big Powers who wanted to increase their presence in his strategically positioned kingdom, balancing India against China, the Soviet Union against the United States. While he recognised Communist China and accepted its *de facto* suzerainty over Tibet, he also allowed CIA-backed Khampa guerrillas fighting on behalf of the Dalai Lama to operate from Nepalese territory.

Mahendra revelled in his diplomatic games and attended many international conferences. He was the first of Nepal's kings routinely to cast aside traditional Hindu objections against crossing the 'black water' so that he could travel extensively abroad. The official purpose of these visits was to boost Nepal's diplomatic status throughout the world, but his hosts usually indulged the King's passion for hunting and arranged for him to shoot whatever game was locally available. A visit to the United States, for example, afforded him the opportunity to bag a mountain lion. In Scotland he stalked red deer; in Germany wild boar. A tour of East Africa yielded up two dozen trophies including lion and leopard, rhinoceros, giraffe, various species of antelope and wild dog. At home in Nepal he continued to spend every winter season hunting tiger, leopard, rhino and bear.

It was, in the end, typical that Mahendra should die of a heart attack while on a hunting expedition in Royal Chitwan National Park. As his former Prime Minister and closest confidant, Kirthinidi Bista, recalls: 'He was so passionate about hunting that whenever he saw wild animals, he couldn't resist. It was a tremendous temptation, even after he had his first heart attack. That actually happened when I was with him in a hunting hide. I held him in my arms until help came. But even after that he didn't give up his sport.'

King Mahendra was only fifty-one when he died. He had been

warned many times by his doctors; and he was all too aware that heart disease ran in the family. Only one Shah king in two hundred years had made it past his sixtieth birthday. Yet Mahendra continued to rule in person and keep up a fast and furious lifestyle. For a reigning monarch, that might be considered irresponsible. But to go out with a bang on a hunting expedition – that all added to his personal legend.

Mahendra's solemn funeral procession marked the passing of the ninth generation of Shah kings who could trace their descent in an unbroken line from the founding monarch, Prithvi Narayan Shah. More than two centuries had passed since the ambitious Raja of Gorkha had thrown that vomited up curd back on to an old hermit's hands, and as a consequence had heard the dreadful prophecy of Gorakhnath. His direct descendants, he had been told, would rule Nepal for ten generations and no more. If the prophecy ran true, the next King of Nepal would also be its last.

King Mahendra's eldest son, Crown Prince Birendra, was not of the same 'devil-may-care' type as his father. He was a more thoughtful, articulate and compassionate monarch. Even his greatest admirers admit, however, that he was not a commanding personality. Cautious and analytical in his decision-making, in his personal manners he approached that very English ideal of a 'true gentleman'. Birendra was the first Nepalese prince to be educated abroad: first at England's prestigious Eton College, before going on to Tokyo University and Harvard. In later life he was more comfortable speaking English than Nepali, though he regretted this and made sure his own son was fluent in the national language.

For the Crown Prince to shoot his first tiger was considered a rite of passage, and Birendra duly did so in Royal Chitwan National Park. But he never relished *shikar* as his father had done. By one of those chances of timing, these gentler tastes reflected changing attitudes to wildlife. Fortunately for the tiger, it was finally recognised as an endangered species in 1973, a year after Birendra ascended the throne, and all over India old *shikars* had begun to put aside their guns and turn to conservation. In Nepal, the new King supported the creation of pro-tected zones under the auspices of the King Mahendra Trust for Nature Conservation.

But old traditions died hard. When visiting royals or foreign dignitar-ies came to Nepal, time-honoured rules of hospitality meant that a tiger shoot had to be laid on. This could lead to embarrassment when a royal guest, such as the Duke of Edinburgh, was closely linked to international conservation bodies. For him to refuse a royal invitation to a tiger shoot would be worse than impolite. But to be photographed pulling the trigger or, worse still, posing beside the kill, would have been a public relations disaster. Calls for his resignation from various wildlife charities would inevitably have ensued. It was a tricky situation, but eventually a diplomatic solution was found. Prince Philip accepted the royal invitation. However, on the morning of the shoot, he emerged with his trigger finger encased in plaster. Obviously, he would be unable to shoot any tigers that day.

Enormous expectations of change and progress accompanied King Birendra's accession to the throne in January 1972. The new monarch was twenty-six years old, Western-educated, and known to be more liberal minded than his father. He made a point of travelling around the country and meeting his subjects so that he could listen to their problems and grievances in person. But for all the hopes of an early shift towards a more democratic regime, Birendra retained the *panchayat* system put in place by his father.

He may well have been influenced by those same senior palace officials who were effectively running the country for him, and who therefore had their own reasons to oppose any liberalisation. Then there was his wife, Queen Aishwarya, who was a Rana by birth and instinctively supported the royal prerogative and the privileges of the elite. A strong-minded though not particularly well-educated woman, Aishwarya exercised a powerful influence over her husband throughout the thirty-one years of their married life.

The *panchayat* system was to remain in place for nearly two more decades. During that time it was constantly tweaked so that, in theory at least, it reflected the 'will of the people'. A 'back to the village' campaign was extended by Birendra to ensure that government stayed in touch with the concerns of Nepal's overwhelmingly rural population. Commissions of Enquiry were dispatched to root out corruption at the local level. An all-powerful Investigation and Enquiry Centre was set up so that complaints could go straight to the top rather than get bogged down in officialdom. King Birendra wanted very much to be informed of the state of his nation; and, whenever possible, he sought to provide a remedy. It was a very personal and benevolent approach to kingship, but it was not very democratic.

Whether King Birendra ever took much notice of the Gorakhnath prophecy is unknown. Early on in his reign he did visit the main centre of the deity's cult just across the border into India, as had his forefathers before him, and paid for special *pujas* (ritual offerings) to be made on his behalf. He must have known about a legend so intimately linked with his own family, and been aware that the prophecy implied that he would be the last Shah king of Nepal. But to function on a day-to-day basis in the knowledge that this was the *fin de ligne* would have been intolerable.

Besides, there were many other prophecies and predictions in Nepal, few of which came to anything. And while Birendra was a deeply religious man, his preference turned towards the teachings of another, living guru, Sathya Sai Baba, and other 'modern' strains of Hinduism rather than the ancestral gods. So the curse of Gorakhnath was conveniently forgotten.

But there were other aspects of Hindu kingship which were less easily ignored. Birendra had no choice but to go along with popular beliefs that he was an incarnation of Vishnu. However, the divine aspect of kingship was not something he felt particularly comfortable with, and whenever possible he tried to play it down. The only exception was perhaps during the festival of Badha Dasain, when the elders in every family place a *tika* of red paste on the foreheads of younger members. Then the gates of Narayanhiti would open and thousands of

Nepalese would flood in and line up for the King to bestow on them the *tika* in the belief that this would wash away at least some of their sins. Birendra may have felt something less superstitious but, for him, more tangible, in this age-old ritual. It was an affirmation of his role as the father of all his people.

On some of the other more vexed issues that surround orthodox Hinduism – the treatment of the 'intouchable' caste of Dalits, for instance, or the prohibitions against people of different castes inter-marrying or even eating together – the King had to walk a fine line between his own liberal views and the minimum requirements of a Hindu monarch. He had little time for caste divisions; nor, for that matter, the issue of cow-slaughter, which is firmly linked with the Gorakhnath cult and is still an issue today.

King Birendra tried to stay above the fray. He was a Hindu monarch, but he was also King to all of his twenty-three million peoples – whatever their race, religion or mother tongue. He was always punctili-ous about attending Buddhist as well as Hindu rituals, and endeavoured to steer a 'middle way' between unthinking traditionalism and the equally uncritical copying of Western customs. 'One should move with the times,' he once said, 'but with roots firmly embedded in a country's soil and the best of its legacies.'

The prospect of being assassinated is something that all ruling monarchs have to live with. It is rather like a stray dog that follows you around and won't be shooed away. Most of the time it can be kept at a safe distance, but its presence is always there, unseen, lurking in the shadows. Should you choose to rule the country in person, as a sort of royal dictatorship, then there is all the more reason for it to rush forward and bite in an unguarded moment. King Birendra was fully aware of this. In fact, from very early on in his reign, he believed that one day he would be assassinated. He never spoke of such foreboding in public: that would be alarmist and self-defeating. It would undermine that 'divinity [which] doth hedge a king'; and in the case of Nepal's monarchs, that divinity was real enough.

For the young King Birendra that 'wake-up call' came in the late summer of 1979 when Lord Louis Mountbatten was blown up by Irish republicans. Mountbatten and his family had been staying at their holiday home on the west coast of the Republic of Ireland, and he was aboard a small boat just outside the harbour of Mullaghmore, in County Sligo, when the bomb went off. The Provisional wing of the IRA claimed responsibility. Security was heightened for the state funeral in London, in which, following tradition, a riderless horse with the dead soldier's boots turned backwards in the stirrups preceded the gun carriage bearing the coffin.

All of this may have happened half a world away, but it had a profound impact on King Birendra. Mountbatten was not only the Queen of England's cousin, he was the former Commander-in-Chief of the Allied Forces which had defeated the Japanese in South-East Asia and the last British Viceroy, who negotiated independence for India and Pakistan. Both he and his wife Edwina had visited Kathmandu. The young Prince Birendra would not have been able to remember that visit – he had only been one at the time – but he had heard tales of this glamorous couple from his older relatives. As a renowned soldier and world statesman, Lord Mountbatten embodied what many backward looking royal rulers believed they should aspire to. Now he had been blown to smithereens.

King Birendra was on a state visit to China when he heard the news. Like his father before him, Birendra favoured a close relationship with China, mainly in the hope that the People's Republic would act as a counterweight to the otherwise overwhelming influence of India, which surrounded his landlocked kingdom from the south and through which practically all imports, including petrol and kerosene, had to be transshipped. The King had recently declared Nepal a 'Zone of Peace', the centre of a strictly neutral area between Asia's two nuclear superpowers which might in time extend across the entire Himalayan region. The Dalai Lama later proposed his own version of a Zone of Peace, with a demilitarised Tibet as its fulcrum.

China's support mattered a great deal to Birendra, which is why he visited not only Beijing but other regional cities as well. The Nepalese royal party had reached Urumchi, capital of the oil-rich province of Xinjiang in China's far north-west. Urumchi is a dusty, windblown, soulless place, most of it newly built to house the influx of Han Chinese immigrants. It is not the most uplifting of cities, and the King's thoughts that evening were sombre. Taking aside his private secretary, he talked first about Mountbatten's unnatural death before declaring that he expected to be assassinated rather than end his days peacefully. 'To be blown up like that, suddenly,' he said. 'Maybe it's not such a bad way to go.'

At the time, there were plenty of people who might have been happy to see Birendra dead – extremists from among pro-democracy movements, for instance. The King was not only 'above the law': any criticism whatsoever could be construed as treason; and in Nepal treason remained a capital offence. None the less, there were people willing to risk imprisonment or death to rid Nepal of the King and his *panchayat* system of government. There were constitutionalists and communists, students and lawyers, an emerging urban middle class and landless peasants. Already trouble was brewing on university campuses and high schools around Kathmandu.

It was the repressive system that these opponents hated, rather than King Birendra himself; but the King stood at the head of the *panchayat* system. All key decisions were referred to him, or at least to the Palace Secretariat which acted in his name. So if someone wanted to topple the system, the quickest way to do so would be to target the head. Which may be why, in a far-flung corner of the People's Republic, King Birendra felt convinced that his life would end bloodily.

By the dawn of the third millennium, Birendra found his role to be greatly altered. Still King of Nepal, he was no longer its absolute ruler. Instead he had become a constitutional monarch. Not so different, in fact, from the Queen of England or the heads of other modern European monarchies.

Since the great changes of 1990, Birendra had proved himself to be the very model of a modern constitutional monarch, always ready to help Nepal's fledgling democracy through its recurrent crises. For the past decade his country had been a multi-party democracy, ruled by elected politicians rather than directly from the palace. As a result, the King was far more popular than he had ever been. There were far fewer potential enemies out there.

The transition from royal autocracy to democracy had not been a tranquil process. In fact, the Shah dynasty was almost overwhelmed by the storm of popular protest against the old *panchayat* regime that had broken out in April 1990, when thousands of Nepalese surged up Durbar Marg towards the reinforced steel gates of the Royal Palace. Riot police fired tear gas first. Then they tried baton charges. When that failed to hold back the crowds, they used live ammunition. Hundreds of unarmed protesters were killed or wounded, and once again a curfew was declared throughout the Kathmandu Valley.

At that stage the King could have called in the Royal Nepal Army, whose loyalty to the monarchy was unquestioned. Instead he chose to enter into peaceful negotiations with opposition leaders and declare the *panchayat* system of government dissolved. He handed over most of his own powers. But Birendra was by nature a moderate and a pragmatist. By stepping back from the brink, he not only prevented his countrymen from spilling each other's blood; he also sidestepped the very real threat that the institution of monarchy would be jettisoned. The moment of crisis passed, and Birendra's moderation ensured the Shahs could at least remain on the throne. In terms of the dynasty's survival, it was a probably a shrewd move.

Not everyone inside the Royal Palace agreed with the King's decision to give way gracefully, however. Some hardliners went into exile until such time as they might be recalled. That was not an option for Queen Aishwarya, who had to grin and bear it while staying at her husband's side. During the *Jana Andolan*, the 'Spring Awakening' of 1990, the Queen had been singled out as a target for anti-monarchist slogans. This was mainly because of her role as head of a special commission which channelled huge sums of foreign aid into the country, much of which had been siphoned off. Indeed, the whole organisation was deemed to be irremediably corrupt.

If anyone had contributed to the monarchy's unpopularity, it was Queen Aishwarya. However, that did not stop her from criticising her husband's 'weakness' in giving in to a handful of self-styled revolutionaries. Aishwarya may not have been the most intellectual member of the royal family, but she had a will of iron; and there were many others in the Palace and among her Rana relatives who supported her stand.

Crown Prince Dipendra was still a teenager and away at school in England when the Spring Revolution erupted in Kathmandu. At the time he supported his father's decision to accommodate change and sent an encouraging fax from Eton. But as the years passed and a series of democratically elected governments came and went in rapid succession, each one of them as inadequate and corrupt as the last, the tides of opinion began to turn.

In the country at large, King Birendra was more popular than ever – if only because the failings of Nepalese-style democracy made people look to the King for leadership again. But within some parts of the palace and the military establishment – precisely those circles in which the Crown Prince spent so much of his time – there was a growing sense of dissatisfaction.

It was not just the failings of the new constitutional monarchy that caused unease. By the beginning of the twenty-first century, the Kingdom of Nepal faced a serious guerrilla insurgency. Maoist rebels promised to rid the country of its corrupt parliamentary leaders and to put an end to monarchy. They controlled entire districts of western Nepal where they had set up an alternative government, and their armed bands controlled more than a third of the country. The police sent out against them were poorly armed and not trained in anti-guerrilla tactics, with the result that many police posts were surrendering without a fight. Only the Royal Nepal Army could take on the Maoists and win, it was argued; and the Crown Prince, who considered himself first and foremost a soldier, sat in on these discussions. With the monarchy itself under threat, surely it was time to act?

But the King was unwilling to countenance either a full-scale civil war in his country, or, for that matter, a military coup d'état. As Commander-in-Chief, only he could order the army into action. He was coming under increasing pressure from his own Prime Minister to do so. Another constitutional crisis loomed, yet the King steadfastly refused to give the green light for deploying the army.

8

Heir Apparent

Even his closest friends say that they did not really know Crown Prince Dipendra. In public, he was always affable, charming, self-controlled. There was a spontaneity about him that had not been apparent in previous generations of Nepal's royal family. He liked a good joke and his broad, unmistakably Nepali features were always ready to break into a smile. He had what one courtier described as 'the common touch' – the ability to stretch beyond the restrictive formalities of his royal status and make some sort of direct contact, however fleeting, with ordinary citizens.

The Crown Prince liked to go trekking into the more remote and mountainous areas of Nepal. He often preferred to travel in disguise, passing himself off as an army officer on leave. This enabled him to talk to villagers far more openly than would have been possible had they known that the Crown Prince was in their midst. It allowed him to become a different person, a 'man of the people', and he liked that sensation. He also enjoyed seeing the surprise on people's faces when they finally realised who he was. Since he was a child Dipendra had a weakness for practical jokes.

Of course, as Crown Prince he was expected to attend all manner of formal receptions, state dinners and religious ceremonies. Generally he was conscientious about carrying out these royal duties. He may have found standing around at some of the lengthier ceremonial functions tedious, but he got through them by downing a few large scotches beforehand. It did not seem to affect his public behaviour in the least. He could drink like a fish and still show no outward signs of intoxication.

If something was troubling him, he simply went quiet. There were no outbursts of temper or falling over or excessive affability.

Those palace officials responsible for ensuring that public functions went smoothly admired the prince's capacity for 'seeing things through' without causing any embarrassment. This kind of self-discipline is one of the prime requirements of being a royal. For no matter what you get up to in private, when in the public's gaze you are expected to keep up the image, show interest and concern as appropriate, and never, ever, 'let the side down'.

This is not something that junior royals have any choice over. It is a completely different situation from those people who run for President or Prime Minister. They generally choose to do so, and accept the personal costs of holding high office. For them, there is always the prospect of honourable retirement. Not so for crown princes. From the moment they are born they have a fixed responsibility and it is a job for life. The only ways out are to abdicate, be declared insane, or commit suicide. Or, in Nepal, to marry into a beef-eating caste – which, from the standpoint of most traditional Hindus, amounts to another form of insanity.

The boy child who was to be King of Nepal was born on 27 June 1971. The precise location and time of his birth – down to the last minute and second – were carefully recorded, and along with other requisite details taken to the Royal Astrologer, Mangal Raj Joshi, so that he could draw up the infant prince's birth chart. As always, the finer details were kept secret to prevent other unofficial astrologers from making their own predictions. It was important to get all the details right, for on the accuracy of that birth chart depended not only the fortunes of this boy child, but the future of the royal dynasty and the well-being of all the people of Nepal.

At his naming ceremony the boy was given an old Sanskrit name, Dipendra, or 'Lord of Candlelight'. The next major rite in Hindu households would normally be the first rice eating ceremony. Not only does this mark the infant's progression to solid foods; it confirms their acceptance as full members of the family's caste, since traditionally boiled rice can only be eaten together with those of the same caste. But before he followed that important rite of passage, his father King Birendra ascended the throne and the one-year-old Dipendra was declared Crown Prince of Nepal. Security worries about the King played a part in this, for only when the heir presumptive had been confirmed as Crown Prince was the royal succession secure.

Dipendra grew up in the new Narayanhiti Palace that had been almost completely rebuilt during the 1960s by his grandfather, King Mahendra. It was completed in somewhat of a rush so as to be ready for the royal wedding of Birendra and Aishwarya in 1970. The architecture is a strange mixture of traditional and modern, though from a child's point of view the overwhelming impression would have been how very new everything was. The interior furnishings conformed to the tastes of those times, with extensive use of vinyl and other synthetic materials. Despite the oversize portraits of royal ancestors staring down from the walls, there was little real sense of continuity.

The young prince spent most of his time in the royal couple's more homely private apartments, looked after by his devoted nurse and specially assigned servants whenever he was not being shown off to admiring royal uncles and aunts. The palace's artfully landscaped gardens, with their sculpted lawns and ornamental ponds, were his to play in – though there was always a watchful attendant to make sure he came to no harm. When he could scarcely walk he was presented with his first pony, good horsemanship being considered an essential quality in a prince. There were fancy-dress parties with his royal cousins. But for most of the time his world was circumscribed by the stout brick walls and steel gates that surround Narayanhiti.

As is often true in such large households, the child spent more time with servants than with his own parents. King Birendra was preoccupied with ruling the country – he was a distant figure whom the young prince was taught to address as 'Your Majesty'. Queen Aishwarya was herself deeply involved in palace politics and running the Social Services National Co-ordination Council. She was chairperson or patron of many charities – all time-consuming duties – and liked to keep some time to herself, writing lyrical poems under the pen name Chandani Shah, some of which were set to music.

In addition, there were new family members to care for. A sister, Princess Shruti, was born in 1976, and a brother, Prince Nirajan, two years later. Whereas Dipendra was brought up to be tough enough to handle his future role as King, his younger siblings were deeply indulged. Queen Aishwarya was also keen on philanthropic projects, one of them being to look after an orphan boy who was taken into the palace and showered with affection. None of this can have made Dipendra feel secure about his mother's feelings. Add to this the absence of both his parents on state visits to other countries and it is perhaps understandable that the young prince felt left out. While the King and Queen were abroad, Dipendra was left in the care of Queen Mother Ratna and his uncle, Prince Gyanendra, who may well have understood the boy better than his parents. Gyanendra also stood in for the King as head of government.

The Crown Prince was sent to his first school when he was three. The Kanti Ishwari kindergarten is named after the two sisters who married King Tribhuvan. It stands beside the Bagmati River, not far from a statue raised in honour of that royal revolutionary who freed Nepal from the Rana autocracy and so restored the Shah dynasty to meaningful power.

After the peculiarities of palace life, the freedom to play with other boys and girls must have seemed like a breath of fresh air to Dipendra. Naturally, the heir to the throne was driven to school by armed ADCs who then hung around as inconspicuously as possible until it was time to escort their charge back to the Royal Palace. But during school time he was supposed to be treated the same as other children, though naturally everyone was aware of his standing. On the school's open days, the King and Queen held the place of honour; and before long Dipendra was joined by other royal siblings, first his cousin, Prince Paras, and then by his sister, Princess Shruti. Although thoroughly exclusive, the school provided a first taste of normality for Dipendra. He retained fond memories of his time at Kanti Ishwari, and later helped form its alumni association.

From there he went on to Budhanilkantha School, set up in the hills to the north of Kathmandu. The school takes its name from a nearby shrine to the Sleeping Vishnu, at the centre of which is a gracious figure of the recumbent deity, carved in pale stone and surrounded by a sunken pond. Since the Kings of Nepal were themselves considered to be incarnations of Vishnu, it was deemed extremely inauspicious for them to set eyes on the statue of Vishnu in his sleeping form. In fact, it was forbidden them. But despite these warnings, the young prince still wanted to enter the temple.

Modelled on a British boarding school, with a house system and prefects, Budhanilkantha deliberately aimed to circumvent the intricate class and caste hierarchies that still survive in Nepal. Students were not known by their surnames. Instead they were given numbers, like serving members of the armed forces. So the eight-year-old Crown Prince Dipendra Bir Bikram Shah was known as plain Dipendra, No. 832.

Life was not wholly untroubled for No. 832, who was occasionally subjected to the school's strict discipline for his misdemeanours – such as raiding the kitchens when he felt hungry in the middle of the night. During his eight years at the school, several new masters were taken on who were not professional teachers at all, but high-ranking army officers. This was partly to ensure the Crown Prince's security, but it also had a lasting impact on Dipendra. His history teacher, Dharmapal Thapa, captivated his students with stories of Napoleon and Prithvi Narayan Shah. These appealed to the bright but intellectually lazy prince, who grew to hold military and martial values above all others. He also took up boxing and other 'manly' sports. On his eighth birthday, Dipendra's parents gave him his first real pistol.

Dharmapal Thapa established a lasting relationship with the Crown Prince, who regarded him as a sort of guru. After his spell of school teaching, Thapa returned to the army and rose to become Commander-in-Chief. Even after he stood down from the post, he remained one of Dipendra's closest confidants.

Even though Budhanilkantha School was established along British lines and had an English headmaster, it was still a departure from royal tradition to have the Crown Prince educated alongside commoners in his own country. Previously there had been private tutors within the palace, while King Birendra's own schooling had been mainly abroad – first at St Joseph's, an elite Catholic college in Darjeeling, in India, and then at Eton. Dipendra's was the first generation of young royals to be educated mainly at Nepalese schools. The King, however, wanted his son to have some experience of the wider world. He valued his own time at Eton and it was decided that Dipendra should follow in his footsteps. So, at the age of fifteen, the Crown Prince bade farewell to his Nepalese schoolmates and flew to England.

Eton has been educating the English ruling classes for nearly six hundred years. It is a royal foundation, having been established near Windsor Castle by the same King Henry VI who first lost half of France in the Hundred Years War and then, after a bitter civil war, the crown itself. Since when Eton has produced eighteen British prime ministers, countless generals and admirals, novelists and poets, ambassadors, bankers and, of course, landed magnates. Old Etonians, it is said, manage to convey a sense of 'effortless superiority'. Nor was there anything unusual about princes attending the school. The heirs to the House of Windsor, Prince William and Prince Harry, were sent to Eton – partly because the school has a tradition of treating royals the same as other boys. In such company it would be far more difficult for a Nepalese prince to make his mark than back home in Kathmandu.

Things did not get off to a good start when Dipendra smuggled alcohol into the school and another pupil sold the story to the newspapers. Headlines about exotic oriental princes selling booze to his upper-class friends did not go down well with the school authorities. The other boys nicknamed him 'Dippy', with its connotations of being either slightly mad or a dipsomaniac. (His father, Birendra, had been known at Eton as 'Nipple', a crude corruption of Nepal.) A somewhat chastened Dippy decided to concentrate on what he was best at – the martial arts, target practice on the shooting range and playing at being soldiers in the school's Combined Cadet Force.

Everyone acknowledged that he was 'a crack shot' as well as being one of the best students of karate in years. Some found him slightly frightening. In one incident, when a fight was brewing between a group of Etonians and local boys in the town, Dipendra showed no fear whatsoever as he advanced into the melée. But when he lifted a fellow pupil by the jaw because he thought he was being laughed at, he had crossed the line of acceptable courage. He had a habit of punching people 'as a joke', which some Etonians did not find so funny.

Dippy did not excel in any of the school's major sports such as cricket or rowing, which bring popularity. Though bright enough to sail through his examinations, he lacked the intellectual polish to make much headway among the arty, slightly louche set whose authority derived from acerbic wit rather than physical prowess. As a result, Dipendra was never asked to join Pop, the self-electing society – not so very unlike the traditional Nepalese aristocracy – which sits at the pinnacle of Eton's hierarchy and whose members have the right to wear fancy waistcoats. Instead, Dippy tried to win friends by bragging about his possession of a loaded revolver or how he could have any girl he wanted back in Nepal. The fact that he returned from one Christmas holiday with the status of a god – because his 'coming of age ceremony' had been celebrated – meant that he was excused from going to chapel. It also marked him out as being even more peculiar. He enjoyed the freedom that went with living in Britain but he often felt very lonely.

On weekends he would usually stay with Lord Camoys, his guardian in England, who had previously looked after Birendra when he had been at Eton. But Dipendra also sought out the company of his fellow Nepalese, driving down to the barracks of the British Gurkhas near Aldershot so that he could talk and join in Nepali singing and dancing. He often told friends that he missed his homeland. He also missed the company of women. At the age of nineteen that is hardly surprising, and back in Nepal he had a girlfriend, Supriya Shah, whom he very much wanted to marry. Towards the end of his time at Eton he met Rosella Scarcella, an equally lonely Italian girl who was working in a shop in Windsor. The two of them went for long walks together, and he confessed that, while he expected to go through with an arranged marriage, he hoped that love would also be involved.

Dipendra left Eton with a small circle of English friends who would stick with him through thick and thin. He had passed his O and A Level examinations with reasonable grades, but whereas his father had gone on to study at Harvard, it was thought best for Dipendra to return to Nepal. He enrolled as a student at Tribhuvan University in Kathmandu, where he took an MA in Geography. At the same time he was being groomed for his kingly duties. The waiting years had begun.

It has always been the fate of crown princes to wait, sometimes for decades, before they can assume any meaningful role in life. There is no choice in the matter. From early childhood they are aware that only one road is mapped out for them — to be King and the father of future Kings. Nor do they have much say in when they take up those responsibilities. That depends on the previous King's health, the chances of war, or the assassin's bullet.

Keeping the heir apparent usefully employed has always posed a problem. Some dynasties granted them private estates, principalities or duchies, to rule over. Others gave them command of armies and fleets — even when, as was often the case, they showed little natural military ability. It was all good training for their future role, made them feel important and, if nothing else, kept them occupied.

Neither of these options was open to Nepalese crown princes. Prithvi Narayan was the last Shah king to have commanded troops in battle. He also introduced strict laws of succession whereby all lands were held directly from the King and could be transferred only to his eldest son when he died. While this preserved the Kingdom of Nepal's unity, it left future generations of princes without lands or a meaningful role of their own.

Martial values continued to be fostered among the Shah kings, though campaigning itself was deputed to generals rather than princes of the blood. Besides, the opportunities for winning military glory all but vanished once Nepal was hemmed in by British India. Apart from the occasional punitive expedition against Tibet, the Royal Nepal Army has not fought on its own account for nearly two hundred years. Only Switzerland and Sweden have maintained perpetual peacetime armies for longer.

Although largely inactive, the Royal Nepal Army has been kept up to strength and enjoys a privileged position in society. The officer corps is still dominated by Ranas. In recent years Nepalese units have been part of UN-sponsored security forces in East Timor and other trouble spots, but otherwise the RNA's chief concern is internal security. Its allegiance is directly to the King himself, and the Crown Prince is customarily given the title of Colonel-in-Chief.

Here was an institution, with its own archaic codes of duty and honour, into which Dipendra could throw himself wholeheartedly. He volunteered for tough infantry training and parachute courses that were not strictly necessary to fulfil his honorific duties as Colonel-in-Chief. He learned to fly helicopters. He became involved in testing small arms. He liked the military-style banter down at the Army Club, and preferred the company of Sandhurst-trained ADCs to civilian courtiers and palace officials.

His was an exalted idea of a soldier's duty. He expressed this in one of the few poems of his that he allowed to be published. It is entitled 'Soldier', and in it he imagines himself in Nepal's high hill country, cold and exhausted, missing the city lights and the one he loves. And yet he is determined to do his duty:

Left bonds of love and affection, having duty understood
If needed soaked in blood, be ready to fight I would,
To flames reduce, will lightning halt, spray with blood I will,
On this uniform, the country's vermilion, shake this earth I will.

Here is a strange and darkly apocalyptic sense of a soldier's duty. Precisely what 'enemy' he is called on to combat is never made clear. Maoist guerrillas? Invading armies from India or China? Perhaps the confusion stems from the fact that, if Nepal ever were attacked by an external enemy, the best its small and poorly equipped army could do would be to go down fighting. That kind of suicidal last stand seems to be what the Crown Prince imagined as a soldier's duty.

Writing poetry, sketching and painting were encouraged within Nepal's first family. Following his mother's example, the Crown Prince planned to have a collection of his own poems published to mark his thirtieth birthday. King Birendra preferred sketching and painting in the abstract manner. The whole family believed that self-expression rather than formal values counted for most. As King Birendra put it, 'the highest form of literature is always ingenuous'. He held that 'such literature emanates from the vibration of people's heart where a rock articulates, a mountain drips, and everybody gives full expression to his or her inner-self'. In that, at least, his son followed in the family tradition.

The Crown Prince's fondness for music extended to playing the piano and electric guitar as well as the hand-held traditional Nepali drum. He wanted to excel in all he did — as soldier, poet, musician, scholar, lover. In this he followed the model of a well-rounded and accomplished prince. He spent time grooming himself to become a statesmanlike monarch, setting himself all manner of self-improving goals.

After completing his MA at Tribhuvan University, Dipendra went on to enrol as a Ph.D student. His thesis was on 'Demographic Factors Affecting Fertility Among Migrants and Non-Migrants in Kathmandu' — a down-to-earth topic for which the research materials were conveniently at hand. He rarely appeared on campus. Instead his thesis supervisor, Dr Bal Kumar KC, came to the Royal Palace and taught him in his private apartments at Tribhuvan Sadan.

Very often it seemed that Dipendra's quest for self-improvement only thinly disguised a more basic hunger for excitement. The Crown

Prince took up paragliding. He pursued his earlier interests in the martial arts under a Japanese master. He earned his pilot's licence and then used any excuse to practise his skills flying around the country. He insisted on taking an advanced driving course on the pretext that, as with his firearms training, such skills might contribute to his personal security in an emergency. The reality was that he liked to drive extremely fast. He knew he was good at it. He also knew that not a single police officer in the entire Kathmandu Valley would ever try to stop him. As Crown Prince, he stood above the ordinary laws of the land.

Dipendra spent much of his twenties being quietly initiated into the skills and procedures of kingship. He sat in on meetings with his father and top palace officials during which key policy issues were discussed. He learned about all the correct procedures and how the Palace Secretariat functioned. But when it came to decision-making or face-to-face discussions with the Prime Minister and other political heavyweights, the Crown Prince was generally excluded. Such things were the King's business.

Learning about the real conditions in which people lived was an important part of this 'grooming' process. Dipendra had access to all manner of reports and privileged information, to which he added his own personal experience. He was forever making flying visits to different corners of the realm, some of them official tours of inspection, others private excursions for trekking or hunting. As a result, he gradually built up a thorough knowledge of his country and its peoples.

Most certainly he did not like everything he saw. The grinding poverty in which most of the population lived, the shortage of schooling and medical facilities, the persistence of feudal-style landlordism and bonded labour, the fact that every year some six thousand young Nepalese girls were sold to become sex-workers in India or Arab countries – that was then, as it is now, as much the reality of modern Nepal as rhododendron forests and mountain vistas. Dipendra's response was to set about creating a charitable foundation that would both raise funds and channel them into the kind of integrated development programmes that from previous experience worked best in rural Nepal. It was to be loosely modelled on the Prince of Wales Trust in Great Britain.

Dipendra threw all his energies into the project. He had found a new role for himself, and one which fitted well with his idealistic nature. It offered him, the Crown Prince, the chance to do real good for his people. Plans were at an advanced stage when, for unexplained reasons, the entire project was dropped. Those closest to the Crown Prince suggest it was vetoed by somebody at the very top of the palace hierarchy, possibly Queen Aishwarya herself. If so, it can only have made worse the relationship between mother and son.

Any real warmth in the Crown Prince's relationship with his father was artificially constrained by palace protocol. Dipendra continued to refer to him as 'His Majesty' and did his utmost to be an obedient and respectful son. It was his duty to comply with the King's wishes, even when he disagreed with them. Occasionally, as in the Hindu spring festival of Holi, the normal pattern of respectful behaviour was abandoned. Everybody would deliberately get drunk and let their hair down – in the fairly certain knowledge that whatever was said would be buried in the next day's hangover. But even these rare opportunities for airing differences were bound up in tradition and ritual. In the absence of any other, less formal conduits for expressing disagreement, it was only to be expected that tensions would build up as the Crown Prince grew older and more entrenched in his own opinions.

That has always been the case with hereditary monarchies. The Hanoverian kings of England, for instance, were all cordially loathed by their successors-in-waiting. This often has less to do with the personalities involved than the frustrations that go with being a Crown Prince. Differences of opinion emerge – over policy, the use of the army, or whom the Crown Prince should marry. While such matters can be discussed privately, ultimately the King's decision cannot be questioned. The only option for the heir apparent is to bide his time until the power structure has changed. Pushed into such a corner, one does not have to hate the King personally to wish sometimes he were dead or at least out of the way.

What is certain is that by the late 1990s a deep frustration was building up within the Crown Prince. Every time he tried to do something positive it was blocked. The only public role he could call his own was as head of the National Sports Council and his work on Nepal's Olympic Committee. He liked sport, but the administrative side meant putting in a lot of not very entertaining hours. Nor did such mundane duties fulfil his own sense of high purpose. The years were slipping by and he had nothing to show for them. He was still living in the same bungalow in the grounds of Narayanhiti that he had moved into when he was eighteen.

Above all, he was frustrated in love. At the age of nineteen he had asked permission to marry his first love, Supriya Shah, but his mother had told him he was still far too young. Having obediently accepted his mother's decision, his affections would eventually turn to another beautiful and aristocratic young woman called Devyani Rana.

Like most of the younger members of the royal family, Dipendra had been smoking hashish since he was a teenager. That is not unusual in Kathmandu. The Crown Prince even had palace servants to roll his joints for him and kept a special Cartier cigarette case to carry them – hashish on one side, marijuana on the other. It was around the same period of disillusionment that Dipendra declared to friends that he was 'serious' about Devyani, even though his mother had voiced opposition to their relationship, that those closest to him started noticing how much his drug consumption had increased. He stayed clear of hard drugs – against which he held very firm opinions, blaming the growing number of chemical substances available for the corruption of Nepal's youth. None the less, when Dipendra started smoking ten to fifteen joints a day even his closest friends started worrying about his state of mind. Especially when he started waving around one of his guns.

The Crown Prince had always been fond of shooting, but his collection of guns had recently expanded far beyond what might be considered normal – even in a family whose male members customarily carried sidearms and had for generations been addicted to the pleasures of *shikar*. His private arsenal comprised not only shotguns and hunting rifles, but various sidearms and a machine pistol issued for his personal security. As Colonel-in-Chief of the Royal Nepal Army he had access to all the weaponry to be found in a modern armoury – especially since he had responsibility for assessing infantry weapons as part of the RNA's procurement programme.

Dipendra was therefore able to sign for and obtain from the palace armoury a 5.56 calibre Colt M-16 automatic assault rifle with a laser-equipped telescopic sight that was capable of firing up to 1,000 rounds a minute. There was also his 9mm Heckler & Koch MP5K sub-machine gun (nine hundred rounds a minute), a single-barrel twelve-bore SPAS shotgun made in Italy, and his customary 9mm Glock pistol.

It was all too easy for the Crown Prince to assemble this private arsenal. The M-16 was requisitioned from the Royal Nepal Army arsenal on 31 May 1999 and handed over at the *kotkhana*, the armoury within Narayanhiti Palace, to the royal guard military police, who in turn handed it over to the Crown Prince. The Heckler & Koch sub-machine gun was obtained through a different route, from the ADCs' office, on 27 July 1999. For nearly two years, therefore, Prince Dipendra had both of these lethal weapons in his possession. That might have been acceptable if they had been kept in a secure place; but, as his personal ADC Gajendra Bohara admitted, the Crown Prince was accustomed to taking weapons directly from the Royal Palace armoury whenever he wanted to.

Dipendra liked to keep his guns with him practically all the time. He usually carried at least one pistol, sometimes two, either openly in a military-style holster or in a concealed shoulder holster. He took the M-16 with him whenever he went trekking in the mountains, on the grounds that he might be a target for Maoist terrorists. While driving about town in his Toyota Land Cruiser he had the M-16, his weapon of choice, together with a Heckler & Koch G36 carbine mounted in a gun rack especially designed for easy access, beside the gear shift. Since he drove extremely fast and kept his 9mm Glock loaded and ready to fire, palace security were worried about the very real possibility that he might be killed or injured if a weapon went off accidentally. Kathmandu's notoriously potholed roads only increased the likelihood of an accidental discharge. But as one palace official put it: 'Who was going to tell him not always to be carrying so many guns? He was the Crown Prince. Only his father could have ordered him not to.'

9

Behind Palace Walls

The lack of control over the Crown Prince's access to weaponry was symptomatic of a much larger problem within Narayanhiti Palace. Nobody was really in control. The King worked long hours in his private office but avoided taking any difficult decisions. Too often he used the excuse of work to absent himself from family discussions, especially when he knew disagreements would be aired.

Since the smooth working of any monarchy depends on there being a clear chain of command, King Birendra's reluctance to become too closely involved left a void at the very top of the palace pyramid. This caused some confusion, for the royal family and its servants and advisers abided by the same patriarchal values as most other extended families in Nepal. There needed to be a strongman at the top, ready and able to enforce his authority. Otherwise rival power centres would establish themselves elsewhere within the palace, and family unity would be displaced by faction.

The layout of Narayanhiti Royal Palace may have encouraged this disintegrative process. Within its enclosing walls, a whole complex of buildings – offices, barracks, temples and private residences – had gradually been added over time with little concern for architectural coherence. The broad driveways leading straight in from the main gates to the south and west soon gave way to a tangled network of internal roads linking all the different parts. The grounds were similarly divided up between private gardens around each of the royal residences, which reflected the tastes of their particular inhabitants, and more formal, 'public' lawns with artificial lakes and fountains upon which ordinary citizens could peer through the massive steel bars of the southern perimeter fence. Seen from the air, the palace complex more closely resembled an exclusive holiday resort, with its separate villas and service areas, its private helipad and stables, than a palace occupied by a single royal family. As with some metropolitan cities, it was difficult to identify exactly where its centre lay.

The main body of the palace was used for state occasions and formal receptions. It was built to impress rather than to be lived in; though beautifully maintained by servants, it remained empty for much of the time. Apart from Prince Nirajan, who still occupied part of the private wing, all other royal family members had moved out to their own separate residences dotted around the palace grounds.

The King and Queen lived in Sri Sadan, a comfortable but modest three-bedroom house to the south-east of the main block, its beautifully kept flower gardens shielded by trees and an internal wall from the main entrance to the palace. The Queen Mother had her own residence nearby, named Mahendra Manzil, after her late husband. As for the Crown Prince, since his coming of age he had occupied a residential bungalow to the north of the main palace, part of a complex of buildings known as Tribhuvan Sadan. His private quarters were linked by a little bridge to the rest of Tribhuvan Sadan, which was formerly used for private audiences but had since been equipped with a billiards table, bar and dining room, for entertaining family and friends.

It is understandable that each member of the royal family wanted their own space to retire to. Living on top of each other in the residential wing of the main palace would have been intolerable. More-over, the modernist architecture of Narayanhiti's main block made it far from cosy. Its rebuilding had been ordered by King Mahendra during the 1960s as a deliberate break from the Rana past. So the stately neo-classical pile originally built by Prime Minister Ranaudip Singh Rana during the 1880s was demolished, and a new palace rose up in its place.

It was supposed to express a marriage of modern and traditional

Nepalese architecture, though the results are unconvincing. With its pagoda-roofed throne room flanked by a needle-thin and thoroughly modernist tower, its austerely plain frontage broken up by a fanciful double staircase adorned with statues of elephants, peacocks and other auspicious animals, this new Narayanhiti presents a confusing assemblage of contradictory styles.

The immense state rooms are filled with great mirrors and chandeliers, stuffed tigers and other sporting trophies, glass-fronted cabinets to display gifts of porcelain and crystal, and oversized portraits of kings of the Shah dynasty. The effect is to create an impressive backdrop for ceremonial occasions such as the swearing in of a new government or receiving the credentials of foreign emissaries. There is a great deal of rather heavy-handed symbolism that is meant to convey how a traditional Hindu monarchy is embracing the modern world. The throne room has a tapering false roof designed to resemble that of a Hindu temple, while the throne itself is supported by carved lions and elephants, its arms covered with golden serpents and its canopy by an umbrella with the royal symbols of the sun and moon. The divine aspect of Nepalese kingship is conveyed by having the guardians of Lord Vishnu standing on either side of the royal emblem. Yet, for all this carefully thought out symbolism, there is little sense of either the mystery or the majesty of kingship.

Just visible from the palace's upper floors, hidden in the south-east corner of the grounds, is a temple dedicated to Narayan, the same avatar of Vishnu which the King of Nepal is commonly held to embody. It is from this temple and the *hiti*, or water spout, which stands beside it that Narayanhiti derives its name.

As usual, there is a myth surrounding this temple, which concerns one of the Licchavi kings who ruled in the fifth century AD. According to the legend, the King sought the advice of a tantric priest as to how the terrible drought afflicting his lands might be ended. The priest advised that the holiest man in the land, one endowed with all the auspicious qualities, be offered as a sacrifice. After much searching it became apparent that there was only one person fit for such a role, and that was the King himself. He ordered his son to go to the Narayan Temple the following morning and kill the person he would find sleeping there. The Crown Prince obeyed, and no sooner had he carried out the sacrifice than great thunderclouds gathered and water gushed from the spout beside the temple. The drought was over, as had been foreseen. But when he discovered that he had killed his own father, the new King was filled with such remorse that, according to Newar traditions, he founded the great stupa at Bodhnath to expiate his terrible sin.

Unsurprisingly, that particular story of royal parricide is not celebrated among the religious symbols that adorn Narayanhiti Palace. But the legend has survived.

In contrast to the megalomaniacal grandeur of its centrepiece, the working parts of the palace were designed to be austere and strictly functional. The barracks that house the royal guard are no better built than other army installations, while the Palace Secretariat operates from a sparsely furnished whitewashed block down by the West Gate that is already showing its age. Yet, despite its unremarkable appearance, this is still the nerve centre of much that goes on both inside Narayanhiti and far beyond its walls.

The principal royal secretaries and their countless assistants perform many roles. They act as the eyes and ears of their master, ferreting our information from sources it would be inappropriate for the King to meet in person. They also filter information received and carefully screen anyone seeking a royal audience. Their internal procedures are shrouded in mystery, and they are accountable only to the King himself. Very often their functions go far beyond what might be implied by their official titles. They tend to recruit from a close-knit group of families. For all its modern façade, Narayanhiti is heir to an ancient court culture.

This is partly because the same families have served the Shah dynasty from one generation to the next. Household positions are usually held by Newars, the original inhabitants of the Kathmandu Valley, while royal secretaries and advisers are chosen from the same families of *bharadars*, or 'burden-carriers', who accompanied the first Shah king on his campaigns of conquest two hundred and fifty years ago. The names of the same Gorkha clans – Pandey, Thapa, Basnet – appear among today's palace officials, just as they did throughout the eighteenth and nineteenth centuries. Of course their roles have changed over time, but the traditions of loyal service and absolute discretion live on.

Some key positions have been held on an overtly hereditary basis, the job passing automatically from father to son. That has certainly been true of the Royal Preceptors, whose role as personal spiritual advisers or gurus to the King and other members of the royal family gave them enormous influence within the palace and the country at large. Until the codification of Nepalese laws in the nineteenth century, the Royal Preceptors were responsible for interpreting the holy *shastras* and then pronouncing legal judgements. Although their powers have since been reduced, they continue to have authority over cases involving caste rules and their infringements.

As the recently retired Royal Preceptor Nayan Raj Pandey pointed out, there have been some changes of late. It is now required that the Royal Preceptor be proficient in Sanskrit and complete his studies up to or beyond the official requirements. But continuity is much valued in a role similar to that of a family priest. To prove as much, faded sepia portraits of previous Royal Preceptors adorn the walls of Nayan Raj Pandey's living room, all of them ancestors who had fulfilled the same duties as he had.

Since the times of King Surendra, every Nepalese monarch has had as his Royal Preceptor a member of Pandey's clan. They have anointed successive kings on their coronation days, recited the appropriate texts at their coming of age ceremonies, and in between exerted an invisible influence over the Shah dynasty. If anyone is responsible for promoting the godlike status of Nepal's kings, it is this line of Royal Preceptors. For Nayan Raj Pandey there is no room for doubt; the King is indeed the incarnation of Vishnu.

Another prominent member of the royal household, the Master of

Ceremonies, is equally proud of the way in which his family have served Nepal's rulers over the centuries. Chiran Thapa points out that a family member has been present on every state visit to Britain since Jung Bahadur Rana led the first one in 1850. His branch of the Thapa clan came to Kathmandu before the Gorkha conquest, and possibly for that reason did not rise to become prime ministers under the early Shah kings like Bhim Sen and his nephew Mathbar Singh Thapa. For the same reasons they survived the bloody purges that decimated the more illustrious branch of the Thapa clan, and have served successive Rana Prime Ministers and Shah kings.

Chiran Thapa rose to become one of King Birendra's closest advisers during the *panchayat* years, when the Palace Secretariat was effectively running the country. So closely was he identified with royal absolutism that, after the democratic revolution of 1990, Thapa left for England where he resumed his studies at Trinity College, Cambridge. But once things had settled down in Nepal, with King Birendra building up his new role as a constitutional monarch, his old confidant returned to become Master of Ceremonies. As always in the palace, the official title does not necessarily limit either the functions or the influence of the incumbent. What matters more is whether one enjoys the confidence of the King.

A more recent court position, although one which has been held by the same family since its inception, is that of Royal Photographer. The Chitrakars are an ancient Newar family who have been painters, sculptors and makers of ceremonial masks to the wealthy of Kathmandu for generations. One Bhagu Man Chitrakar was attached to the state visit to Britain in 1850, during which he made numerous paintings of Jung Bahadur's progress, one of which survives in the British Library.

It was his grandson, Dirga Man Chitrakar, who expanded the family's artistic traditions into photography. Dirga Man accompanied Prime Minister Chandra Shamsher Rana to London in 1908 and made good use of the opportunity to buy the latest photographic equipment and learn how to use it. He also painted a portrait of King Edward VII for which he was offered the then enormous sum of £10,000, but which was refused on his behalf by the Nepalese Prime Minister who insisted it be a gift. Upon returning to Kathmandu he set up a photographic studio at his family home in the Old City; but since there was no electricity, the glass plates were exposed on to contact sheets by opening a small hole in the roof for sunlight to come in. For all that, the results were impressive, and very soon an indoor studio was installed for taking artfully arranged portraits, complete with painted backdrops to suggest the sitters were in front of a mountain range or some magnificent palace.

While the Chitrakars were, as court photographers, responsible for recording coronations, tiger hunts and other important events, most of their everyday business came from wealthy Rana families, so that, after the Rana regime was overthrown, this family of royal photographers was not invited back to the palace for a number of years. Eventually they were reinstated, and the current generation of Chitrakars are still official photographers at enthronements and other royal ceremonies. But it is only occasional work, and their main employment these days is as TV cameramen.

The royal adviser who claims his family have worked in the same profession for longest is the Royal Astrologer. According to his own calculations, Mangal Raj Joshi believes that thirty-two generations of his family have practised oriental astrology. He operates from a run-down town house in one of the older districts of Patan. But, despite the dismal surroundings, there can be no doubt that this is a thriving business. Customers arrive for consultations so early in the morning that he often stays overnight in a flea-ridden bed rather than return to his much more comfortable family home. An entire floor of the house is occupied by assistants who squat on the floor, rapidly scanning birth charts and pumping the data into computers and pocket calculators.

Joshi's reputation for delivering accurate predictions used to be second to none, or at least that was true within the Kathmandu Valley. How far that depended on his being astrologer to Nepal's first family, and whether his failure to predict their untimely demise will affect his other business, is uncertain. Mangal Raj Joshi explains away this glaring gap in his astrological predictions by claiming that his royal clients cancelled a crucial series of calculations before their demise. Be that as it may, the Royal Astrologer is currently touting for new business. Among the many horoscopes in his in-tray was one labelled 'Nancy from Seattle'.

The Royal Astrologer's technical qualifications are impressive. Not only has he mastered Sanskrit, the classical language of oriental astrology, he has also studied geology, meteorology, mathematics and modern astrology so as to bring together scientific accuracy with eastern traditions. He claimed to have predicted the outbreak of the Gulf War in 1991, right down to the day and time of the first attacks, and to have given timely warnings of several major earthquakes. But on his dealings with the royal family, and the knowledge he still holds of their birth charts, the wily old astrologer will not be drawn. Partly this can be put down to professional ethics, though Mangal Raj Joshi is also imbued with that discretion which is the hallmark of any royal adviser.

Loyalty, continuity of service, discretion – these are the qualities which have kept the same families as servants and advisers to the Crown for generations. It has not always been easy. The Brahmins and *bharadars* have had to survive three revolutions – Jung Bahadur's usurpation of royal authority in 1847, King Tribhuvan's triumphant return in 1951, and, most recently, the 'Spring Awakening' of 1990 that ushered in democratic rule. But no matter who was in power, these palace officials somehow remained in place, survivors from an *ancien régime*.

Despite the fact that the Royal Palace no longer governs Nepal, the size of the Palace Secretariat remains much the same as before 1990. Its role has shifted from deciding national policy to information-gathering and analysis, but it is none-the-less a well-oiled machine. Some would say that for the purposes of a constitutional monarchy it is excessive – rather like taking a Rolls-Royce to the supermarket. It marshals established procedures to cover every eventuality, both human and divine, or so it was thought.

So when a dreadful warning came in the spring of 2001 from eastern

Nepal, where a statue of the god Bhimsen was found to be 'perspiring', the palace checked on the appropriate response and dealt with the matter expeditiously. The piece of cloth soaked in the deity's sweat was duly accepted, the eyewitness report of this miraculous event noted, and the appropriate articles of worship together with a he-goat were dispatched to the temple in order to ward off this ill omen. In the past, earthquakes and other calamities had followed shortly after Bhimsen had given such a warning. That potential danger was recognised; but having taken all the appropriate steps, there was nothing else that the palace officials could do about it.

For much of the time the Palace appeared to be running on autopilot. Deprived of a meaningful role, too much of its energy and analytical capacity became turned in on itself. In an echo of the past, palace politics appeared to become distanced from events going on outside the walls. Internal matters acquired an artificially exaggerated importance. It became a claustrophobic world, heavily laden with petty intrigue: which may explain why Crown Prince Dipendra was forever trying to cut loose from it all.

King Birendra was no fool. He knew that all was not well within the Palace, but he was too indulgent a monarch to dismiss faithful servants, let alone undertake a wholesale purge. Besides, he still thought of the Palace Secretariat as his personal power base.

Instead of overhauling the machine, Birendra decided to lead by personal example. He had gradually been steering the royal family towards a more informal style. Many old practices had not changed since his grandfather Tribhuvan's time, and court etiquette still decreed that the King and Queen never smile in public because such expressions of human emotion were deemed unfitting for living gods. All formal portraits, both of the royal family and the Rana aristocracy, would show them unsmiling – if not actually scowling – at the camera. Halfway through his reign Birendra abandoned the old habits and began to smile in public – a gentle, considerate smile that is hard to forget. So, too, did his Queen and other members of the royal family. For ordinary Nepalese it was a revelation, and one which they soon learned to appreciate.

Other changes were introduced behind Narayanhiti's high walls. Whereas previously outsiders only met the King during formal audiences or dinners with liveried bearers and court officials at hand, now they were invited to informal gatherings at which the royal family themselves handed round drinks and hors d'oeuvres. It was a quiet revolution, but a revolution none-the-less. Nepal's royal family were becoming more approachable, more human.

Whenever possible King Birendra also preferred to dress casually — either in the Western style or, more often, in the loose wrap-around shirt and jodhpur-style trousers which is Nepalese national dress. He usually sported one of the multi-coloured and typically Nepali cloth caps known as the *topi*, and encouraged other family members to do the same. As 'father of the nation' he believed he should at least look Nepalese. Some of the younger generation found this regressive and preferred Western clothes, but in this, as in everything else, Birendra sought to bring about changes gradually.

Another radical departure was the opening up of the state rooms of Narayanhiti Palace to the general public. Queen Elizabeth II had done the same with Buckingham Palace in 1993, after all, so why not in Kathmandu? One argument against this is that most of the furnishings, from cabinets stuffed with over-gilded Sèvres bowls through to the extraordinary room where everything — table, chairs, lightstands and ornaments — is made of frosted glass, all bear witness to royal extravagance rather than good taste. None-the-less, the decision was taken to go ahead. Nepalese citizens could visit one day each week, foreigners on another. No one in Nepal would previously have dreamed of entering Narayanhiti. It was hoped that opening it up would signal the monarchy's new-found approachability to the ordinary citizens of Nepal.

Crown Prince Dipendra continued to show the greatest respect for his father. He would not say a bad word about him, even behind his back, but he was increasingly frustrated that he was not being allowed to build a meaningful role for himself. For this, Birendra was at least partly to blame. So concerned was he to abide by the rules of being a constitutional monarch that he was wary of allowing his headstrong son any official status other than that of heir to the throne. Even if he were running a charitable trust, the Crown Prince might be tempted to speak out, for example, on the lack of rural development in Nepal. That would be overtly political, and it was the King's intention that the new constitutional monarchy should always stand above politics. It was therefore safer to do nothing.

At times, Birendra appeared to be a 'reluctant monarch' who carried on because it was his duty to do so, and not because he particularly enjoyed it. He preferred simplicity to pomp and circumstance. Birendra would dutifully dress up in military uniform when that was required of him, in complete contrast to his son who positively revelled in it and seemed ready to burst the buttons of his uniforms with suppressed energy and pride.

There were other differences between father and son. While Birendra tried to live up to the highest ideals personally, in domestic and family matters he would generally defer to his wife's opinion, even when this meant upsetting his eldest son. In the political arena, he preferred to look at situations from every angle, to listen and refer to his numerous advisers, rather than take any really tough decisions himself. In short, he dithered.

He had none of the hallmarks of a dictator – which is how some of his opponents tried to portray him. Rather, his instinctive sense of moderation made him an ideal pathfinder in Nepal's first experiment with democracy combined with a constitutional monarchy. All who knew him remember King Birendra as a 'true gentleman': courteous, well-meaning, self-contained. At times it was hard to remember that this soft-spoken man was indeed a king.

Had the democratic system of government of which he approved worked better in practice, Birendra's quiet, benign style might have proved ideal. But the experience of the 1990s was of unstable and swiftly changing governments – there were ten in all – each more corrupt and self-serving than the last one. So while the King's lack of forceful decision-making was seen by some at court as weakness, the institution of the monarchy was gaining in popularity – if only because it had distanced itself from government and could no longer be blamed for the mess.

Birendra's lack of natural authority led to muttered criticism within the Palace, where there had always been a conservative clique, including Queen Aishwarya and most of the older generation of royals, that regretted Birendra's decision to surrender so much power to elected politicians. Senior army generals shared these views and some of them were close to the Crown Prince. They were particularly worried about the Maoist insurgency spreading from western Nepal. The Maoists had gained effective control of parts of the eastern hills and much of the countryside around the Shah dynasty's ancestral home at Gorkha.

More than a thousand lives had already been lost in what threatened to become the all-out civil war that Nepal had successfully avoided throughout the Shah dynasty's rule. The generals argued that if they had only been given the order back in the early days, when the insurgency was still growing, the entire problem could easily have been nipped in the bud. But for whatever reasons, the order never came. The King was still taking advice.

The waiting game, however, carries its own hazards. King Birendra suffered a heart attack late in 1998 and he was flown to London for a bypass operation. Queen Aishwarya accompanied him, and during their absence the Crown Prince stood in for his father in meetings of the royal council and at formal occasions. By then Dipendra was twenty-seven – a year older than his father had been when he ascended the throne.

The very real possibility that the King might die suddenly – the history of recurrent heart problems in the Shah family was known to everyone – had the effect of a minor earthquake being triggered beneath Narayanhiti Palace. Courtiers, royal relations, palace officials, indeed anyone with an eye on the future, looked carefully at how they stood with the Crown Prince and started shifting their positions accordingly.

None dared to declare openly that a 'Crown Prince's Party' existed. While the King lived, that could be construed as disloyalty. Disloyalty was unthinkable. It would also run against deeply ingrained habits of discretion. Sensitive topics are not, as a rule, discussed openly within Narayanhiti's walls. Possibilities are hinted at; undesirable consequences merely implied. The subtle shifting of allegiances is signalled by the swiftness with which a request is carried out, by the apparent sincerity of a smile.

When King Birendra returned from London after his successful heart operation, the people of Kathmandu came out in their thousands to cheer him home. It seemed that with each passing year he was becoming more popular. Birendra settled back into a period of gentle recuperation. His doctors had told him to give up smoking, strong drink, going on high-altitude treks, and many other pleasures of his youth. He was prescribed pills to counter his natural tendency to high cholesterol. The following spring, both the King and Queen Aishwarya went down to the royal retreat in Pokhara so that he could convalesce in peace. But while he was there, another government failed, another general election was called, and Birendra felt it his duty to return to Kathmandu.

Even after his heart attack the King continued to put in long hours at his office. He needed to be kept informed, especially since the whole process of democratic change which he had embraced seemed to be falling apart at the seams. He was typically circumspect when it came to discussing Crown Prince Dipendra and the royal succession. He noted that whenever he himself travelled outside Nepal, his son automatically took over as chairman of the Council of Royal Representatives. Birendra expressed neither praise nor enthusiasm for his son and heir. Instead, he simply stated that Dipendra had been groomed to assume the responsibilities of kingship, that he had been exposed to all the requisite analytical and decision-making processes. 'It is a role he knows he has to take on. But in the end, each individual must make his own job of it.'

With hindsight, those might seem like fateful words. But King Birendra preferred to contemplate the long-term future of monarchy in Nepal rather than any immediate problems. Kings, he explained, had to think through decisions and their consequences over a much longer time frame than elected politicians.

'Each one of us,' he said, 'must make a step, and be sure that it is solid enough to build the next one.' In doing so, he expressed a thorough understanding of the true nature of monarchy, which is not so much about any individual's performance as the continuance of a relationship between a ruling family and the people of a country across many generations.

Naturally, the marriage of the Crown Prince and the provision of further heirs to the throne entered into the equation. But at the time this did not appear a pressing concern. The King had two grown-up sons: his youngest, Nirajan, as well as the Crown Prince. On that front, at least, the succession seemed secure. The royal ladies were in charge of the matter, after all.

IO

Love and Marriage

On 8 May 1997 Princess Shruti, only daughter of Their Majesties King Birendra and Queen Aishwarya of Nepal, was married to Kumar Gorakh Shamsher Rana. It was a splendid wedding. Representatives of the royal houses of Europe and Asia flew into Kathmandu. The young princess was borne aloft in a palanquin, a gold-flecked veil of transparent fineness covering her head. The timeless Hindu rites were performed. No expense was spared at the sumptuous wedding feast. All of Nepal's royal family were present. For Birendra, there might have been a tinge of sadness. Shruti had always been very much her father's favourite.

Like him, she was an accomplished artist and a skilled equestrian. At school, first at St Mary's in Kathmandu and then at the elite Mayo College at Ajmer in India, she had revealed only average aptitude; but her unassuming ways won her many friends. She was kind, self-disciplined, considerate – even to the point of helping out servants with washing the dishes. But Shruti was no pushover. She had firm opinions, and among her qualifications was a black belt in judo.

In time a slightly gawky young girl had grown to be a beautiful woman, a true princess. 'Even when wearing a sari,' a friend commented, 'she had the poise of a Botticelli Venus.' She was twenty when she was married.

It was some consolation to her father that the newly-weds were setting up house in Kesar Mahal, only a short distance from Narayanhiti's West Gate. The marriage, of course, was an arranged one, and Shruti would never have challenged her parents on that account.

But the relationship between the newly-weds blossomed. A year later Shruti gave birth to the first royal grandchild, a girl, who was named Girvani. A second daughter was born the following year.

There was a constant coming and going between the palace and Kesar Mahal, for Birendra delighted in his granddaughters. Sometimes the King and Queen would stroll over to visit them, to the immense surprise of ordinary pedestrians, though generally Shruti brought the children to their grandparents. She remained very close to her parents. In all respects, it seemed an ideal marriage.

Crown Prince Dipendra might well have had mixed feelings about his sister's marriage. More than five years her senior, by rights he should have been the first of his generation to marry. With each passing year he became less comfortable about being the country's 'most eligible bachelor'.

Of course the Crown Prince had had the occasional 'affair of the heart' – not to mention fleeting liaisons when his royal duties took him abroad. But by 1997 more and more of his friends and contemporaries seemed to be married. Being virtually the only bachelor in the group was becoming something of an embarrassment. Not that he had anyone particularly in mind. He still saw his teenage sweetheart Supriya Shah from time to time. They remained good friends, but they were no longer in love. Besides, there were many other good-looking girls whom he counted as good friends. One in particular had caught his eye – the daughter of Pashupati and Usha Rana. There could be no denying that Devyani Rana was one of the brightest stars in Kathmandu society's firmament, limited though it admittedly was.

Dipendra and Devyani Rana had first met not in Kathmandu (although they lived within minutes of each other), but at a far more cosmopolitan party in England, at Stonor Park, near Henley-on-Thames, the country house of Lord Camoys. Devyani was accompanying her elder sister Urvashi, who in 1995 married into one of India's wealthiest families, the Khemkas, since when she has spent much of her time at their London town house in Eaton Square. In many ways the Rana sisters were much more sophisticated than Dipendra, even though he was Crown Prince of Nepal.

Quite apart from her aristocratic beauty, there were many things about Devyani that appealed to the Crown Prince. She had a natural exuberance that set her apart from other girls of similar class and background. She was decisive and straightforward – qualities which the Crown Prince found a pleasant change from the artful ambiguities of the Palace. There was a refreshing frankness about her, though of course Devyani was also bound by the constraints of Kathmandu's conservative and extremely gossip-prone society. Like others of her generation, she complained of only being allowed to go out when accompanied by a relation or, when she did meet up with friends, that it had to be at their parents' houses. For Dipendra, who had to live within even tighter constraints, she was a breath of fresh air.

Devyani was also brighter than most of her contemporaries, having graduated near the top of her class from Welham Girls High School in Dehra Dun, India, before completing her university degree at Lady Shri Ram College in New Delhi. After returning to Kathmandu, she helped her father run both his political career and the family's extremely lucrative bottled gas business. It helped that Pashupati Rana was also then Nepal's foreign minister. But she still carved out a role for herself – not the easiest thing for an unmarried woman in Nepal. She had the knack of making herself indispensable. As a fund-raiser for her father's political party, she could always be relied upon to wangle contributions out of even the most hard-nosed businessmen. She had charm, and she knew how to deploy it. So perhaps it is no surprise that, after nearly three years' platonic friendship, the Crown Prince should fall ever more deeply in love with her.

By his twenty-eighth birthday he was telling friends that he was serious about Devyani. From then on, Dipendra would force the pace. It was he who was ready to throw caution to the winds; she who reminded him of the need for discretion. It was as important for her reputation, as an unmarried Hindu daughter of a high-profile politician, as it was for him that their relationship was conducted in secret.

They used all kinds of subterfuge so that they could be together alone. They would often arrange to meet at a supermarket where they might not so easily be noticed. It helped that the Crown Prince's ADCs cooperated and even assisted with his clandestine assignations, often driving over to her father's house in Maharajganj and whisking her off to Dipendra in his private apartments inside the Royal Palace. At other times they used a friend's house in Patan for their assignations; or the ADCs would hire an upstairs room at the Shangri-la Hotel, midway between the palace and Maharajganj. When Devyani accompanied her father to some public function, the Crown Prince would turn up just as it was ending. Sometimes he would not even be able to talk to her because there were press photographers around, or simply because the risk of so many people seeing them together was too great. Whenever they could not meet up, the two of them were forever on their mobile phones – sometimes just chatting, but as often planning their next assignation. The intrigue only added excitement to their romance.

But before long, half of Kathmandu's chattering classes were talking about their affair, so they started to meet openly and went out for meals together. Their favourite place was a pizzeria called Fire & Ice, handily located on the road from the palace's West Gate towards the backpackers' district of Thamel. The restaurant was more popular with tourists than locals, which meant there was less chance of being recognised. Whenever he was in the mood, Dipendra would ask for a table at a few minutes' notice and drive over in his old Land Rover. A corner table would be cleared for him and Devyani. The ADCs who always had to accompany him sat at a separate table between them and the rest of the diners. Dipendra invariably ordered pizza – Capricciosa with extra cheese, ham, salami, but no olives. She liked spaghetti *alla carbonara*. He would have a few beers and on one occasion was invited to try grappa. Throughout, the ADCs kept a watchful eye on the exits and on other diners.

What Dipendra was trying to achieve though these impromptu outings was a sense of normality. He simply wanted to go out for a meal with his girlfriend and talk, and enjoy for an hour or two the illusion of being an ordinary person having a good time. They would share each other's food; then he would order an ice cream, which he loved, and try and persuade her to have some. Whenever he could not find his mobile phone or cigarettes, she always seemed to know which pocket they were in; and though they would not be seen holding hands or having any physical contact, since this was a public place, they talked and laughed together until the meal was over. They seldom left later than nine-thirty: Dipendra had to get back to the palace.

For the Crown Prince, however, such interludes were all too rare. Most of the time he did not enjoy the freedom to be himself rather than to act out some preordained role. It had been like that for as long as he could remember.

His parents had selected boarding schools for him where he was, in theory, treated no differently from commoners in order to 'toughen him up'. Certainly it was a stark contrast to his pampered existence during the school holidays, when palace servants and functionaries were always at hand. His life became compartmentalised, and he had to assume a different persona in each compartment. Dipendra 832 at Budhanilkantha School had to abide by different norms from HRH Crown Prince Dipendra Bir Bikram Shah at home. Dippy the Etonian had to learn to abide by yet another set of rules – not just the school rules, but those subtle codes of behaviour laid down by other boys.

Back in Nepal, he was taught to assume a different persona when he appeared at formal occasions in public. Yet another side of his personality came to the fore when he was training with the army or socialising with fellow officers. Even his relations with his parents involved an element of role-playing. Indeed, so much of his time was spent in acting out a variety of roles that he may have wondered sometimes which of them was the real Dipendra.

The question of the Crown Prince's marriage was by now becoming a matter of some urgency within the Palace. Many people considered that, at nearly thirty, he was getting too old to be a bachelor and really should settle down with a good wife who could produce further heirs to the throne. Queen Aishwarya decided to take things in hand. She asked her mother, Sri Rajya Laxmi Rana, to find a suitable bride for Dipendra.

The possibilities were eventually narrowed down to three names. One was Dipendra's old flame, Supriya Shah, despite the fact that Queen Aishwarya had previously forbidden their marriage on the grounds that, when they had first courted in the early nineties, Supriya and Dipendra had been deemed too young. But Supriya was of good family, a great-niece of the Queen Mother, and although her relationship with Dipendra had cooled the two of them still got on together. Second was Garima Rana, a bright young lawyer who was related to Princess Shruti's husband. She was probably the Queen's preferred choice, and Garima and Dipendra went out together for several months until both decided it would not work out. The third name on the shortlist was Devyani's.

When discreet enquiries were made about an arranged marriage, Devyani's mother, the formidable Usha Rana, replied that her daughter was the granddaughter of Vijaye Raje of Gwalior and famously wealthy, a response which could be said to imply that Nepal's royal family were less well off. Indeed, that was almost certainly the case, since the former ruling family of Gwalior, the Scindias, were major industrialists and owned extensive properties in New Delhi. However, Queen Aishwarya did not like to be reminded of the fact that the Shahs were not the wealthiest of royal families, and she appears to have taken Usha Rana's message as a snub. She was a strong-minded woman and sensitive about her own royal dignity. To be sneered at by a commoner was something she would not forgive, regardless of the consequences.

Aishwarya had shown the same unbending spirit before. At a summit meeting of South Asian leaders in 1989 she apparently had a run in with Sonia, the Italian-born wife of Indian Prime Minister Rajiv Gandhi, over who should take precedence. India may have been by far the largest country represented; but as Queen and wife of the Head of State, Aishwarya thought she was above a mere Prime Minister's wife.

One of the unfortunate consequences of that spat was that it strengthened Rajiv Gandhi's determination to teach the Shahs a lesson they would not forget. An economic blockade was imposed on landlocked Nepal, using the pretext that negotiations over the trade treaty between the two countries had reached deadlock. The blockade of such essentials as petrol and kerosene caused real hardship for ordinary Nepalese and within a year, in 1990, the 'Spring Awakening' was taking place in Kathmandu.

Queen Aishwarya's exaggerated sense of royal dignity led her to stir up trouble with the Gandhis and it ended up undermining Nepal's monarchy. She would not, however, learn from past mistakes. Instead, when the widowed Sonia Gandhi announced a visit to Kathmandu after the assassination of her husband in 1991, the Queen saw to it that she was denied entry to Nepal's holiest temple at Pashupatinath on the grounds that she had been born a Catholic and only later became a Hindu. A feeble enough way to exact revenge, but, as head of the Pashupati Area Development Committee, the Queen at least knew she would have her way. It did not matter to Aishwarya that this slight might damage relations with the leader of India's Congress Party, the woman who might one day become that country's Prime Minister. So much the better, as far as she was concerned. In imagining she had somehow defied the 'Indian juggernaut', the Queen was only too happy to drape herself in the folds of strident Nepali nationalism.

The episode reconfirmed Aishwayra's already strongly anti-Indian sentiments. She had long suspected that Indian intelligence was behind the riots in 1990 that led to democracy and, as she saw it, the emasculation of Nepal's ancient monarchy. Like other ex-*panchayat* conservatives, she was swift to blame India for Nepal's problems. Now, with the marriage of her eldest son under discussion, Usha Rana, the daughter of some Indian maharaja, was bragging about their family's wealth. It would never do.

There were plenty of other reasons put about – some more imagined than real – as to why Devyani was unsuitable as a bride. The most tangible was that the Queen would not tolerate a woman as independent and tough-minded as Devyani becoming her daughter-in-law. What others found spontaneously charming in Devyani, the Queen saw as calculating and manipulative. Such personal antagonisms, however, were not enough to deny the Crown Prince happiness. There had to be other, more tangible reasons for objecting.

First, it was suggested – without any medical evidence whatsoever – that Devyani was unable to bear male children. Since producing a healthy male heir is one of the prime qualifications for becoming a Crown Princess, this automatically ruled her out. The Queen and other 'antis' also pointed to the fact that Devyani had no male siblings. Even her name, Devyani, was considered inauspicious. It was, according to the Hindu scriptures, the name of the daughter of a renegade Brahmin who had assisted the demons in their battle with the gods, and she herself had ended up marrying someone not of her priestly caste.

Given that Queen Aishwarya was becoming increasingly religious with age, any such warnings of unsuitability coming from the ancient scriptures only confirmed her instinctive hostility towards Devyani Rana. Nepal's royal family did not want the heir to the throne – and therefore an incarnation of Lord Vishnu – to commit himself to a mismatch comparable to that of the legendary Devyani.

There were also doubts about the purity of Devyani's lineage. On her father's side she was descended from the Shamsher Ranas, and some genealogists claim there was an improper intercaste marriage in the distant past. She was also the great-granddaughter of the last Rana Prime Minister, Mohan Shamsher, a man not fondly remembered by either the Shahs or the Queen's family of Juddha Ranas. On her mother's side, as Usha Rana had been all too quick to point out, Devyani was descended from an extremely wealthy and influential Indian princely family, the Maharajas of Gwalior. But objections could be raised against such wealthy ancestors: they were, for example, dispossessed princes and not of pure Rajput stock. Such subtle distinctions of clan and caste are increasingly overlooked in the modern world, but they still mattered to Queen Aishwarya who set great store by purity of caste and blood lineage. If nothing else, they provided her with good excuses for continuing to oppose her son's desire to marry the woman he loved.

On this the Queen was absolutely determined. If the Crown Prince refused to marry either of the other two perfectly suitable girls whose names had been put forward, wedding plans could be suspended. To justify further delay, a rumour was circulated that an astrologer had predicted great harm would come to the King and the Kingdom as a whole if the Crown Prince married before he was thirty-five. For him to go ahead regardless would therefore be both selfish and irresponsible.

The official Royal Astrologer denies ever making such a prediction, and its true source (if indeed one ever existed) has never been revealed. But the story was soon buzzing around Kathmandu, and those who knew what was going on inside the palace could read these astrological rumours for what they were – yet another salvo aimed at sinking Dipendra's plans to marry Devyani.

The atmosphere inside Narayanhiti became increasingly sour as the 'marriage question' continued to divide the family. The Queen had most of the elder relatives on her side. The King generally went along with her on family matters. The Queen Mother was close to Dipendra: he frequently went to see her at Mahendra Manzil. But as for what the former Queen Ratna really thought, one could never be certain.

Dipendra could at least count on the support of his younger brother Nirajan and his cousin Paras. In their company he dispensed with the old-fashioned formalities. He insisted they call him *dhai*, or elder brother, rather than by his official titles. They went out drinking and to restaurants together. They all assumed a similar irreverence towards their hidebound elders. But Dipendra always made sure the young bloods looked up to him.

Of the younger generation, Princess Shruti was most strongly opposed to her brother's relationship with Devyani, perhaps because she was a close friend of Supriya Shah. In a traditionally male-dominated society like Nepal's, her opinion would not normally have mattered a great deal; but since she was a happily married mother Shruti could claim to know how things work out in marriages.

Dipendra did not appreciate this opposition from his younger sister Nor did he appreciate the conversations about him and Devyani going on behind his back. At his twenty-ninth birthday party, held at Tribhuvan Sadan, he went public about his feelings, and in spectacular fashion.

Dipendra had been steeling himself for a showdown all evening, slipping back to his bedchamber several times to smoke another of his 'special cigarettes'. He waited until after the older family members had left before dropping his bombshell, suddenly declaring to the assembled company that he was going to marry Devyani. If anyone opposed the idea, they could leave straight away. Those who agreed could stay. Anyone who wanted to speak their mind should do so immediately.

The message was clear enough: 'you're either with me or against me'. His guests, most of them royal cousins, fell into an embarrassed silence. But Dipendra had not finished yet. He openly threatened to kill anybody who opposed his marriage, his own parents included. At this, Shruti went over to speak to him, accompanied by her husband Gorakh, who would later claim to have had sharp words with the Crown Prince. Others dispute this, saying that he would never have dared to do such a thing and was simply building up his own role in the fracas. What is clear is that Dipendra was in an uncontrollable state. He slapped his sister, who was heavily pregnant at the time, sending her falling to the floor. The Crown Prince had to be led out of the room by his younger brother and cousin Paras.

His behaviour that night had been unworthy of a future King of Nepal. Worse still, Dipendra apparently thought *he* was owed an apology because his sister had been 'disrespectful' towards him. The birthday party provided the clearest possible warning of a confrontation ahead, one that would be extremely bitter.

In fact, the Palace was fully aware that Dipendra's behaviour had become increasingly erratic. He was drinking heavily and had been abusive to servants and palace officials. He himself recognised that he had a problem. The previous spring a thoroughly depressed Crown Prince had sought psychiatric help. He had been prescribed a course of antidepressants which required that he give up alcohol. Given his previous consumption of up to ten beers and a dozen whiskies a day, this must have been a shock to the system. Dipendra 'compensated' by smoking more grass and hashish.

As their affair intensified, Dipendra and Devyani became increasingly reckless. They were seen out together more often in Kathmandu. The gossips went into overdrive. Articles linking their names appeared in the local press – apparently to the Queen's intense displeasure. It was also rumoured that a secret tantric ceremony had been held in Devyani's house, that a spell had been cast upon a ring to bind the lovers together, and that the tantric priests who officiated had been invited from India to perform these arcane, power-enhancing rituals by one of Devyani's mother's Indian relatives. For those Nepalese who believe in tantrism's mystical and life-transforming potential, there was something slightly sinister in this appeal to supernatural powers.

Whatever was fuelling their passion, they both felt that simply seeing each other for an occasional hour or two was not enough. What they wanted most of all was to spend whole days together, alone and unrecognised. That was clearly impossible to arrange within Nepal because the Crown Prince was known everywhere. So they decided to meet up abroad.

An opportunity arose not long after the disastrous birthday party. Dipendra had for many years been involved in sport and athletics, and not merely as patron of the National Sports Council and various other organisations. He had put in some hard work on the South Asia Federation Games and Nepal's Olympic Committee. Now he had been invited to the Olympic Games in Sydney as head of the Nepalese delegation. The secret plan was that Devyani join him there.

This required as much subterfuge on her part as on his. She told her family she was off to London to visit her elder sister – Urvashi could be relied upon to keep a secret. In fact, Devyani obtained a visa from the Australian Embassy in Kathmandu and booked a separate flight to Sydney. The two of them stayed in the same hotel, revelling both in each other and their new-found anonymity. Dipendra had squared things with his ADCs and the sports officials staying in the hotel. Nobody needed to know anything about the Olympic Games assignation.

It was an unrealistic hope. Inevitably, word trickled back to Kathmandu. At first Devyani's family could not believe it. When confronted by an angry relative she lied, insisting she had been in London with her sister. Only when her presence in Sydney was confirmed by the Australian authorities did Devyani admit being with the Crown Prince.

Dipendra's parents made it clear they were not amused by this latest escapade, which they considered nothing short of scandalous. All kinds of 'special favours' and effort had been needed to hush things up. It was no way for the heir apparent to conduct himself. If anything, the episode reinforced the convictions of Queen Aishwarya and those who shared her views that Dipendra could never marry such a shameless woman. Confrontation loomed ahead.

Sharp words may have been exchanged in private, but on the surface, at least, life at Narayanhiti Palace continued as before. Dipendra still regularly joined his parents for meals and ran errands for the Queen Mother. His sister Princess Shruti turned up with the grandchildren. The appearance of being one big happy family had to be maintained.

Beneath the surface, however, hostile coalitions were assembling. Some kind of showdown over Dipendra's wedding plans was inevitable. The Queen relied on the moral indignation and prejudices of the older generation; the Crown Prince on the fear that he inspired – not least because he knew exactly what his younger brother and cousins got up to in private. The art of gentle arm-twisting is perhaps the oldest of royal sports and, in more brutal times, the key to survival.

After the Australian jaunt, Dipendra reverted to the tactics he had clumsily announced at his twenty-ninth birthday party. He no longer seemed to care what other people thought. He was going to marry

Devyani, and that was the end of it. Who could prevent him? It would be contrary to the Royal Constitution to force him to stand down as Crown Prince. It was his birthright. If threatened with that, he would just 'blow them all away'. Or so he boasted when he was among friends, far away from any figure of authority.

It was dangerous talk, though none of his friends believed him. It was just 'CP' – the abbreviation by which he was referred to among close friends – showing bravado. They all laughed at the absurdity of it all. CP liked jokes.

If anybody realised how serious things were, it was Devyani. She knew Dipendra better than anyone. She knew how to mother him as his own mother never had. She saw that he ate properly, sending him home-prepared low-calorie meals because she knew he shared the inherited cholesterol problem. She reassured him. When he had to make a parachute jump, Devyani was there with him. She had also been present when he was so drugged with hashish that he covered it up by announcing 'let's not talk about anything serious now'. Devyani knew him well enough to realise whether he was joking or not.

One of their closest friends described them as 'soul mates', as they were, at a certain level, though the relationship resembled that between a nurse and an emotionally needy patient. It was always Dipendra who demanded that she marry him. On one occasion he produced a phial of what he claimed to be poison and threatened to commit suicide if she refused him. On her side, Devyani was conscious of the need to keep the increasingly volatile prince more or less on the rails. For his sake she had already rejected a raft of marriage proposals from eligible young men – including one belonging to an Indian princely family who flew up to Kathmandu and waited in vain for her response. Devyani was also painfully aware that time was slipping by. But as long as Dipendra's parents remained implacably opposed to their marriage, she reasoned, nothing could be done about it.

In taking this line, Devyani was the more realistic of the two. Where Dipendra looked ahead to an idealised future together, she was more grounded in the realities of the present. She tried to 'improve' him, urging him to lose weight and cut down on the drink, drugs and cigarettes. She knew that if Dipendra continued to consume at the same pace, he would burn out sooner rather than later. History told her that little joy awaited her as a Nepalese prince's widow. And he had put on so much weight recently that he was beginning to lose what looks he ever had.

What kind of love or affection Devyani and Dipendra shared was conditioned both by his position as Crown Prince and by all the rows between families and within families that ensued. But once he had declared his intention to marry her, Dipendra was determined to win, whatever the cost. This may have been driven as much by old-fashioned *amour propre* than 'true love'. He certainly did not stop seeing other women – including his old girlfriend, Supriya Shah – because of his love for Devyani. In fact, he had both their photographs in his wallet beside each other. He telephoned Supriya regularly up to the end. But then, as Crown Prince, he stood above ordinary conventions.

11

Star-Crossed Lovers?

The Crown Prince combined a strongly romantic streak with a remarkable memory. Since his schooldays he had been in the habit of memorising entire poems or scenes from Shakespeare. Predictably, *Romeo and Juliet* was among his favourites, for it seemed to deal with matters very close to his own heart. When he toured Verona, therefore, he made a special point of visiting the balcony where Juliet is said to have listened to Romeo's impassioned pleas. The graffiti that despoiled the courtyard annoyed him: such lack of respect was not fitting in a shrine to romantic love.

Astrology was also of great importance to Dipendra, especially when it came to his choice of bride. Although determined to marry Devyani, he still wanted to be certain that the marriage would be auspicious. He needed assurance that they would prosper and have male children, that Devyani and he would have a long and harmonious life together. An appropriate date for the wedding ceremonies needed to be found, and so Dipendra followed the normal course and consulted the family astrologer about their horoscopes.

In arranged marriages, the two sets of parents would normally organise the comparing of astrological charts. These were deemed to be extremely valuable and sensitive documents that would normally be kept locked in a safe. Dipendra's situation, as a young man seeking to marry against his parents' wishes, was somewhat different. As with everything else it seemed, it required secrecy and subterfuge. Somehow Dipendra got hold of both sets of charts and took them to an unprepossessing house up a side lane in Dilli Bazaar. This was the residence of his (and the royal family's) personal guru, Nayan Raj Pandey.

As Dipendra related the incident to his friends, Nayan Raj Pandey was only too pleased to assist in such a delicate matter. The Brahmin studied the two birth charts, compared the alignment of the stars and planets in each case, and concluded that they were very beautiful. These two young people were compatible astrologically. Indeed, they seemed to be unusually well matched. Their union would be fruitful.

Dipendra was elated by the news. It was true: he and Devyani really were star-crossed lovers. They would be married after all. He and Devyani pencilled in a date for the forthcoming winter wedding season.

But for Nayan Raj Pandey, this unsolicited consultation was not the end of the matter. His first obligation was not to Dipendra but to the King, whose foremost spiritual adviser he was. His wife was guru to Queen Aishwarya. It was Pandey's duty to tell them both about the Crown Prince's visit to his house. In the account he gave to the King and Queen, his judgement was that Dipendra and Devyani's horoscopes were exceedingly ill-matched. He knew this was precisely what they, or at least the Queen, wanted to hear.

Quite understandably, Dipendra was furious when he heard what Nayan Raj Pandey had done. His confidence had been betrayed. Worse than that, he had been set up. In his anxiety, he felt that his status within the palace had been reduced to that of a star-struck fool.

Among his own circle the Crown Prince railed long and hard against that two-faced old priest who 'was nothing better than a bat'. It was a telling jibe, because in Hindu mythology the bat was forever changing sides in the epic battle that is supposed to have been fought between all the animals of the earth and the birds of the air. The bat vacillated: when the animals were winning it proclaimed itself to be one of them, and when the birds looked dominant it argued that, since bats can fly, they must obviously be counted among the birds. From this legend stems the idea that the bat is synonymous with cunning, deception and selfishness. They never joined in the fight themselves, but prospered by joining the winners of the contest. As an insult, it is particularly fitting for brahmanical priests like Pandey who neither fought nor tilled the soil, but always prospered by hanging on the coat-tails of princes.

The Crown Prince may have decided unilaterally that he would marry Devyani, but his equally strong-willed mother continued to stand resolutely against their union. The more frantic and outrageous Dipendra became, the easier it was for the Queen to gather support for her stand among other members of the royal family. Thinking that the whole matter was on hold, she turned her attentions to another prospective marriage – that of her youngest child, Prince Nirajan.

Nirajan had always been Queen Aishwarya's favourite, and she took pleasure in indulging his whims. Perhaps it was his more delicate features and winning smile that made the Queen prefer him to his elder brother. His character was more straightforward and easygoing. From the Queen's perspective, he was simply much less trouble than her first-born.

That said, Prince Nirajan had got himself into some embarrassing scrapes. He had disappeared from Eton for several days to go on a drink and drugs binge in London. The Queen and the Crown Prince had immediately felt compelled to fly to England to take him back to school and persuade the authorities that the boy really should not be expelled for one transgression, however serious.

But after that incident, Nirajan had turned out reasonably well. He was a fine athlete, a competition-level swimmer, and seemed to be studying hard for his college degree in commerce. He was well liked by his friends and possessed none of the erratic and domineering traits that were becoming all too apparent in his brother. When compared side by side, some thought that Nirajan would make the better King – especially in a constitutional monarchy, where the skills most in demand were tact and diplomacy. But Nirajan was only the younger brother: the Royal Constitution stated unequivocally that the eldest son had to inherit.

There was nothing, however, to prevent the younger brother getting married first. He had turned twenty-two and his mother felt it would be good for him to settle down once his final examinations were over in June 2001. Queen Aishwarya and the other royal ladies already had matters in hand. Ayushma Rana, a girl of good family, who would suit him admirably. The astrologers pronounced them compatible and they seemed to get on well together. Their engagement could be announced after Nirajan's graduation and the wedding would take place during the winter season, once an auspicious date had been secured.

For the Crown Prince these were disturbing developments. If Nirajan went along with an arranged marriage, Dipendra would become even more isolated. It would be humiliating still to be unmarried and to be compelled to attend the wedding of a brother more than seven years his junior; doubly humiliating, in fact, since everyone there would know about his rash and unfulfilled promise to marry Devyani.

There was another, even more disquieting historical undercurrent. What would happen if his own marriage prospects remained deadlocked and Nirajan went ahead and produced an heir? Of course nobody would dare to suggest that the Crown Prince be removed from the royal succession. That was not how things were done in Narayanhiti. But if Dipendra openly defied his parents in marrying Devyani, the possibility of an alternative succession was always a silent threat.

The Crown Prince did not have the time or the inclination to analyse the situation carefully, as his father would have done. That was not in his nature. He had many other distractions. Through the early months of 2001 he was very much involved in preparations for the country's biggest sports event, the Fifth National Games. The administrative load was more than he had anticipated, and there would be a round of site inspections and last-minute details to attend to in June.

Such administrative duties were time consuming, but not nearly as stressful as Dipendra's dealings with the army's top brass. It was a highly sensitive role, entrusted to him by his father; and by the spring of 2001 the question of whether to deploy the Royal Nepal Army against the Maoist guerrillas could no longer be avoided. The King was against the idea, and one of the few real powers left to him as consti-tutional monarch was to order the army into action. Prime Minister

G. P. Koirala wanted to deploy the troops. A constitutional crisis loomed.

Birendra dealt with the Prime Minister and other politicians in person, but other key roles had been delegated to the more active members of the royal family. His youngest brother, Dhirendra, had the delicate task of maintaining lines of communication with the Maoists. Dipendra's role was to liaise with the generals and report back to the Palace what they were thinking. If the situation across the country deteriorated, some of the hardliners might be tempted to act on their own and impose martial law without the King's consent. The Crown Prince was chosen as the conduit because he had always been close to the military, but the role was taxing. For the first time in his life Dipendra found himself with seriously high-pressure responsibilities.

The Crown Prince did not respond well to stress. A heavy drinker and smoker, he justified his sometimes prodigious drug consumption as necessary to help him 'de-stress'. Dipendra also had a weight problem: he had been greedy since early childhood. In his early twenties he tried to stay reasonably trim by jogging and hard physical exercise. But more recently he had let things slide and had become so overweight that his doctors suggested he had a medical examination. Dipendra may well have dreaded the results, being only too aware that he was seriously out of condition and growing old before his time.

In early May, just after returning from his official visit to Japan, the Crown Prince asked a much older courtier how he managed to look so young. 'I dye my hair, Your Highness' was the response. Dipendra jokingly replied that that would not do much good for him as his own hair was coming out. At which he pulled off his *topi* and pointed to all the loose hairs inside the brim. He laughed it off at the time, though in private he worried about yet another sign that his youth was behind him. What concerned him most, however, was how unfit he had become. A forthcoming demonstration karate match with his Japanese teacher required that he train especially hard if he was not to make a complete fool of himself in public. He promised he would start on a strict regime – no cigarettes, alcohol or drugs, just plenty of disciplined exercise. He never quite got round to it.

Underlying all the day to-day pressures there remained, as ever, the 'marriage question'. The fact that Dipendra was deeply depressed about this, and in an increasingly unstable frame of mind, was known even in England. Early in May 2001 his former guardian, Lord Camoys, faxed a private letter of warning to King Birendra about the Crown Prince's mental state generally, and in particular his unhappiness at being denied both a meaningful role in life and the right to marry. Whether or not the King took notice of this letter is unknown.

Dipendra's mood swings subsequently grew still more erratic. As spring turned to summer he at first seemed to be in a much more buoyant frame of mind. He seemed convinced that there were signs that his father was finally coming round to the idea of his marrying Devyani. Around the middle of May the King confided as much to his former Prime Minister Kirthinidi Bista. For the first time in years Dipendra believed he might finally have gained his father's blessing. With the King's support, all the other family members would eventually fall into line. In the meantime, he dutifully kept calling on the Queen Mother – though her views on the matter remained as inscrutable as ever.

At least for a short while, Dipendra believed that he had almost won through. He felt confident enough about the likelihood of a wedding to advise some of his closest friends in England to keep their diaries free for December 2001. Although an auspicious date still had to be found, he told them that the marriage ceremony would definitely take place during the coming winter season.

But then mysterious wheels inside the palace began to turn again, this time against Dipendra. That the Queen led the counterattack is taken for granted, though precisely how she brought Birendra over to her side is not known. But now there was an added twist. Queen Aishwarya knew her son well enough to realise he would go ahead and marry with or without their permission. Dipendra was therefore presented with the ultimate deterrent. If he persisted in defying his parents, he would be stripped of both his royal titles and his financial allowance.

Dipendra had always been kept on a tight budget by his father. He was not extravagant, but for the money to dry up completely would be a disaster. Unless he was carrying out official duties, the twenty-nine-year-old Crown Prince would effectively be confined to his bungalow inside the Royal Palace.

The threat was a testament to Aishwarya's strength of will and determination. And also to her insensitivity. Having come so close to his goal, Dipendra felt utterly betrayed by his father. He also found himself boxed into an untenable position. He had made a semi-public commitment to Devyani which he could not now reverse. His closest friends had practically been invited to the wedding. If it was cancelled, his credibility, his reputation, his unusually developed sense of personal honour – all would lie in tatters. There was only one honourable course of action open to him: he would marry Devyani anyway, even if by doing so he lost his royal birthright.

There are various reports on how Devyani responded to Dipendra's proposed solution to his predicament. Some say that when Dipendra told her he would give up his royal titles – that they would be happy together anyway, that between them there would be enough money on which to get by – Devyani went 'white with rage'. Her own family deny this strenuously, and understandably so. The clear implication is that Devyani was determined to be Queen of Nepal and that she would not accept Dipendra's throwing away that future simply because he was having a monumental fit of pique.

A more generous interpretation is that she was angry about the way in which he was being treated by his own family. For, despite entrenched differences over the 'marriage question', Dipendra had always spoken respectfully of his parents and remained loyal to them. Yet, however understanding Devyani was of the Crown Prince's problems, he was still trapped in a corner from which there seemed no acceptable way out.

Unsurprisingly, when the results of Dipendra's medical check-up were returned, his blood pressure was found to be abnormally high, as was his cholesterol count. Although these were hereditary ailments, in Dipendra they were present much earlier than might normally have been expected. The diagnosis gave yet another reason for the Crown Prince to be profoundly depressed.

Of all his forthcoming official engagements, the one that Dipendra looked forward to with least pleasure was in his diary for the afternoon of 1 June 2001, when he was expected to accompany his parents to the house of the royal guru, Nayan Raj Pandey, and congratulate him on his seventieth wedding anniversary. The Crown Prince would be obliged to offer his felicitations, despite the fact that the old priest had deceived him over his and Devyani's horoscopes. Worse still, such an occasion would allow his mother to put on her religious airs and graces and be quietly triumphant. Dipendra initially tried to avoid the entire affair.

His sister Shruti had been excused because she was busy with her two little daughters; Nirajan was allowed to stay at home because he was tired after his final examinations. Dipendra's day included a full morning at the office, lunch with his parents, followed by an inspection tour of the sports facilities for the forthcoming National Games – the swimming complex; the new squash courts; the shooting ranges. He would have to be full of encouragement and at the same time satisfy himself that all was ready for the grand opening in two days' time. Then, in the evening, he was hosting the family's regular Friday night reunion. There was not room in this schedule to spend even a few minutes together with Devyani. Yet it was Devyani who finally persuaded him that he really should accompany his parents. His failure to join them would otherwise provide another opportunity for them to criticise him.

So Dipendra dutifully followed behind his parents in their armour-plated Mercedes as the royal motorcade made its way through Kathmandu's narrow streets towards the priest's plain-fronted, three-storey house in Dilli Bazaar. The usual security arrangements required he travel in a separate vehicle. They were greeted in the front yard by the old priest who performed a welcoming ceremony, throwing silver coins on the ground in offering to Birendra as an incarnation of Vishnu. The King left them untouched, for he could never accept an offering from his own guru. Then, as Pandey's family and neighbours showered rice flakes and flower petals from the balconies above, the royal party climbed the narrow stairs and were ushered into a sitting room.

Tea was served and four generations of Pandeys filed into the room and made their respectful greetings. There were many of them, for this line of royal priests had prospered in the seven decades since the twelve-year-old Nayan Raj had been married to a little girl called Jeev Kumari. Though it had only been a simple ceremony, King Tribhuvan had graced that occasion with his presence. Now his grandson Birendra and great-grandson had come to celebrate his anniversary. It was a touching scene.

Dipendra sat apart from his parents and scarcely uttered a word throughout. When food was served, Queen Aishwarya tucked into black lentils and potatoes, fried breads and pickles, and especially the sweet rice pudding flavoured with saffron. She was obviously in good spirits. The King ate sparingly, explaining that his heart condition demanded he keep to a strict diet. Dipendra did not touch a thing, not even the Coca-Cola he had been served. He sat there, unsmiling, as the priest recited a religious poem and then entered into an involved conversation with his monarch.

For the best part of an hour the Crown Prince was surrounded by people enthusing about tradition, religion and families; he might as well not have been there at all. His eyes remained expressionless, his mind obviously somewhere else.

Towards the end of the visit, Aishwarya went into the family shrine room and offered a prayer to the assembled Hindu gods. The royal party then took its leave. The Crown Prince remained silent and impassive. Only when he was back in his car did his face break into a smile. The motorcade drove down to Durbar Marg and then turned right towards Narayanhiti's main entrance. The massive steel-barred gates opened and then closed behind them. The journey had been covered in less than five minutes. For Nepal's royal family, that was their last journey through the outside world,

12

The Family Reunion

The invitations to the habitual Friday *soirée* at Tribhuvan Sadan had been sent out by the Palace Secretariat, as usual. Only members of the royal family and their in-laws were on the list. It was to be an informal family gathering: first drinks, and then a late buffet dinner at which everyone helped themselves. No ADCs or bodyguards would need to be present, since this was a strictly private occasion held in the safest cordon of the palace. Servants came only to bring in the food or refresh the ice as required. The King and Queen, their three grown-up children, and some twenty other royal relations were expected.

There was nothing unusual. Such informal family reunions had been going on for nearly thirty years. The tradition had been started by King Birendra himself, shortly after he ascended the throne. It was a good way, he thought, to keep the extended royal family together. The gatherings were usually held on the third Friday of the Nepalese month. In the Nepalese lunar calendar, the due date fell on 1 June.

The venue for the family gathering shifted around the palace complex according to who was host that evening. Sometimes it was held at Sri Sadan, the private apartments of the King and Queen. At other times it was at the Queen Mother's residence. On 1 June it was the turn of the Crown Prince to play host, so the guests were invited to his private residence at Tribhuvan Sadan, the cluster of buildings that had grown around the hall where the King's grandfather had formerly received guests. Since it had been converted into a billiards room, with a music centre and an adjacent sitting room, it was a comfortable enough spot for family gatherings.

That evening, the six sofas in the billiards room had thoughtfully been arranged in two semicircles — one at each end, so the more elderly royals could sit and chat apart from the more boisterous younger members of the family. When dinner was served, usually quite late on in the evening, they would move to the dining room next door. It was very informal. For the immediate members of the royal family, who as part of their 'jobs' had to attend endless banquets and receptions, such cosy informality was a welcome relief. It was good to be able to talk without always having the servants around.

The only slight deviation from routine practice was that the guests had all been telephoned personally by the Crown Prince's ADC for confirmation that they would be attending. Normally the Queen's ADC, rather than the Crown Prince's, would have been responsible for this: but it was only a minor change to the custom and nothing worth dwelling on.

The evening light was fading as the Crown Prince crossed the bridge from his personal apartments to the main part of Tribhuvan Sadan. He had showered and changed since returning from the tea party with Nayan Raj Pandey, and seemed to be in a much better mood. As host for the evening, it was incumbent upon him to be there well before any of the guests arrived. He was accompanied by his usual ADC, Major Gajendra Bohara. He poured himself a stiff whisky at the bar — The Famous Grouse, his favourite brand.

Dipendra told his ADC to remain with him while he waited for the first guests to arrive. He moved down to the billiards table where he practised shots with his ADC. Servants were laying the tables for dinner in the adjoining room. The hands of the clock moved inexorably towards seven-thirty, when his guests were due.

The first to appear was Maheshwar Kumar Singh. It was his habit to arrive early. Maheshwar was born into an Indian princely family and had married one of King Birendra's aunts. He had lived in Kathmandu for more than forty years and was a regular at the Friday night gatherings. A dapper figure in his Nepali cap and tight-fitting trousers, he bowed respectfully to the Crown Prince upon entering the room. Dipendra poured him a whisky with ice and water. At this point, the Crown Prince appeared to be 'completely normal', smiling and making small talk.

Next to arrive was another of the King's uncles by marriage and a member of Nepal's aristocracy, the seventy-four-year-old Rabi Shamsher Rana. A retired general of the Royal Nepal Army, he too was a regular guest, though since his wife's death four years earlier he attended the family reunions alone. As barman for the evening, the Crown Prince served him a large scotch. Rabi toyed with it as other guests arrived, for the tumbler had been filled to the brim and he could no longer drink as he had in the old days. Dipendra asked Rabi to join him in a game of billiards, to which the old general replied that he could not play properly because he had hurt his hand in an accident.

The Queen appeared wearing a red sari just as the King's three sisters, Princesses Shanti, Sharada and Shobha also arrived. Next, Prince Nirajan wandered in with a CD in his hand. Princess Shruti was accompanied by her husband, Kumar Gorakh, but without their two young daughters. There had been another party for the children the previous week; this was for adult royals only. Besides, it was only a short distance to the palace from their family house in Kesar Mahal.

By now a stream of vehicles bearing assorted royal cousins and aunts was entering the palace's West Gate. Smartly uniformed guards snapped to attention and saluted as they drove first up a tree-lined avenue towards the main palace before turning left, past the back of the Palace Secretariat buildings, to Tribhuvan Sadan. The royal guests were dropped off outside the ADC's office, from where it is only a short walk through a flower-filled garden to the veranda entrance to the billiards room. Cousin Paras arrived with his mother, Princess Komal, his sister Prerana, and his elegant Indian-born wife, Himani. He was escorting all the ladies this evening since his father, Prince Gyanendra, was away from Kathmandu.

The King's other brother, Dhirendra, arrived with his three daughters and son-in-law, Captain Rajiv Shahi. Following his divorce, Dhirendra had lost his royal title and all the privileges that went with it. But plain Mr Dhirendra Shah was back in favour with the King, who still considered his youngest brother very much a part of the royal family. Moreover, recently he had been on better terms with his ex-wife, Princess Prekshya, who had also been on the invitation list for that evening. But she was unable to attend.

Another royal divorcee, Mrs Ketaki Chester, arrived, as did her mother Princess Helen and her tiny but immensely sharp-witted sister, Princess Jayanti. Princess Helen was there primarily to talk to her sister-in-law, the Queen Mother, and they were to spend almost the entire evening closeted together in a separate room.

The Crown Prince had been busy welcoming guests and dispensing drinks. The younger crowd sat at the end of the room furthest from the billiards table, where they could smoke without being noticed. Although Dipendra smoked, even at thirty he dared not do so in the presence of the King or Queen Mother. It was contrary to protocol. If he was smoking when his father appeared he would immediately stub out the cigarette and have it removed surreptitiously.

Dipendra joined the young set and started talking with Paras. As ever, the 'marriage question' was in the air and Dipendra had been called in by his parents to discuss it. Paras knew about this meeting, but did not mention it for the time being because it seemed obvious to him that the Crown Prince had been drinking. 'What will you have?' asked Dipendra, still acting the host. Paras said he was thinking of having a Coke. 'You just want a Coke? I've been drinking whisky.'

Others present had begun to notice oddities in the Crown Prince's behaviour. Dipendra was a hardened drinker, capable of downing a dozen whiskies apparently without his composure becoming ruffled. 'He certainly wasn't drunk,' commented Ketaki. 'Normally when he'd been drinking he just went quiet. This time he was putting on an act, bumping into tables and so on.' Something abnormal was going on.

Paras asked the Crown Prince what had happened during the talk with his parents. 'Oh nothing,' he replied. 'We've been talking about the marriage. I talked with my mother and grandmother and they both said no. I will talk about it to His Majesty on Sunday.'

Dipendra was closer to his cousin than to most of his own immediate family. He admired Paras's recklessness and envied his 'bad boy' reputation, while he had to play the 'Model Prince'. Paras had backed him over his decision to marry Devyani and remained Dipendra's closest confidant concerning his troubled marriage prospects.

At around eight o'clock Dipendra left his guests to drive to the other side of the main palace to Mahendra Manzil, the Queen Mother's residence. As host, it was his duty to greet his grandmother and escort her to the party. Whether anything was said between them concerning the marriage situation is not known, for to this day Queen Mother Ratna has remained resolutely silent on the subject. But it was clear to everyone present that, on his return to the party, the Crown Prince's mood had changed for the worse.

The Queen Mother went straight to the smaller room known as Baitho Bathak where she was accustomed to receive visitors. The older royals trooped in to perform the ritual *darshan* on entering the Queen Mother's presence and then to pay their respects. Dipendra stayed behind in the billiards room, took out his mobile phone and called Devyani.

They talked for a little over a minute. The contents of their conversation remain Devyani's secret to this day. It could well have been no more than small talk. They were in love and, because they could not see each other as often as they wanted to, they talked incessantly on their mobiles. Devyani was preparing to go out to a party hosted by wealthy Indian friends, Sanjay and Shilpa Dugar. If the Crown Prince could get away early after the family dinner party had ended, it had been tentatively agreed that they should meet up afterwards. But something said during their conversation appears to have upset Dipendra. After speaking to Devyani, he called his ADC and commanded him to bring him his cigarettes.

Gajendra Bohara had received such orders many times before and he asked a royal orderly, Ram Krishna KC, to make up a packet of five of the prince's 'specials' containing the usual mixture of hashish and, it would later be reported, a mysterious black substance. ADC Bohara then proceeded to walk over to the billiards room. Rather than enter a room full of members of the royal family, he stopped at the east door and entrusted the cigarettes to Prince Paras. It seemed the right thing to do, since Paras was all too aware of the Crown Prince's smoking habits.

Only six minutes passed between Dipendra's ordering his 'specials' and the next call. It was incoming and it was from Devyani's personal landline. Dipendra did not accept the call, which was transferred automatically to his ADC. Devyani said she was worried about the Crown Prince. His voice had sounded slurred. Could Bohara check out the situation? Curiously, she asked the ADC to look for him in his private rooms because he might not be feeling well.

Devyani was obviously very anxious about something. Once she had spoken to Bohara, she telephoned another of Dipendra's regular ADCs, Raju Karki, on his home number. He was off duty and preparing to fly to the United States for further military training. Devyani insisted he go immediately to the palace. She must have been persuasive: he put on his ADC's uniform and drove over to Narayanhiti at once.

Perhaps Devyani knew more than she was letting on. She was familiar with Dipendra's sudden mood swings and how he behaved when on drugs. But why ask the ADCs to look in his rooms? After all, he had just called her from the party.

At precisely the same time that Devyani was talking to Raju Karki, the atmosphere within the billiards room had become unsettlingly bizarre. The Crown Prince began to fall about as though he were roaring drunk. He then slumped to the floor and appeared to have passed out. It was as out of character as it was embarrassing. Fortunately, most of the older family members were with the Queen Mother in her separate chamber. The King had not yet arrived but was expected at any minute. For the Crown Prince to be found unconscious would be a catastrophic breach of protocol, made worse by the fact he was supposed to be hosting the evening.

Paras tried to revive Dipendra. 'Not here, it's inappropriate,' he declared. 'The King has arrived.' But it was no use. The Crown Prince appeared to be out cold. Four of the younger generation decided it would be best to get him out of the billiards room immediately. They staggered under the deadweight, his brother Nirajan and Captain Shahi taking an arm each while Paras held up his feet. Princess Shruti's husband, Kumar Gorakh, followed behind as this bizarre cortège lurched over the little bridge and up the steps leading to the Crown Prince's private apartments. They hauled him to his bedchamber and placed him on a low divan. Switching off the lights, they left Dipendra to sleep it off and returned to the party in time for the King's arrival, as was only proper.

King Birendra had been working late, as usual. This particular evening he had been closeted with his principal press secretary, Mohan Bahadur Panday, going over the details of a rare interview with a magazine editor. After years of self-imposed seclusion, Birendra was becoming more open with the press. As the discussion drew to a close, Panday asked and was granted permission to leave at about eight-thirty.

Rather than be driven around to Tribhuvan Sadan, Birendra chose to walk. Since his heart attack two and a half years earlier, the King had been advised to take more exercise. It was only five minutes' walk from his office, but even so he was accompanied by one of his ADCs, Colonel Sundar Pratap Rana. When he reached Tribhuvan Sadan, the King went straight to the small chamber where the Queen Mother was holding court, so that he could immediately pay his respects. Colonel Rana left him at the entrance, knowing, like the other ADCs, this was a 'family only' evening, then walked on to the ADCs' office, less than a minute away. Both he and the other officers on duty could easily be called, if needed.

The Queen Mother was surrounded by royal relations when the King entered. They hurried to greet him, then everyone raised a toast to Queen Mother Ratna's health. She responded by suggesting that they replenish their glasses. In the world of palace etiquette, where things are said indirectly, this was a clear hint that she wanted a private conference. Most of the royal uncles and aunts departed, leaving only King Birendra, Queen Aishwarya and Princess Helen with the Queen Mother. The four of them remained talking in the private chamber for twenty minutes. What precisely they discussed is not known, though with three senior royal ladies present the subject of marriages – and not just Dipendra's, but plans for his brother Nirajan to marry a suitable Rana girl – may well have received their attention.

There are many reasons why Dipendra, intoxicated or not, should have wanted to absent himself while this kind of conference was going on. It was humiliating to be talked about in such a manner. Besides, he knew that none of the three royal ladies supported his plans to marry Devyani. He did not need to hear echoes of their disapproval. It was preferable to absent himself entirely, even if it meant acting the drunken idiot.

The opinion of many who saw him falling about – that he was only acting rather than physically intoxicated – seems be borne out by what happened next. He had been left in his bedroom, apparently fast asleep on the divan, at a little after eight-thirty. He must have roused himself almost immediately, for just a few minutes later two servants sent by ADC Gajendra Bohara after he received the telephone call from Devyani found the Crown Prince trying to undress himself on the bedroom floor. Together they helped him, after which Dipendra went to the bathroom and was apparently sick. One of the servants believes he heard retching noises through the bathroom door. The Crown Prince then returned to his bedchamber and ordered the two servants to leave.

The next thing he did – just seven minutes after being deposited apparently unconscious on the divan – was to call Devyani again. Vomiting may have helped to clear his head but he seems to have made a remarkably swift recovery. She took the call on her mobile phone. Her memories of their conversation are confused: 'He said he'd call tomorrow; then he said good night.' Next, according to Devyani, he asked again about something he had already mentioned earlier, but hung up before she could reply. She says she then called back and Dipendra told her: 'I am about to sleep. I'll call again in the morning.'

Strangely, there is no record of that second call in the otherwise meticulous log kept by Nepal Telecom; only of an attempt to reach him from the landline of Devyani's friend, Debina Malla, which was automatically transferred to the palace switchboard. Whoever was calling in hung up after one second. Obviously they wanted to talk to Dipendra and no one else.

In his last conversation with Devyani, the Crown Prince seems clearly to have intended to return to bed. In fact, he did no such thing. He began to get dressed again, this time in military fatigues: camouflage vest, black socks, ill-matching camouflage combat jacket and trousers, his army boots and a pair of black leather gloves. His next move was still more sinister. He assembled and checked his weaponry: the favourite 9mm Glock pistol; a stubby MP5K sub-machine gun; his preferred assault rifle, the Colt M-16; and a Franchi twelve-bore pump-action shotgun, along with the magazine pouches and webbing for carrying spare ammunition.

As Dipendra was about to leave his rooms, his orderly Ram Krishna called out: 'Shall the emergency bag be brought, sir?' The 'emergency bag' contained weatherproof clothing, insect spray, a torch, spare batteries and other items that might come in handy when the Crown Prince went trekking. Seeing his master dressed up in military gear and carrying guns, Ram Krishna quite reasonably assumed he was going on some overnight sortie outside the palace. 'It's not necessary now' was Dipendra's curt response.

Once the King had ended his private conversation with his stepmother he rejoined the rest of the guests in the billiards room. The talk among the older men was about the army and whether it might be deployed against the Maoist guerrillas – all in a guarded, indirect manner, of course. The King, eschewing alcohol, was drinking Coca-Cola on his doctor's advice; but he none-the-less sent for a cigar. It was one of the pleasures he still allowed himself occasionally.

One of the royal uncles, Rabi Shamsher Rana, engaged him in small talk. Another uncle, Maheshwar Kumar Singh approached the King and apologised for his wife's absence from the party because of her arthritis. Birendra commented that many family members suffered from gout, uric acid and high cholesterol.

He was still holding forth about the family's tendency to high cholesterol when something moved just beyond the French windows. At first, nobody noticed the 'dark figure' dressed in camouflage fatigues, a peaked cap, black combat boots and black leather gloves.

General Rabi claims he recognised the Crown Prince first and realised he was carrying at least two guns. 'I thought he looked at me,' the old general recalls, 'and I think he smiled.' Others describe Dipendra's face as expressionless throughout. Everyone present agrees that he never said a word.

'The King was standing by the billiard table,' Ketaki remembers. 'I was nearer the door than the others and saw Dipendra walk in.' At first she thought he was playing some kind of practical joke. 'Isn't he too old to be dressing up like this?' she asked her sister, Princess Jayanti.

Most of the people in the room thought Dipendra had come to show his father something. General Rabi saw the little MP5K sub-machine gun and assumed it was a replica or toy. At first King Birendra stood motionless beside the billiards table, the glass of Coke still in his hand. Then he took a step towards his son. Without uttering a word, Dipendra advanced with a gun in each hand and released three rounds at the King.

The retort of the sub-machine gun in such a confined space was deafening. Maheshwar Kumar Singh, who was standing near the King, at first thought it came from the TV. 'It was very near my ears and I thought my eardrums had burst. I blinked. I turned to see what was happening.'

Others were better placed to observe as events moved rapidly on.

'The gun rode up and some bullets went into the ceiling,' says Ketaki. 'It didn't seem that dramatic. There wasn't lots of ceiling coming down on us or anything.'

'There was a burst of three shots,' specified General Rabi. He knew his firing drill: bursts came in fives, in threes, or just single shots. But he had no idea how to react to the situation unfolding before his eyes. 'I just stood there watching. I knew he was a happy-go-lucky person, but this was no way to fool around. Then I saw the blood rushing out of the King's side. I screamed for an ambulance; but it seems no one heard.'

During that first attack King Birendra was struck by two 9mm bullets from the stubby German-made sub-machine gun. For a few moments he remained standing, long enough to put down his glass very slowly. Looking towards his son, he said very quietly: *Kay Gardeko?* – 'What have you done?'

According to General Rabi, who was standing beside him, King Birendra started to collapse towards the left. Blood was already seeping out of a wound to his neck. The Crown Prince meanwhile retreated through the garden windows and out on to the veranda.

Still no one in the room moved. They could not believe what had just happened. 'We did not think that he intended to kill,' said the King's youngest sister, Princess Shobha. 'We thought the gun had gone off by mistake.'

Once Dipendra had returned outside, the wave of stunned silence that had engulfed the room evaporated. General Rabi and others rushed to assist the King. Dhirendra's son-in-law, Captain Ravi Shahi, was a trained army doctor. 'His back!' he cried out, calling for assistance to support the King who by then had collapsed on the floor and was bleeding profusely.

Suddenly there was total confusion. 'People were in a complete panic about who or what was going on,' Maheshwar testified. 'I felt the Queen had left. Perhaps she went outside? Maybe to the back? But she left. Then Princess Shanti began waving both her hands, wanting to know what had happened, and immediately went outside. Probably to call for help, what else? And as I recall, Princess Sharada also followed her.'

Although King Birendra had taken two heavy calibre bullets fired at point-blank range, he was still alive. Captain Ravi tried to staunch the flow of blood from the neck wound. 'I am also hit in the stomach,' murmured the King.

At that moment Dipendra strode back into the billiards room. Outside, on the veranda, he had swiftly rearmed. The Italian-made pump-action shotgun had been discarded. This time he carried the M-16 in his right hand, the machine pistol in his left.

He must have seen the group trying to help the King, heard his father's voice, and realised that his mission was not yet accomplished. 'If the Crown Prince had not returned at that precise moment,' a palace secretary said later, 'he might have thought the King was dead. Then things would have turned out very differently.'

The Crown Prince threw down the sub-machine gun he had been firing. Perhaps he thought it had jammed, though later it was found to be in perfect working order. More probably he wanted someone else in the room to pick it up. That way their fingerprints would be left on the weapon used against the King, not his, since he had taken care to wear gloves throughout. Or perhaps, through some twisted sense of personal honour, he wanted to give his victims a chance to strike back, to justify what was coming.

It was the wounded King who made a move to pick up the fallen sub-machine gun. But as he reached for it, Princess Shobha stopped him. 'I said "leave this" and snatched it. The magazine came out and I threw it away.' It was a snap decision, no doubt based on her desire to prevent further bloodshed. It was a decision she has lived to regret. She had mistakenly thought that she was disposing of the only weapon in the room. As the magazine fell free and clattered to the floor, the last realistic chance of stopping the killing had been thrown away.

Ketaki recalls how careful Dipendra was not to allow anyone to come around behind him. With hindsight, she sees the way in which this first phase of attack was executed as being 'coldly calculated'.

Dipendra had, after all, selected his prime target: his father, the King. With him out of the way, the Crown Prince would by the Royal Constitution of Nepal automatically be proclaimed King — whether he was a murderer or not. 'The King is dead; long live the King' still applies in such cases, for the throne can never be left vacant. And if Dipendra had been declared King, then someone else could have been made a scapegoat for the royal murder. With all the other family members placed under house arrest, they could be cowed into agreeing to the official version of events. And Dipendra would finally be in charge.

Certainly Dipendra's subsequent actions show he needed to be certain he had killed the King. Now armed with the M-16 assault rifle, he fired off a burst at his father from point-blank range.

The King's youngest brother, Dhirendra, was the first to make a move towards the Crown Prince. 'Baba, you have done enough damage,' he said. When his appeal to reason failed, Dhirendra tried to restrain him physically. He was a powerfully built man and had been trained in karate, but he was unarmed. Before he could get near enough he too was cut down by a burst of automatic fire through the chest.

Any warped logic or planning that might have explained Dipendra's actions so far seems to have been abandoned completely at this stage. Two others were caught in the fusillade that killed the King's brother. Kumar Khadga, Princess Sharada's husband, went down with bullet wounds to the chest that were to prove fatal. Princess Shruti's husband, Kumar Gorakh, was shot in the neck but survived. He recalls being targeted by the light on the M-16's telescopic sight. 'When he held up the gun there was a flash. I thought "this is the end". That was when I was hit.'

Princess Shruti was rushing to her father's aid when she heard her husband mutter 'I also have been hit'. She changed directions and tried to comfort her husband, cradling him in her arms. 'Baby, you too have been hit,' she said. Sadly, that was enough to attract the gunman's attention. He fired again. Princess Shruti was wounded through the elbow and sustained internal injuries that would prove fatal.

Kumar Khadga has also fallen out in the open. His wife Princess

Sharada went to him and lay over his body, sobbing 'What has happened to you, what has happened to you?' Blood spread across the floor.

For a second time Dipendra retreated through the doors to the veranda. He was only outside a few seconds before advancing once more. Now he let off long bursts of gunfire, spraying the room indiscriminately. Three of his aunts, Princesses Shanti, Sharada and Jayanti, went down in the hail of bullets. Princess Sharada was trying to shield her husband with her own body. Princess Jayanti was trying to retrieve a mobile phone so that she could call the ADCs. Her action may have inflamed the gunman even further. He fired another burst into the fallen bodies. All of them sustained fatal injuries.

Ketaki was luckier, in some respects. She took one bullet through the lower arm and another that blew away the top of her shoulder, but she lived. 'I didn't realise it at the time,' she said, 'but the blood had spurted all over my face and head. It must have looked like I had taken a bullet in the head, which is probably why I am still alive.' Another of Dipendra's aunts, Princess Komal, had a bullet pass through her left lung. It missed her heart by centimetres; she was extremely fortunate to survive. As the wife of King Gyanendra, she is now Queen Komal of Nepal.

Most of those hit had been standing or lying out in the middle of the main hall, where there was no furniture to hide behind and any movement would immediately draw the gunman's attention. Another group had taken cover behind tables and a sofa at the far end of the sitting room. It was Paras who had urged them to take cover there, shouting to others still out in the open to duck and stay out of the line of fire.

Meanwhile, the killer was moving about the room. He approached the body of the King and kicked it with his booted foot, to make absolutely sure his father was dead. He did the same to the body of his younger sister. Her wounded husband, Gorakh, recalls how methodically Dipendra 'returned and picked out those who had been hurt, took aim and shot, took aim and shot'. It was chilling. Ketaki saw him 'swing the gun so casually and just shoot them again. It was deliberate. You could tell by the look in his eyes.'

Then Dipendra walked over to where most of the survivors lay huddled. Cousin Paras saw him standing by a tall chair in front of them. 'We fell in his direct gaze,' says Paras, who began pleading for their lives. 'What have you done, sir? . . . *Please* leave . . . What are you doing? . . . Only we are here . . . just us . . . Please go.'

'Well, if he had hit all of us . . .' Paras left the ensuing bloodbath to the imagination. Besides himself, there was Maheshwar Kumar and General Rabi, his sister Prerana, his wife Himani, and three of Dhirendra's daughters. One of them, Princess Sitasma, was hiding behind the sofa. She had recently returned from studying in Scotland, and only seconds before had narrowly escaped a bullet that went past her forehead. From her place of hiding she looked up to see her gun-toting cousin looming over them all. 'Dipendra came, looked at us, and left' is how she put it.

For the gunman it was a bizarre exercise in absolute power, holding the lives of these people in his hand. But with a toss of his head, as though to signify 'you may live', he left the room. If he had decided to fire again at that group the eventual death count would have been doubled.

The bodies of the King and twelve other family members lay dead or wounded inside the billiards room. But so far Queen Aishwarya and her younger son, Prince Nirajan, had been spared. Shortly after the firing had started they had both gone outside. Ketaki remembers seeing the Queen 'marching out of the door' in pursuit of Dipendra. At the same time, the badly wounded Dhirendra said 'either she'll disarm him or she'll get shot too'. It was an all too accurate assessment.

'I called out to her twice,' Ketaki recalls. 'I said no, don't go.' She also saw Nirajan running after his mother. 'It was the last I saw of them. Then I heard some shrieks.' What exactly happened outside is not clear, for none of the main protagonists lived to tell what happened. Other witnesses only saw or heard things from a distance, and their accounts are confused and at times contradict each other.

The King's ADC on duty that night says he 'heard gunshots and Her Majesty's, a woman's voice, saying "call the doctor"'. The Queen's ADC, who should have recognised her voice, is not so certain. 'It could have been Shruti's or Her Majesty's voice,' he testified. Neither of these senior ADCs moved from their office to investigate the firing. Instead, they both say they immediately tried to call the doctor. One used the ADC's office line; the other was on his mobile. Neither of them was successful.

The shooting was all over in three to four minutes. During that critical period not one of the ADCs, whose office was less than a hundred and fifty yards away, made it to the scene of the slaughter quickly enough to intervene. The junior ADC to the King, Captain Pawan Khatri, called up the military police on his radio set and then 'ran forward'. By the time he reached Tribhuvan Sadan the firing had stopped. He did see 'a man in combat fatigues leave from the back door, on the garden side, with a gun whose light was still on'.

Several palace servants, including kitchen boy Santa Bahadur Khadka, saw a 'lady in a red sari' running through the garden. Queen Aishwarya was wearing a red sari that evening. He also saw the Crown Prince moving backwards with guns in two hands. As he was moving back-wards, the woman in red confronted him. 'The two were not talking, they were running, shouting, screaming. I cannot say who was speaking. The women in the billiards room were [also] screaming.'

Santa Bahadur Khadka may not recall what was said, but others within the palace that night apparently can. For besides the public report on the 'palace incident', two other secret reports were drawn up concerning what actually happened that night – one for the King's principal secretary and the other for the head of palace security. Neither has been made public. Their contents are, however, known to senior palace officials.

It appears that, after the shooting inside the billiards room had stopped, the gunman retreated across the gardens towards the Crown Prince's private apartments. Queen Aishwarya pursued him, followed by Prince Nirajan. She had always been a tough-minded woman, and now she was furious enough to confront the armed man in camouflage fatigues even if he carried a loaded weapon in each hand. She kept screaming at him, using a Nepali phrase whose meaning was the equivalent of 'you filthy bastard'. It was the ultimate act of confrontation. Perhaps she felt she was invulnerable, that her own son would never dare touch her. It was a serious misjudgement.

Two bursts of automatic fire were subsequently heard coming from the garden. It seems that Prince Nirajan was shot first. That view is supported from the position in which his body was discovered and the location of the spent cartridges, since no eyewitness to his death has come forward.

Nirajan may have been trying to protect his mother against his elder brother's fury. If so, it was a supremely brave action, since Nirajan was unarmed. His own pistol, the same model 9 mm Glock that his elder brother used, was later found inside the billiards room. It had not been fired that night.

The twenty-two-year-old prince was shot a dozen times. Two gaping bullet wounds to the head must have killed him instantly. He collapsed on the lawn in a pool of his own blood. His body was so riddled with bullets that when rescuers finally arrived they could scarcely lift it intact.

Now the Queen faced Dipendra. With his father, sister and brother all dead or dying, only his mother lived on to challenge him.

Even now, in this eye of the storm, and after all the violence unleashed on those around her, Queen Aishwarya displayed a degree of self-belief or recklessness that is hard to understand. Rather than flee for her life into the surrounding darkness, the Queen again approached the gunman. She ran across the garden and up the marbled steps leading to Dipendra's bedchamber, screaming as she went. The Crown Prince seems to have been backing off, or at least walking backwards. Perhaps she believed that he could not bring himself to shoot his own mother. Or perhaps she was heading for Dipendra's rooms so that she could seize one of the other weapons he kept there, either to defend herself or kill the man who had murdered her husband and two other children.

While the gunman continued to withdraw up the stairs that led to the Crown Prince's bedchamber, she confronted him face to face. The Queen must have climbed seven steps before she realised what would happen next, for suddenly she turned round as though to flee. The gunman fired a long burst, hitting her from behind. Her skull was blown apart and most of her brains scattered over a wide area. Fragments of brain tissue, jawbone and teeth, the red *tika* she had placed on her forehead, her ear pins and broken red glass bangles, were found in different places close to where she fell. As with Nirajan, her body was also pumped full of bullets. Expert opinion confirms that she was shot from behind.

No one witnessed the Crown Prince killing his own mother. Nor did anyone actually see the final act of this tragedy. For this, Dipendra must have walked back towards the billiards room, crossing the small bridge over a stream feeding into the ornamental pond. Around this time somebody claims to have heard him shriek out, 'like a madman'. The next thing they heard was a single shot. Having murdered all his immediate family, Dipendra apparently turned his gun on himself.

At that very last moment perhaps even he was scared, for the clinical efficiency displayed in the shooting of so many relatives was markedly absent in this attempted suicide. Did he lose his nerve? Or was it because, for some reason, he had held the pistol in his left hand? That should not have made a great difference because, although Dipendra was right-handed, when it came to firing guns he was 'effectively ambidextrous'.

Whatever the cause, a single bullet entered just behind his left ear and went right through the brain, leaving a massive exit wound slightly higher on the right side of his head. But it was not enough to kill Dipendra outright. He was found lying on the grass, groaning loudly, near the edge of the ornamental pond. A statue of Buddha stood nearby.

Only slowly did the full extent of the carnage inside the billiards room become apparent. The bodies of the dead and wounded lay huddled together on the blood-soaked carpet, while those lucky enough to come through unscathed were still cowering in shock. The floor was a mess of scattered articles of clothing, much of it blood-smeared, along with broken spectacles and slippers and hastily discarded whisky glasses. After all the noise of gunfire, there now followed an eerie silence.

'King Birendra was the only one who moved at all, making signals with his hands. All the others were quiet,' said Ketaki, who by then had already lost a great deal of blood. 'Nobody was crying out for help,' she explained, 'because we knew help would come from somewhere. Then I heard Paras's voice.'

The younger cousin with a bad reputation seems to have been the only person capable of doing anything. Ketaki in particular thinks that 'Paras was very, very controlled. If anyone came out alive in that room, it is due to him.'

After Dipendra had walked away into the gardens, in pursuit of or pursued by his mother and brother, Paras got up from behind the sofas and began moving around the scene of devastation. He remembers how 'there were people on the floor. I approached Dhirendra to find out what happened. He said: "Paras, my feet don't move, I can't move my feet, please move them." I moved them a little but he couldn't feel it. The badly wounded Dhirendra then said: "I can't see straight, look after your Aunt Ketaki." Then he told me to look for the children.'

At that point Paras was still unaware that his own mother, Princess Komal, was among the fallen. Then he saw her try to raise herself up and slump back down again because the dead Princess Shanti had collapsed on top of her. He helped his mother into an upright position and she said 'I'm not well, I'm not well', all the while holding her bloodied forehead. 'At first I thought she'd been shot in the forehead,' he confessed. But on closer inspection there was no wound there. He soon ascertained that the blood was from Princess Shanti's wounds and not his mother's.

After that, Paras ran to the Queen Mother who had remained in her separate room throughout the massacre. He had heard more gunfire outside the billiards room and initially thought it came from the Queen Mother's private chamber. 'I ran over there,' he said, 'but nothing had happened.' He briefly explained to his grandmother and Princess Helen that the King and many others had been shot, though sparing the elderly ladies all the details.

He next went outside to find the ADCs, who had finally arrived. He explained to them 'there were dead people as well as wounded ones. Ignore the dead, but immediately rush the wounded to hospital.' He ordered them to break down the glass panes in the French windows to permit easier evacuation.

In the event, the King was carried out first, although in Ketaki's opinion he was by then 'definitely dead'. But from there on Paras insisted that rescuers evacuated the wounded first, helping to get them into whatever vehicles were available and taking them to hospital. Some, like Ketaki, were completely disorientated. She was losing a great deal of blood from her shoulder wound, but still she insisted on finding her shoes because she was worried about cutting her feet on the broken glass.

With the evacuation underway and more help arriving, Paras moved on to those still unaccounted for. 'I told three people to go and look for the Crown Prince, the Queen and Nirajan,' he says. The Crown Prince's ADC soon came back to report that Dipendra had shot himself but was still alive. Both the Queen and Nirajan were beyond hope. So Paras and ADC Gajendra Bohara loaded the two royal princes, Dipendra and Nirajan, into the same vehicle and drove them to hospital. It was a macabre situation, the killer and victim both propped up in the back seat together.

13

The Sounds of Silence

The trauma room at Chhauni Military Hospital was already crowded when they arrived. Doctors and nurses were still trying to resuscitate the King, though there was evidently no hope. He probably died on the way to the hospital, in the back seat of a Jaguar which got stuck behind a truck and somehow managed to take a full fifteen minutes to cover less than five miles. The body of the Queen had been placed on a trolley. It was left unattended because, with half her skull blown off, it was obvious nothing more could be done for her. Princess Shruti and her husband Kumar Gorakh lay side by side. She was very pale, her pulse almost imperceptible, while Gorakh had walked in unassisted; yet the woman doctor on duty saw to him first before moving on to Shruti who was haemorrhaging badly and died within the hour. By the time that Dipendra and Nirajan were brought in on stretchers there were no trolleys left unoccupied, so their stretchers were laid down on the trauma room floor. Dipendra was breathing noisily. His brother was declared dead on arrival.

The duty staff were overwhelmed as more casualties arrived. The dead were laid down beside the dying and those still struggling for life. Ventilators were strapped on; intravenous drips inserted; pressure bandages applied; adrenalin injected. But for many of the arrivals there was nothing that could be done.

Three royal princesses, Shanti, Sharada and Jayanti, were declared dead on arrival, all of them from head wounds. Kumar Khadga, the King's uncle by marriage, died from chest injuries as hospital staff tried to resuscitate him. The King's youngest brother, Dhirendra, was still conscious despite multiple chest wounds sustained when he had tried to stop the killing. He was given suction and oxygen before being operated on – to no avail, for he died the following day. Princess Komal had a bullet through one lung and multiple rib fractures. Although the bullet had passed so close to her heart, chest tubes were inserted and she was operated on successfully.

Meanwhile the hospital switchboard had been desperately calling in specialists from all over Kathmandu. Cardiologists, plastic surgeons, radiologists and neurosurgeons were summoned from their homes or Friday night parties. The Royal Physician, Dr Khagendra Bahadur Shrestha, had been alerted directly by the Palace and was among the first to arrive. He immediately went to the King and, after a brief examination, declared his condition hopeless. Even then efforts to resuscitate him continued. The Queen Mother arrived and gave directions. Nobody wanted to be the one to declare Nepal's god-King dead.

Some of the civilian specialists were hard to track down. A royal ADC was dispatched to bring in the country's top neurosurgeon, Dr Upendra Devkota. He was needed for a very special patient: the man blamed for the killings, but who might technically now be King of Nepal. The ADC drove fast towards the private hospital where he was told he would find Devkota, smashing into two vehicles on the way. When he arrived he marched straight in and demanded to see the doctor, who had just completed an operation. 'The Crown Prince has bullet injuries,' he announced. The doctor immediately knew these must be head wounds. They set off for Chhauni Military Hospital at terrifying speed.

Neither he nor any of the civilian specialists had yet been told what had happened earlier that night in Narayanhiti. His immediate supposition was that there must have been a one-off assassination attempt. On entering the trauma room, it became obvious that something far worse had occurred. The place was so full of badly wounded that it seemed a full-scale attack by Maoist insurgents must have taken place. Either that or a military coup.

Devkota stopped beside a trolley where an army doctor was

attempting resuscitation on a patient in bloodstained national dress. The patient wore a locket bearing the image of Sai Baba, the Indian guru especially revered by Birendra in recent years. Dr Devkota felt for a pulse before moving on, leaving the dead King to the junior medic's useless ministrations. Although he had met Birendra before, this time he had not been able to recognize him. Only when the Royal Physician took him aside and explained that practically the entire royal family had been massacred did the gravity of the situation sink in. His immediate responsibility was to operate on the Crown Prince.

Trying not to imagine the circumstances that had led to such carnage, Devkota changed into his surgical gown and went straight into the operating theatre. Blood and brain tissue oozed from the entry and exit wounds on either side of Dipendra's head. The army medics had already fixed up an intravenous line and put an airway down his throat. Heart rate and blood pressure were satisfactory, his breathing was being assisted by bagging and, although the pupils were fixed and dilated, he still responded to pinching. Dipendra was not brain dead.

The neurosurgeon's assessment was that on the Glasgow Coma Score – where fifteen is normal and three equates to a vegetative state – the Crown Prince scored four. Only a miracle would restore him to consciousness, but the operating team went ahead none the less. They enlarged the entry wound, removed dead brain tissue and bone fragments, cauterising and leaving an opening in case of future infection. The plastic surgeon on the team then provided skin cover.

Only after the operation was completed did Devkota learn that the person upon whom he had just performed surgery was responsible for the massacre. A brain scan showed there was continued bleeding between the ventricles, but the body was resilient. Crown Prince Dipendra, eleventh in direct line of succession from Prithvi Narayan Shah the Great, was still clinging to life.

Nobody at the military hospital was sure what to do next. Should post-mortems be carried out? This posed a tricky constitutional problem, since the incident had occurred within Narayanhiti Palace. They knew the normal medical procedures; but it was not clear whether these should be followed when members of the royal family were involved. So there were no post-mortems, no screening for drugs and other substances. Instead the Royal Physician ordered that a list of injuries sustained be drawn up.

By now, dawn was breaking over Kathmandu. Prince Gyanendra, now the senior male member of the devastated royal family, was said to be arriving at any minute. Somebody had to take charge.

Army personnel had gone to find Gyanendra at the royal family's retreat in Pokhara, just forty minutes' flying time west of the capital but at least five hours by road. They took him to the airport under armed guard. He was told that he must return immediately to Kathmandu, with no further explanation. A helicopter was sent for him.

At first he too thought there must have been a military coup. When he contacted a close friend and business colleague, Prabhakar Rana, he was still ignorant of what had happened inside the Royal Palace. Only when his son Paras finally spoke to him by telephone was he made aware of the true situation.

The helicopter had been forced to turn back because of bad weather so Gyanendra set off for Kathmandu by car, travelling through the night under heavy armed escort. By dawn the convoy had covered only half the distance. Another helicopter was dispatched to rendezvous with the motorcade and fly the dead King's brother to the capital. The Kingdom of Nepal was without a king. Every minute counted.

News that something terrible had happened inside Narayanhiti was spreading fast. Through the small hours of the night, telephone calls and e-mails had been going out notifying family relations and friends as well as public officials. Amazingly, Prime Minister G. P. Koirala was not informed until after nearly two hours had elapsed. He was taken first to Narayanhiti to be briefed by palace officials on what had happened there and the immediate security implications. Only then did he continue to the hospital. The army chief was already present, as were the head of the Royal Privy Council, the country's Chief Justice, and the Speaker of its Parliament.

Urgent discussions were held in the relative calm of the hospital's library. Should the death certificates be completed? That was normal procedure. But if King Birendra's death was officially recorded and no successor announced, that would imply the throne of Nepal was vacant for the first time in two and a half centuries. According to the Royal Constitution, this was an impossibility. 'The King is dead; long live the King' was enshrined practice for royal successions.

But who was King? Should the Crown Prince now be declared King of Nepal, even though he had apparently killed his own father and was in a comatose state? No precedents could be found, not even in the bloodiest episodes of Nepal's turbulent history. Since any decision would have the gravest constitutional implications, it was thought best to wait until after Prince Gyanendra's arrival.

On being helicoptered into Kathmandu, the oldest surviving royal prince went straight to Chhauni Military Hospital where he was shown around the intensive care units. There were more dead than living, and among those clinging to life was his own wife, Princess Komal. An ashen-faced Gyanendra then called a series of brief meetings in the hospital's library. First he saw the Royal Physician and Dr Devkota, to be informed at first hand of Crown Prince Dipendra's condition. He was told that, although he was still alive, the prognosis was extremely poor. The Royal Physician asked if standard procedures to assess whether the patient was brain dead or not should continue. Prince Gyanendra told them to proceed with the tests and let him know the results.

Next into the library went the Prime Minister and other officials to discuss the thorny question of the royal succession. The head of the Privy Council was to summon all one hundred and twenty-five members to an emergency meeting within two hours. By then the tests on the Crown Prince would be completed. The possibility of Gyanendra becoming Regent was raised for the first time. But it was up to the members of the Raj Parishad, the royal privy councillors, to determine on matters of succession. They duly met and, on being told that medical tests showed the Crown Prince was technically not brain dead, they decided that the unconscious body being kept alive on a ventilator be solemnly declared His Majesty King Dipendra Bir Bikram Shah Dev of Nepal. He was of the eleventh generation to Prithvi Narayan Shah to be named king, though Dipendra can never have been conscious of the fact

That the same person who had cold-bloodedly shot his own father be declared his heir, a serial killer assume the semi-divine status of Nepalese kingship, may seem bizarre if not grotesque. The members of the Raj Parishad were fully aware of this; but according to the laws and ancient customs of Nepal they had little choice in the matter. King Birendra was dead; his appointed successor still lived; therefore Dipendra had to be named as the new King. They did add the provision that he was 'physically and mentally unfit to rule'. His uncle, Prince Gyanendra, should therefore exercise all the new King's authority and act in his place as Regent.

Their decision had other, equally far-reaching, implications. The King stands above the law of the land so whatever he has done – no matter how heinous the crime – he cannot be prosecuted. In fact, so long as Dipendra was King of Nepal there could not be any investigation of what he had allegedly perpetrated inside the Royal Palace. No one had the authority to order such an investigation apart from the King himself. In the interests of being constitutionally correct, time itself was put on hold.

But outside, in the real world, news of the massacre was travelling fast. By the time Dipendra was proclaimed King of Nepal nearly sixteen hours had elapsed since the slaughter. Most people in Nepal already knew their beloved King Birendra and most of the royal family had been killed. But they burned to know *who* had done the shooting. And outside those circles with access to palace information, there were few ready to accept that the Crown Prince could have murdered his own father.

Normal broadcasts on Nepal's state-run radio and television channels were replaced by funereal music and the reciting of religious verses. Most newspapers that appeared next morning failed to mention anything unusual had happened. But this atavistic attempt at imposing a total news blackout could not succeed in the twenty-first century – not with the BBC, CNN and Indian TV and radio stations all reporting a terrible massacre in the palace.

Households with access to a television simply switched to one of many satellite channels. Reports from India had by far the greatest impact, since most Nepalis can understand at least some Hindi. In thousands of isolated villages where there is no electricity, people tuned their battery-powered radios to short wave frequencies and picked up the news from foreign broadcasts. The fact that panicking officials in Kathmandu tried to prevent ordinary Nepalis from learning about the catastrophe suggests a staggering ignorance of how news travels in the real world.

The royal funerals had to be arranged in a hurry. It is Hindu custom to cremate the body as soon as possible after death, and for the eldest son to light the pyre. Since Dipendra was incapable another male relative, Deepak Bikram Shah, stood in for him.

The trappings of royal ceremonial accompanied the funeral procession as it passed through Kathmandu on its way from the military hospital to the burning *ghats* at Pashupatinath, on whose stone-clad steps leading down to the sacred Bagmati River the royal dead would be cremated. Bandsmen played solemn music; the cavalry escort's hooves clattered on the city's broken pavements; the Gurkha infantry marched in slow time.

King Birendra's flower-covered body was carried on an open bier by white-clad Brahmin priests. Queen Aishwarya's was placed in the same palanquin in which she had once been taken to her wedding ceremony. Her head was held together by a doll's mask and wrapped in cloth to conceal the terrible injuries. The bodies of Prince Nirajan and Princess Shruti followed.

An estimated half a million people came on the streets to pay their last respects. They clung to every rooftop and building along the route, many of them throwing flowers as the dead King passed by. There was sadness but also anger in the air.

That anger erupted when the crowds spotted Prime Minister G. P. Koirala's armoured Mercedes. Some suspected he was behind the massacre. If not a perpetrator, as head of government he was still held responsible for allowing the dreadful tragedy to occur. Angry young men began chanting slogans. They demanded that the King's murderers be hanged. Stones were thrown at the Prime Minister's car. Its windows were broken and Koirala had to escape under armed guard, continuing his journey in a military vehicle. Soldiers started firing in the air to prevent the rioting from spreading.

The procession made its way to the Pashupatinath Temple, set amidst a green park on the banks of the Bagmati River. The pagoda-roofed temple is Nepal's holiest site and is dedicated to the Hindu god of both creative and destructive energy, Lord Shiva, in his manifestation as 'Lord of the Beasts'.

Darkness had fallen by the time the King's body was brought to Aryaghat, the riverside cremation ground that is reserved for high dignitaries, and placed next to where sacred waters from within the temple flow into the river. The bodies of his wife, his two younger children, and four other close relatives were set on separate pyres stretching down the burning *ghats*. They were first sprinkled with water drained from Shiva's *linga*, the phallic-shaped stone symbolising his power. Then the great piles of logs were lit and the flames fed with clarified butter until all was consumed. The ashes were committed to the waters of the Bagmati which flows down into India and eventually joins the sacred Ganges. A few drops of rain fell, heralding the coming of the monsoon. To those watching from the Bagmati's far bank it seemed that an entire era had passed away before their eyes.

Half of Kathmandu had witnessed the funeral procession, but still there was no official statement from the palace. When it finally came on Sunday morning, the wording was so obtuse that listeners were more confused than ever. An official spokesman was reported to have said that the killings were caused by 'an accidental discharge of an automatic weapon'. In fact this was a mistranslation. What had really been said was 'a *sudden* discharge of an automatic weapon'. The effect on Nepalis grieving the loss of their royal family was to make them angry that such a tragedy could be dismissed as an accident. Moreover, they felt insulted by such transparent misinformation. Modern automatic weapons did not go off 'accidentally' or even 'suddenly' all by themselves. They sensed that they were being fed double-speak and thereafter conspiracy theories as to what really happened spread like wildfire.

Palace officials admit that they were not particularly happy with this half-cocked explanation, but protocol forbade them from naming the culprit because that man was now, in name at least, the King of Nepal. To label him a mass murderer was technically treasonable. At the same time they were under immense pressure to say something. Many hoped that a fuller explanation would follow shortly, since the condition of their comatose monarch was apparently deteriorating. By the evening of 3 June, the specialists' opinion was that Dipendra's brain was dying and that the chances of survival were nil.

Dr Devkota was asked to explain the prognosis in a private meeting with Prince Gyanendra. There remained only two alternatives. The life-support machines could be switched off, but only with the full consent of the family. Alternatively, nature could be allowed to take its course and King Dipendra would be declared dead only after his heart had stopped beating. The Regent replied that he would discuss the matter with the Queen Mother. Together they decided to let nature take its course. Treatment was continued through the night until the heart stopped around three-forty in the morning of 4 June. An attempt at resuscitation apparently failed, and King Dipendra was declared dead after a reign lasting less than two days.

A new round of urgent consultations was held early the next morning. The doubts and fears now rising across the nation had to be addressed. It was decided to proclaim Gyanendra as King of Nepal and then immediately afterwards announce an official enquiry into the 'incident' at the palace. The long official silence about events on the night of 1 June could be broken now that the constitutional restraints had been removed.

Preparations for Gyanendra's enthronement ceremony got underway at Hanuman Dhoka Palace, but by mid-morning the mood on the streets was turning ugly. The citizens of Kathamandu, still awaiting an official account to explain the loss of their royal family, came out in their tens of thousands. Many were still dazed by recent events; others were angrily joining in organised protests and shouting anti-Gyanendra slogans.

In the absence of any credible explanation, they had come up with their own ideas about who was responsible for the killings. At first, most people had feared that the perpetrators were either the Maoists or the army. Now a different rumour began to circulate: the new King Gyanendra and his 'evil' son Paras were behind the slaughter. They appeared to have emerged with the spoils, after all. After every previous massacre in Nepal's long history, some group of conspirators had always benefited from the bloodshed.

Of course they must have had willing accomplices. The chief suspect was G. P. Koirala, who was already under investigation for gross corruption. Foreign agents who wanted to destabilise Nepal were also blamed: the CIA and the Research and Analysis Wing (RAW) of Indian Intelligence. Their involvement at least made more sense than the suggestion of a gun going off 'accidentally' and killing the entire royal family.

Some of these versions of events were deliberately promoted by the Maoists and other left-wing groups who believed that they stood to gain from rioting and the collapse of law and order in Kathmandu. The spectre of a vast conspiracy involving anti-communist 'hardliners' – the new King, the Prime Minister and foreign intelligence agencies – suited their purposes admirably. They anticipated that even committed royalists and nationalists would join demonstrations against that kind of threat, swelling the numbers of hard-core protestors being bussed in from outside the city.

Many of the protestors had shaved their heads, as required by Hindu custom of sons mourning a dead parent. And that is precisely how most Nepalis felt about the deaths of their King and Queen. They grieved as though they had lost their own father and mother. If they joined in demonstrations it was because their grief had turned to anger, and not necessarily because they agreed with the hard-core anti monarchist protestors.

As the day wore on, the streets of Kathmandu were flooded with a volatile mix of emotion and politics. The proclamation of Gyanendra as the third King of Nepal in four days sparked off another bout of rioting. His enthronement ceremony could scarcely have taken place in less favourable conditions.

The time had now come for a show of strength against the oppressive elite. As soon as the crowds looked like getting out of hand, armed police moved in to clear the streets with tear gas and baton charges. The army was out in force to maintain order in the streets. Those citizens who had come out to see their new King were unusually silent. There was none of the cheering and clapping that normally accompany a royal coronation. King Gyanendra himself looked extremely solemn, his head shaved beneath a black *topi*, a light checked jacket over a pale cotton tunic and tight-fitting trousers known as *daura suruwal*. The ceremonial enthronement was performed in the open air at Nasal Chowk, the main courtyard of the early Shah kings' palace of Hanuman Dhoka, and followed ancient rites that date back to Vedic times.

A fine drizzle descended on the assembled dignitaries, the Prime Minister and Commander-in-Chief of the army among them. Seated on the golden, serpent-headed throne of Nepal, his head now bared, King Gyanendra remained motionless as the Royal Priest ascended the dais and placed the glittering crown with its plume of bird of paradise feathers on his head. Officials and generals then advanced to convey their felicitations and, as is customary, to offer the new King a silver coin as a solemn token of their allegiance.

The ceremony over, King Gyanendra rode through the narrow streets of Kathmandu's Old City in an open carriage drawn by six grey horses. Beside him was the Commander-in Chief. Normally the Prime Minister would also have ridden in the carriage, but because of the death threats he had received it was thought best for security that he travel separately.

The mood among the watching crowds was sullen. There was little cheering and many did not even press their palms together in the traditional Nepali greeting. As the procession moved into New Road, groups of shaven-headed protestors ran out from side alleys shouting 'Death to Gyanendra'. Even after the royal carriage had disappeared into Narayanhiti Palace, crowds continued to gather outside the gates crying 'Death to Gyanendra' and 'Hang the Murderer'. Angry young men threw stones and set tyres on fire as police tried to contain the situation. At first they fired tear gas into the crowds. But as rioting broke out across the capital the order was given to use live ammunition. A blanket curfew was declared to clear the streets until the following morning. Anyone who refused to disperse after one warning would be shot.

There were many fearful citizens that night who thought the Kingdom of Nepal was coming to an end.

Another royal funeral – that of the late and still widely lamented Dipendra – had also to take place. It was so low key as to be almost invisible. The body was carried to Pashupatinath on an open army truck. To avoid further demonstrations, the truck was routed not through central Kathmandu itself but around the Ring Road. With a curfew declared and security forces clearing the streets, Dipendra's white-draped corpse was taken without ceremony to the Aryaghat and swiftly cremated. It was scarcely the most honourable of ends. Even as this was going on another royal victim, the dead King's brother Dhirendra, finally succumbed to his wounds in hospital. He too needed to be cremated. In less than a week, Kathmandu had witnessed ten funerals and an enthronement.

The new King addressed the Nepalese nation on the evening of 4 June. He announced the death of King Dipendra and explained that this now removed those constitutional impediments – namely the impossibility of declaring the ruling monarch to be a mass murderer

– which had earlier prevented any explanation of events. He also appointed a three-man commission of enquiry comprising the Chief Justice, the Speaker and the Leader of the Opposition in Nepal's Parliament, and granted them wide-ranging powers to investigate the events surrounding the palace massacre.

Only the King could empower this commission, since the entire incident had taken place within the Royal Palace and there was no provision under the constitution for civilians to intervene in anything that went on within its walls. But King Gyanendra was all too aware that the people of Nepal were owed a detailed explanation. And so, for the first time, the veil of secrecy surrounding Nepal's royal family was pulled aside and civilian investigators allowed into Narayanhiti Palace. They were given three days to report their findings.

The announcement was meant to clear the air. It tacitly acknowledged what people had already heard from foreign broadcasts. Dipendra was responsible for the killings. But the air was already so troubled with alternative explanations and conspiracy theories that most Nepalis simply could not accept the official version of events. For a son to kill his own father and mother was an unimaginable crime, especially in Nepal where filial duty and obedience to one's elders are so deeply ingrained. Even as it became increasingly apparent that the palace massacre was strictly 'a family affair', many still could not bring themselves to blame the Crown Prince. To them he was just a scapegoat, a victim along with the others.

Bewildered Nepalis took no comfort from the fact that, throughout history, entire royal families had been massacred before. The executions of Czar Nicholas and his family in Russia in 1918 was a case in point, but that had been a state-inspired killing, a means to a very dramatic end. It was very different from what was supposed to have happened inside Narayanhiti Palace.

For Nepalis with some knowledge of their own history, the murder of Bahadur Shah by his half-brother some two hundred years earlier was a clear parallel. This too had been an inter-family affair, apparently carried out in a suicidal fit of rage. Comparisons were also drawn with the infamous Kot Massacre of 1846.

But there are important differences. No member of the immediate Royal Family had been killed during the Kot Massacre. At Narayanhiti, *only* royals had been shot. In the aftermath of the Kot Massacre a clear victor had emerged in the form of Jung Bahadur Rana. What seemed so inexplicable about the massacre in Narayanhiti Palace was that it seemed to profit no one. Unless, as many still suspected, the new King Gyanendra and his son were behind it all.

Some Nepalis were quick to point the finger at this 'new royal family'. Unsurprisingly, one of the first to do so was the chief ideologue of the Maoists' political wing, Baburam Bhattarai. He wrote that the massacre was in fact part of a broader political conspiracy including both 'feudal' and 'foreign' elements – the first term signifying the new royal family and their allies, while the second was taken to mean India. He also drew direct comparisons between the recent killings and the Kot Massacre.

Baburam Bhattarai praised the late King Birendra, both for his liberalism and for being a true nationalist. He warned, however, that there now existed an unholy alliance between a pro-business King, a corrupt Prime Minister, the army generals, Indian intelligence and business interests and, of course, the CIA. The time was ripe to proclaim a People's Republic. In summing up, he called on ordinary soldiers in the Royal Nepal Army to rise up in mutiny.

His signed article appeared in a leading Nepali language newspaper two days after Gyanendra had been proclaimed King. It was deliberately inflammatory, but the government's response to this challenge was heavy-handed. In arresting the newspaper's editor and two directors, the authorities flouted the freedom of the press as enshrined in the constitution. They also revealed just how far panic had set in at the highest levels.

For many Nepalis, the arrests served only to confirm the abundant conspiracy theories. Democratic rights were being taken away by a high-handed and secretive regime. The government responded by

rounding up Maoist sympathisers and imposing further night-time cur-
fews throughout the Kathmandu Valley.

Although Dipendra had now been named as responsible for the palace
killings, no further details emerged as to what had really happened
inside Narayanhiti that night. The facts would come out only when the
official commission of enquiry had completed its work. Hopes that it
would report within three days, as instructed, were dashed when one
of its members, the Leader of the Opposition, was forced to resign by
the rank and file of his United Marxist-Leninist Party. The two remaining commissioners continued with their investigations, but the report
was delayed indefinitely.

With no official report forthcoming, the wildest rumours were able
to flourish. Some claimed that, quite apart from the ten members of
the royal family slain, an unspecified number of ordinary commoners
– waiters, kitchen boys, palace guards – had also been killed. Why?
Because these commoners were eyewitnesses to what had really gone
on, and their testimony might not tie in with the official version of
events. Smoke had been seen coming out of a chimney at Chhauni
Military Hospital where the civilians' bodies had supposedly been taken
for incineration. Such reports might be unconfirmed, but they made
more sense than having to believe not a single person had been killed
apart from the royal family.

Nothing could be done to redress this situation as long as the commission of enquiry continued with its work. The Chief Justice and
Speaker were taking statements from survivors of the massacre, though
otherwise they and other material witnesses were not allowed to speak
out. But it did not take long for one of the key witnesses to break
ranks.

Captain Rajiv Shahi, the man who had rushed to assist King Birendra
only seconds after he had been shot, decided to give his version of
events. An unauthorised press conference was held at the Military
Hospital, with Captain Shahi in T-shirt and jeans taking it upon himself
to explain the palace massacre. He had an outline drawing of the

billiards room in Tribhuvan Sadan to help him run through the sequence of events. He confirmed the official line by blaming Dipendra for the killings. Then he abruptly left, refusing to take any questions.

Rajiv Shahi was only a peripheral member of the royal family. He was married to the daughter of Prince Dhirendra, and it was as a royal son-in-law that he had attended the doomed Friday night gathering. Precisely why he chose to call an impromptu press conference is unclear, though it may well have had something to do with his personal conduct once the bullets started flying in earnest. A trained doctor in the armed forces, Shahi had abandoned his monarch and other wounded relatives at a critical moment in order to make good his own escape. He jumped through a window and ran out into the palace grounds. Rather than raise the alarm or try to organise emergency services, he apparently kept on running right through the West Gate where he jumped into a taxi which took him to the Military Hospital.

Of course none of this was mentioned when he gave the first eye-witness account of the massacre, but others knew about his movements that night. The unfortunate guard who had allowed him to escape from the palace that night was dismissed. Shahi knew he was in trouble and his main reason for going public first was to save his reputation – if not his skin. That same evening, after the press conference, he faced an official board of enquiry; Captain Shahi was subsequently expelled from the Royal Nepal Army.

But in the rumour factory of Kathmandu, some of the things he had said provided new grist for the mill. Dipendra's face, he said, had remained expressionless throughout. He had not spoken a word. Given the reluctance of most Nepalis to blame the Crown Prince, these details were seized upon to construct a new and altogether more convincing explanation.

The gunman who did the killing had worn a mask to look like Dipendra. It was not the Crown Prince who had done it, but a pro-fessional assassin who had already killed Dipendra in his private apart-ments before massacring the rest of the royal family. To back up this version of events, the manufacture and origin of the 'Dipendra Mask' were given in detail. It had been specially made in China and smuggled over the border. Another version of the story insisted there had been several masked men who had come into the billiards room in turn. How else could one explain the wounding or killing of so many people? It appeared that a number of different weapons had been used. How could one man have carried them all? There must have been a team of professional killers, their faces disguised by the ingenious Dipendra masks. And to organise all of that there must have been a far-reaching conspiracy. Such was the gossip that filled Kathmandu's bazaars during the ten long days of official silence.

In the absence of hard facts, rumour has a habit of taking on a life of its own: and nowhere more so than in Nepal, whose citizens have long suspected they are fed only half-truths by those in authority. For them, truth is a variable and often negotiable commodity. There are religious truths, as when a statue of the god Bhimsen perspires, which may seem more credible than empirical truth. There are surface truths, but behind them may lurk the most complex machinations. In a country whose history is so littered with real conspiracies, it is second nature to accept anything at face value with extreme reluctance. The result is an admixture of credulity and distrust which permits no truth to be set in stone. Rather, it encourages the multiplication of different versions of an event to the point where it seems there are as many 'true' variants as there are gods and goddesses in the Hindu pantheon.

As soon as it was rumoured that Dipendra had been driven mad by thwarted love, different localities in this far-flung kingdom came up with their own versions of who had been the 'true love' in his life. In the remote north-east of the country, in a market town populated largely by those same Sherpas who provide guides and porters for mountaineering expeditions, the answer seemed obvious. All the talk about the Crown Prince being in love with Devyani was nonsense. His real love was for a Sherpa girl. Other regions came up with equally self-satisfying variants. Some had a grain of truth behind them, such as the rumour that Dipendra had fallen in love with a check-out girl at a supermarket called Bhat-Bhateni in Kathmandu. (In fact, Dipendra had occasionally used this supermarket for his secret meetings with Devyani.)

Other rumours had far more explosive potential. It was said that Dipendra and Devyani were secretly married, that they had gone to a certain temple in Patan frequented by those seeking fulfilment of their most intimate wishes, and that a renegade Brahmin had placed vermilion on both their heads to signify their marriage. It was also said that Devyani was pregnant. That would explain why Dipendra could not wait to marry her – as a result of which he was forced to have a showdown with his parents. If there was any truth in this there might be an alternative claimant to the throne of Nepal – the direct descendant of kings as opposed to the junior or cadet line as represented by Gyanendra and Paras. Hardly surprising, then, that this was dismissed by both the Palace and members of Devyani's family, though each had their own and very different reasons for doing so.

In truth, there is another reason why Dipendra had to try and sort things out with his parents on 1 June. They were both due to leave Nepal later that month on an extended visit abroad, first to London for further medical tests on the King's heart condition, before continuing on a state visit to Morocco. If the plans he had already announced for a December wedding were to go ahead, it was vital for the Crown Prince to win his parent's consent before they departed.

Whatever version of the 'truth' they subscribed to, the Nepali people were united in disbelieving that Dipendra had first murdered his entire family and then committed suicide. It was too monstrous, too unnatural an act.

Even Westernised Nepalis could not accept what was supposed to have happened. Instead, they shaved their heads and entered a state of deep mourning. Portraits of their dead King and Queen were strung with garlands; incense and butter lamps burned before them. Many refrained from taking salt with their food throughout the thirteen-day period of mourning.

Long after the night curfew was lifted, the streets of Kathmandu remained deserted once darkness had fallen. Areas that would normally have been crowded — the Old City, Dilli Bazaar, even the tourist enclave of Thamel — were emptied of life. No one ventured out because they believed they no longer had a King; and without the King there was no security, no law.

From early morning, however, they lined up in their thousands outside Narayanhiti's main gate, to sign the book of condolences and pay their last respects. Some waited for hours, the men and women in separate lines, all clutching their meagre sprays of gladioli or garlands of marigolds. There was no weeping or outward display of emotion — this in striking contrast to the scenes in London outside Kensington Palace after Princess Diana died in 1997. In mourning the Nepalese contained their grief tightly within themselves.

Similar crowds gathered to pay their respects in town and villages across Nepal. Portraits of the royal family placed at crossroads were heaped with garlands of flowers and swathed in burning incense. In many places separate shrines were erected to Dipendra, and these attracted almost as many mourners as those dedicated to the rest of the royal family. The thousands of sportsmen who had come to take part in the now cancelled National Games marched in orderly lines from the National Stadium past Tundikhel towards the Royal Palace. Many of them — and especially members of Nepal Karate Federation — were determined to pay their respects to their former patron, the late King Dipendra. Like most of their fellow countrymen, they were in a state of denial.

14

Laid to Rest?

On the eleventh day of mourning for King Birendra, a very unusual ceremony was held at Kalmochan Ghat, beside the Bagmati River. The Katto Ceremony is only performed when a Nepalese monarch has died in tragic circumstances. Its purpose is to ensure the dead King's eternal freedom from the hindrances of this world.

For this Katto Ceremony it was necessary to find a Brahmin who was prepared to lose his caste forever by eating what any orthodox and therefore strictly vegetarian Hindu would consider an unclean meal. The ceremonial requirement was for the food to be laced with bone marrow and animal fat. After consuming this meal the Brahmin would become an outcast, unable to practise his priestly duties or even live in the same community as before. Instead, he would don articles of the dead King's clothing, his spectacles and his shoes, along with an imitation crown and ceremonial robes. Thus arrayed, and borne on an elephant, he would process out of the Kathmandu Valley, never to return again. The Brahmin was amply rewarded for accepting so heavy a burden, with money, food and other gifts. By tradition he was also allowed to keep the elephant.

The preparations for the ceremony began inauspiciously. The elephant had to be brought up from the Terai. As it passed through one of the villages on the way, a woman had tried to run between its legs in the belief that this act of daring would guarantee her a boy child. Her sudden movement frightened the elephant, which picked the woman up with its trunk and dashed her fatally against the ground. But otherwise King Birendra's ceremony went off without a hitch. The elephant duly carried the ex-Brahmin across the Bagmati River and out of the Kathmandu Valley.

Since Dipendra had also briefly been proclaimed King of Nepal, another Katto Ceremony was held for him three days later. This time it was harder to find a Brahmin willing to undergo ritual pollution for Dipendra's sake. The first Brahmin chosen declined, and only at the last minute was another found, in the person of the sixty-five-year-old Devi Prasad Acharya.

The canopied enclosure in which he waited to consume the polluting meal was divided into four areas – a prayer room with its *puja* materials; a living room furnished with a sofa, two chairs, a framed photograph of the dead prince and an electric fan; a sleeping area with a camp bed and a wardrobe full of Dipendra's clothes and personal effects; and finally a store room piled high with foodstuffs that the ex-Brahmin could take with him. There were sacks of rice and lentils, root ginger and spices, baskets of fruits and fresh vegetables, bowls of curd and plates piled with fried breads known as *puris*. Mixed in among these were polluting foods, eighty-four ritually prescribed delicacies in all, including a fly-covered leg of goat.

Even as the Prime Minister and other dignitaries arrived there was some unseemly haggling. Devi Prasad Acharya wanted more money and a house for his family if he was to eat the meal prepared for him and lose his caste. A bargain was rapidly struck. The Brahmin hurriedly ate a few morsels of each dish, and then dressed himself in another set of imitation regalia together with some of Dipendra's personal belongings – his wristwatch, dark glasses and running shoes. Then it was his turn to climb on to the waiting elephant for his final journey out of the Valley.

As the elephant approached the rain-swollen waters of the Bagmati it trumpeted loudly and, ignoring the commands of its mahout, abruptly reversed, forcing crowds of officials and dignitaries to scamper out of its path. The elephant then made a dash back towards the ceremonial enclosure before a second mahout leapt up and regained control. The unhappy ex-Brahmin very nearly slid off its back along with his scarlet umbrella, and it was only after much coaxing that the elephant could be persuaded to ford the river.

Those present said that this did not augur well for the peace of the late King Dipendra's soul. The King-killer's spirit seemed troubled still, which explained why it was to make its final exit with such lack of dignity. For all the elephant's splendid trappings, it ended up becoming an unseemly spectacle.

Much the same could be said of the way in which the official enquiry into the palace massacre was announced the following day. The local press attempted to storm the building because they knew there would not be enough room inside for all the TV crews and reporters. The result was an undignified scuffle.

Responsibility for reading out the findings was given to the Speaker, Taranath Ranabhat, one of the two remaining investigators. Ordinary Nepalese were stunned at the revelations and the material evidence on display. The habitual veil of secrecy had not been daintily lifted; it had been torn away. There were photographs and diagrams of where the 'incident' had taken place. The five lethal weapons retrieved from the site were laid out on a table along with specimens of ammunition. The clothes Dipendra had worn, the army boots and camouflage fatigues, were then pulled out of a tin trunk by an orderly and held up for inspection.

Given the magnitude of events, this should have been a solemn occasion, but the Speaker managed to reduce proceedings to the level of farce. Embarrassed laughter followed as he held up the M-16 to the cameras and imitated the rat-tat-tat of automatic gunfire. Even the choice of trunk in which Dipendra's clothing was stored was unfortunate, given that he was supposed to have been intoxicated when he pulled the trigger. The tin box was covered with stickers indicating that it had previously been used to carry liquor bottles for a Nepalese parliamentary delegation's visit to Lhasa.

Most Nepalese were dismayed by the levity with which details of their royal family's murder were made public. The content of the two hundred and sixty-four-page report showed the investigating committee to have done a thorough enough piece of work within the limited terms of their enquiry. Their remit had been to uncover only *what* had happened inside Narayanhiti on that fateful night. There was no attempt to explain *why* the massacre had taken place, or *how* it could have been allowed to happen.

What was made plain from the testimonies of thirteen surviving members of the royal family and many other eyewitnesses is that Dipendra was the lone assassin. The language of their depositions rang true. Some of the accounts varied, but mainly over the precise sequence of events. Amidst the noise and confusion of those dreadful three minutes, it would have been unnatural for the surviving onlookers, many of whom were wounded, to have perfect recall. Crucially, every-one identified the killer as Dipendra: and since most were close family members, it is unlikely they would have mistaken him for another man or someone in a mask. Nor is it credible that they could all have been coerced into telling the same version of events. Their evidence should have laid all the lurid conspiracy theories to rest, once and for all.

But this is not what happened in Nepal. Instead, some of the short-comings of the report gave rise to as many new questions as were settled. Why, for instance, had no post-mortems or forensic drug tests been carried out before the bodies were taken away for cremation? Some of the doctors at Chhauni Military Hospital had asked this question at the time, but they had avoided taking any decision which might subsequently land them in trouble. The absence of properly conducted post-mortem reports left a glaring gap in the evidence.

There were other instances of the investigators' drawing back in the face of authority. Thirteen of the royal survivors gave evidence. But the fourteenth and most senior member of the royal family, the Queen Mother, did not testify before the investigative committee. This might be explained by the fact that she was not, strictly speaking, an 'eyewit-ness', since she had been in a separate room while all the shooting was going on. But she had been close to the Crown Prince. In fact, she had been one of the last people to talk privately with Dipendra, when he had driven her from her private residence to the doomed family gathering. Closeted with the King and Queen for twenty minutes thereafter, their conversation might well have had a bearing on subsequent events. Yet the Queen Mother gave no testimony.

The same applied to the chief of palace security. Not only was he not required to give evidence, he remained in his job despite the manifest failure of security arrangements at Narayanhiti. The Palace subsequently ordered two internal reports be drawn up, neither of which was made public. Disciplinary action was limited to firing four junior ADCs held most responsible for allowing the disaster to happen. There were many in Kathmandu, including those in the highest echelons of the army, who felt these junior officers had been made scapegoats to cover up a systematic failure in the Palace's security arrangements.

Certainly, the accounts given by ADCs on duty that night point to confusion and incompetence – if not the deliberate dereliction of duty. As highly-trained bodyguards, the moment that they heard gunfire they should have rushed to the aid of the royal family. They could have reached them, ready and armed, in a matter of seconds. Instead, the first reaction of the senior ADC on duty, Colonel Sundar Pratap Rana, had been to pick up a telephone and try to get through to the Royal Physician. The Queen's ADC did the same, warning the Military Hospital to be ready to receive casualties from the palace. Orders went out to the Fighting Force, the crack squad which provided an inner ring of defence. Fixed procedures were followed. But the ADCs themselves did not go to their sovereigns' assistance until it was too late.

The Crown Prince's ADC, Major Gajendra Bohara, was the first to reach Tribhuvan Sadan, but he approached the billiards room from the wrong side, could not see anything, and turned back. He says he then saw the Crown Prince, armed and in battle fatigues, and heard the Queen shouting for a doctor. His immediate duty was to protect the Crown Prince, but he did not rush forward. Instead he backtracked and approached cautiously from the garden side along with some of the other ADCs. Precious time was lost. Nobody seems to have formu-lated any concerted plan of action.

What did not emerge in the official report is that the gunman could have been 'taken out' before he had finished his gruesome business. According to those with access to the Palace's secret internal reports, one of the ADCs had been about to shoot the gunman when his arm was pushed aside by a colleague, just before the final shoot-out in which Queen Aishwarya and Prince Nirajan died. If that ADC had wounded the Crown Prince then and there, at least three lives might have been saved.

But it is an awful responsibility to shoot the heir to the throne – even if he did appear to be massacring the rest of the royal family. Those ADCs whose primary duty was to protect the Crown Prince would instinctively prevent anyone trying to gun him down. There were mixed signals and conflicting loyalties as the ADCs advanced through the night shadows towards Tribhuvan Sadan. Because nobody took a decision, nothing was done to save the surviving members of the royal family. Only when the Crown Prince lay mortally wounded on the grass did the ADCs finally arrive and start evacuating the wounded.

Even then, the decision to transfer them all to the Chhauni Military Hospital rather than the nearby and much better equipped Bir Hospital caused further unnecessary delays. Standard procedure was to use the Military Hospital, for security reasons. But King Birendra was appar-ently still alive, if only just, when he was bundled into the royal Jaguar. By the time it reached Chhauni it was already too late.

The failure of palace security to react in anything like an effective manner encouraged the belief that there was a broader conspiracy behind the massacre. Confusion, panic and the inability to take any decisions in a crisis situation are the more likely reasons. One of the first things the new King Gyanendra did was to reorganise his own security arrangements. There were many reasons why he preferred to remain at his private residence in Maharajganj rather than move into Narayanhiti Palace; but security was undoubtedly one of them.

*   *   *

One key witness whom the investigating committee was determined to question was Devyani Rana. The day after the palace massacre she had been spirited out of the country, taking the first available flight to New Delhi, where she stayed with her mother's family. Completely traumatised by recent events, she was kept at a secret location and placed under sedation. Her health deteriorated, her blood pressure dropping far below normal. She also suffered occasional fainting fits. According to a close relation, Devyani's previous good looks were 'completely gone'.

Her Indian relatives were aware that it was impossible for her to return to Nepal, where she was already blamed for being the underlying cause of the royal massacre. Hostile crowds had gathered outside her father's house in Kathmandu. Death threats had been issued. However, when telephone records revealed she had been the last person to speak to Dipendra, the investigating team insisted that she give evidence. An arrangement was made. They empowered the Nepalese ambassador in Delhi, Dr Bhekh Bahadur Thapa, to interview her in the presence of her physician, Dr S. K. Jain.

The results of that interview could have clarified many things that still remain unexplained. Devyani fobbed off the ambassador with vague and inconsequential replies. She claimed she had come to Delhi for her 'treatment'. She said she had no knowledge of events inside the palace, adding 'I had no idea it could be like this'. When asked about her relationship with the Crown Prince, she replied: 'It's personal. I don't want to talk about it.' Her recollection of the last telephone conversations she had with Dipendra was both confused and abbreviated. Finally, when asked whether she had noticed anything different about the Crown Prince that evening, Devyani replied that his voice had been slurred. This alone had worried her sufficiently to call his off-duty ADC at home and request him to find out if Dipendra was all right.

Devyani was in a highly agitated state of mind and possibly incapable of thinking clearly. But the ambassador's tentative line of questioning hardly amounts to a serious interrogation. If the official transcripts contain all that was said in the Nepalese Embassy, it was an astonishingly brief interview. The ambassador's apparently ready acceptance that she should not have to answer certain questions because they were 'personal', and his failure to seek clarification when she did not give a full and frank reply, were enough to provoke outrage and suspicion in Kathmandu. It was suggested that some secret deal had been worked out between Devyani's extremely influential relations and the Nepalese ambassador. Moreover, it was widely suspected that these were only extracts from a much longer and more detailed interview, the contents of which remained under wraps. Also part of the deal was that Devyani should 'disappear' for a while. She should not give any interviews and certainly not attempt to rejoin her father and mother in Kathmandu. Only if she abided by these conditions might she one day be allowed to return to Nepal.

Devyani Rana was confronted by the prospect of a life of enforced exile. Shortly after the interview she left Delhi for Dehra Dun, the Indian hill station in the shadows of the Himalayas in which she had been educated, where she stayed with a close girlfriend. She later returned to Delhi before flying to Moscow, to be with her married sister Urvashi Khemka for a while. By September the two sisters were together again, this time at the Khemka's palatial London residence in Eaton Square.

Devyani enrolled as a student and apparently expected to remain in London for the foreseeable future. But then another tragedy struck her mother's family. Her uncle Madhavrao Scindia, doyen of one of India's most powerful political dynasties and himself a likely candidate for the prime ministership, died when the small aircraft in which he was flying caught fire and crashed. Devyani flew out to Delhi to join the other family mourners, including a sizeable contingent from Kathmandu. She still looked unwell. Her life was in tatters: first she had lost the man she thought she would marry, and now her favourite uncle. As for the future, there was little hope that she would ever marry. Nor did she know when – or, indeed, if – she would ever be able to return to Nepal.

*   *   *

If Devyani's published testimony was inconclusive, the report's findings on whether drugs had been involved was almost deliberately baffling. Witnesses confirmed that Prince Dipendra had been smoking marijuana and hashish for years. He had ordered some of his usual mixture be brought to him in the billiards room while he was still chatting amiably with his guests and pouring them drinks. Approximately ten minutes later he was spreadeagled on the floor, apparently unconscious. According to the official report, 'the special kind of cigarette [was] prepared with a mixture of hashish and another *unnamed black substance*'. The orderly who usually made up these joints said that Dipendra had himself procured both the hashish and the mysterious black substance, though 'it was not known from where it could have come'.

A mystery drug, then, and one acquired from a mystery source. That, at least, is how the investigators decided to leave the matter. Apparently no forensic tests had been carried out on the remainder of Dipendra's drugs collection to identify the 'black substance'. Nor was any blood sample officially taken when he was in hospital and then screened for the presence of either alcohol or drugs. By ignoring these standard procedures, the doctors and investigating committee effectively closed the door on any scientific certainty as to whether the Crown Prince was on drugs when he pulled the trigger. Or whether he was stone-cold sober.

Given that this is central to any understanding of *why* the massacre happened, it is hard to believe that there was some accidental oversight. The investigating committee claimed to have called on narcotics experts and psychologists to give their opinions, but the official report comes to no conclusions on whether or not drugs were involved. Into this vacuum stepped various outside 'experts' who have all suggested numerous drugs or combinations of drugs which could have induced psychotic symptoms combined with frenetic activity.

Prolonged usage of cannabis resin alone – as would appear to have been the case with Dipendra – can result in schizophrenic symptoms, though it does not fit with the speed and precision of the killings. The same is true of opium and its derivatives. Methamphetamine is a possibility, as is phencylidine, or 'angel dust', a drug previously distributed by the military to front-line troops preparing for an attack, which when taken in sufficient quantity can cause vomiting and homicidal behaviour. The drug ketamine, widely available in South Asia, can induce psychotic behaviour and takes effect very rapidly; but it is demonstrably not a 'black substance'. Then there are a number of locally produced compounds, such as those traditionally used by Rajput warriors of Rajasthan to increase their valour in battle, and similar combinations of indigenous drugs often play a role in tantric initiation ceremonies of the kind that are reported to have gone on in Devyani's house. In the absence of forensic tests on physical specimens, however, all these suggestions are no more than informed guesswork.

The question of drugs is important because it determines the degree of responsibility attached to the man who committed so unnatural a crime. At one end of this spectrum, there is the 'blameless prince' who was transformed into a psychotic mass murderer because his usual hashish cigarettes had been spiked with an unexpected and far more powerful substance. This would explain his sudden passing out, his retching in the bathroom, his inability even to get undressed without the help of his orderly and housemaid. But then this same drug – which he had never taken before – started having a very different effect on him. It turned him into an alert, hyperactive, uncontrollable serial killer. And who might have arranged the switch? The special cigarettes Dipendra ordered up on his mobile phone passed through three sets of hands: the orderly Ram Krishna KC, his regular ADC Gajendra Bohara, and his cousin Prince Paras.

There remains the converse view that Dipendra was a cool-headed and calculating killer who imagined he could get away with murder. He targeted the King first because, with his father out of the way, he automatically became King and somebody else could be blamed for the regicide. Most of the other members of the royal family, whom he largely despised, could be coerced into endorsing the official line. No one would dare intervene within Narayanhiti Palace. He would be King of Nepal and then nobody could prevent him from marrying Devyani.

If that sounds like an unlikely scenario, it was none the less the preferred explanation in palace circles a few months after the massacre. Eyewitnesses placed a new emphasis on the Crown Prince's acting up, his pretence at being intoxicated and deliberately crashing into chairs, so that he had to be carried away to the bedchamber which also housed his lethal collection of weapons. His behaviour was cunning; the crime premeditated; the timing dictated by the fact that his parents would soon be going abroad. But his carefully laid plans went astray when he failed to kill the King outright. As other royals rushed to Birendra's assistance or tried to summon help, the Crown Prince went beserk and sprayed the room indiscriminately with bullets. The same man who so longed to be in control of his own destiny had once again lost control of the situation. His attempted suicide was a final note of despair.

There may be some truth in this version of events. It provides a rational motive, though it is hard to imagine that a thoroughly Westernised young man like Dipendra really believed that in the twenty-first century he could commit regicide and parricide and still somehow emerge unscathed. Those surviving members of the royal family who have been advancing this theory may believe they are doing the new King and his family a favour by contributing to the demonisation of Dipendra. Besides which, all of them lost close relatives during the shootings, so they have their own reasons for hating the very memory of the former Crown Prince. Their aim is to portray him as a cold-blooded murderer. The existence of drugs might imply some degree of extenuating circumstances, that at least the Crown Prince was not in his right mind.

As is so often the case in Nepal, the truth may never come out. There does exist, however, physical evidence that could settle the question as to whether or not Crown Prince Dipendra was under the influence of drugs. Somewhere in Scotland, in a medical laboratory, there is a frozen sample of his blood. It was taken by one of the doctors who operated on him and sent abroad for safekeeping. Any traces of alcohol will long since have vanished, but with proper screening and analysis, the presence of other substances could still be detected. Whether permission for that routine procedure will ever be forthcoming depends, as it has always done, on a secret decision taken in Kathmandu.

What else is known by the authorities but not deemed suitable for the public at large? A great deal about the drug habits of other members of the royal family, for a start. Or previous instances of insanity or psychological problems among the intermarried Shah and Rana families. There are many, many skeletons in the royal closet.

Nor did the palace authorities think it necessary to mention that an offer had been made through the British Foreign Office to provide both technical experts and investigators from Scotland Yard, or that a detective inspector had flown from London to Kathmandu, but that this offer of impartial assistance was rejected.

Perhaps national pride played a part in this, for to accept foreign assistance would be to imply that Nepalese investigators and forensic experts were not up to the job. Besides, the Palace thought it had already bent over backwards to meet the need for greater transparency in the wake of the massacre. Enough was enough, it seemed.

The investigators' brief was to uncover what had happened, not to speculate on what was going on inside the Crown Prince's brain as he mowed down his own family. Nor was it to air any more dirty linen than was strictly necessary. Both the Chief Justice and the Speaker had fulfilled their limited brief, if not to the original schedule, at least within a tight timescale. But in no way did their report lay all the suspicions and rumours about the palace massacre to rest.

A New Model Monarchy

It is unusual for a king to be crowned not once but twice. There have in the past been other monarchs who have lost both crown and kingdom, through conspiracy or revolution or civil war, and were later reinstated. But that normally happened after only a brief interlude, and was at their own behest. In the case of Nepal's new twice-crowned monarch, King Gyanendra Bir Bikram Shah Dev, there was a gap of more than fifty years between his first and second coronations.

The first time was in November 1950, after his grandfather King Tribhuvan had fled to the Indian Embassy along with his father Mahendra and older brother Birendra. Left behind in Narayanhiti Royal Palace was the three-year-old Prince Gyanendra; and since he was the only male representative of the Shah dynasty still in Nepal, the last of the Rana Prime Ministers, Mohan Shamsher, chose to set him up as King and so retain some semblance of legitimacy for his government. The young prince was taken by the Prime Minister hand in hand to Hanuman Dhoka Palace and there, in the Nasal Chowk, the Royal Priest placed the diamond- and pearl-studded crown with its fringe of emerald pendants on Gyanendra's head. Or rather, he held it just above the head, for the crown of Nepal was too big for the three-year-old and would have fallen over his eyes.

Gyanendra remained still throughout the elaborate anointing and gift-bearing ceremonies, his eyes full of bewilderment and suspicion. He had 'lost' his parents and the rest of his family, and now this grizzled and fierce-looking Prime Minister had told him that he must be the new King of Nepal. The child-monarch stood erect and played his part, taking the salute from the Rana generals and dignitaries and troops of soldiers as they marched past. He later confided to a lifelong friend: 'I was just a pawn in a big game that I couldn't understand.'

Among those present at the ceremony was another boy, Mohan Shamsher's grandson Pashupati Rana, whose daughter Devyani was to play such a crucial role in later events. As one courtier put it: 'There is a certain irony that after Mohan Shamsher made Gyanendra King first time round, it was his granddaughter who paved the way for it to happen a second time.'

Gyanendra's first 'reign' lasted just over three months. All memory of it has been expunged from the royal annals, since he was never recognised as the legitimate King of Nepal. Instead it was subsumed within the reign of King Tribhuvan, whose triumphant return to Kathmandu restored the Shah dynasty to real authority. Nobody could blame the young Gyanendra for his part in the proceedings, and he was brought up alongside his two brothers by his step-mother Queen Ratna.

Like his brothers, he was sent to the Jesuit fathers at St Joseph's College in Darjeeling; but whereas Birendra went to Eton and Harvard, Gyanendra stayed behind and took his university degree at Kathmandu's new Tribhuvan University. Never closer than third in line to the throne, it was not deemed necessary for him to be groomed to be a future King. His interests turned instead to wildlife – as head of the King Mahendra Trust for Nature Conservation, and on a broader stage through the Worldwide Fund for Nature – and looking after the royal family's business investments.

Shortly after the wedding of Birendra and Aishwarya, Gyanendra was married to Aishwarya's younger sister, Komal Rana, in a quieter and considerably less extravagant ceremony. Princess Komal, as she now became, may have lacked Aishwarya's glamour and literary aspirations, preferring the more domestic pastimes of shopping and flower arranging, but for those very reasons she has always managed to steer clear of controversy. This suited her husband, who preferred to maintain as low a profile as possible. The pair made their home within one of the stately residences in Maharajganj, just off the main road that runs north from Narayanhiti Royal Palace. There they lived together, comfortably though quietly, for nearly thirty years.

There was no reason why Prince Gyanendra should have imagined that one day he would be called upon to take up the duties of kingship. Both Crown Prince Dipendra and his brother Prince Nirajan stood before him in the line of succession; and since they had both reached their twenties unscathed and could, in the normal course of events, be expected to settle down to married life and produce future heirs to the throne, the junior branch of the Shah dynasty as represented by Gyanendra and his son, Prince Paras, were expected to play only a supporting role.

None the less, King Birendra always remained on the closest terms with his younger brother and often asked for his advice, particularly on matters of economics and finance. Gyanendra had stepped in as head of the Royal Privy Council whenever the King and Queen went abroad until Dipendra was mature enough to fill the role; and when he himself visited foreign countries he usually fitted in several official engagements at which he represented the Kingdom of Nepal alongside his business meetings. Other than fulfilling the duties of a 'minor royal', standing in for the King at the weddings and funerals of other royal families, Gyanendra did not seek the limelight.

Gyanendra was unprepared for kingship. 'I never asked for the job' he confided to one of his closest business colleagues, 'and certainly never expected it.' The immediate danger, when he learned of what had happened inside Narayanhiti, was that he would be overwhelmed by so great a loss. Yet in the immediate aftermath of the palace massacre he was kept so busy trying to handle fast-moving events that there was no time to dwell on the personal tragedy that had befallen his family. 'Who knew what I was feeling when I was crowned?' he said. 'I could not shed one tear.'

Unfamiliar with all the duties of being King, Gyanendra took to working sixteen hours a day – much to the concern of his physicians and closest friends, since he did not stop smoking cigarettes and shared his family's history of high blood pressure. Other members of the much diminished royal family rallied round and offered their support. 'We are now but a few,' he said. 'We try to help each other.' Gyanendra and his son were now the only surviving males of the immediate royal family, which left him isolated and lonely. 'I do not have anyone to talk to,' he said. 'I lost my brothers. We were very close. We discussed everything. I now get solace from my mother,' he added, referring to the Queen Mother Ratna. 'She is a tower of strength for me.' Indeed, the Queen Mother – always the *éminence grise* behind Narayanhiti's walls – has become the linchpin holding what remains of the royal family together. The emotional scars may well take longer to heal than the physical wounds borne by Queen Komal and other survivors. As a sign of respect for his murdered brother, King Gyanendra declined to travel abroad until the full year of official mourning had elapsed. 'The healing process,' he observed, 'takes time after such tragic happenings.'

It will take time for many Nepalese to come round to full and unquestioning acceptance of their new King. For most of them, Gyanendra was an unknown quantity. It was rumoured that he had been opposed to the introduction of multi-party democracy back in 1990 and that he held less liberal views than the late King Birendra. Some feared that their new King might be tempted to do away with Nepal's parliamentary system and rule directly, as his forebears had done.

Similarly, Gyanendra's extensive business interests provoked a mixture of suspicion and envy – despite the fact that as soon as he became King he was required by law to resign from all directorships and hand over active control of his and the rest of the royal family's investments. Some Nepalese still felt he was 'pro-business' rather than 'pro-people'.

The new King certainly brought a more businesslike approach to the duties he inherited as a constitutional monarch. The working hours of the Palace Secretariat were changed to fit standard business hours; and while there was no wholesale purge of long-serving royal functionaries, the less effective soon found themselves sidelined.

Initially, Gyanendra was loath to leave his own house and private office in Maharajganj, there being practical as well as emotional reasons for not wanting to move into Narayanhiti. He had to go to the Royal Palace for official ceremonies, but he preferred to do much of his thinking and take counsel in his own home, where he worked on long after most palace functionaries had stopped for the day.

The long hours were necessary because, quite apart from the devastating blow to its monarchy, Nepal was sinking into a state of crisis. Maoist insurgents sought to exploit their advantage and launched a new wave of attacks on police stations. Prime Minister Koirala's government collapsed after an internal revolt within his own Congress Party. The new King found himself being asked to accept the resignation of one government and then swear in its successor, which immediately proclaimed a ceasefire and began a series of dialogues with the Maoists. Their demands included the abolition of the monarchy and replacing the existing parliamentary system with one party rule, so these talks may have been doomed from the outset. But at least they provided a much needed breathing space.

The Maoists used the ceasefire to regroup in the hills and to extend their campaign of intimidation and extortion across the entire country, including the Kathmandu Valley. Protection money was demanded from businesses large and small, from schools and foreign aid agencies that were trying to assist Nepal. Since the police were unable to guarantee security even in the capital, most people who received threats from the Maoists either paid up or shut up shop. Some of these ill-gotten funds were used to purchase weapons, either on the black market or from extremist groups in India sympathetic to the Maoists' cause. Meanwhile, the Royal Nepal Army was making its own preparations for the conflict that lay ahead. King Gyanendra was kept fully informed of these developments. For when the time came to order the army into action, it had to be by his command.

Apart from attending the official mourning ceremonies for their murdered relatives, the new royal family kept a very low profile during the months that followed the palace massacre. Queen Komal, still recuperating from her chest wound, did not appear in public until the end of August, when she attended the annual Teej ceremony at Pashupatinath Temple. Like most Hindu women throughout Nepal, the Queen donned a red sari and fasted for the sake of her husband, making offerings to Lord Shiva so as to guarantee the well-being and long life of the men in the family. She was accompanied by her daughter, Princess Prerana, and by her glamorous Indian-born daughter-in-law, Princess Himani.

King Gyanendra's only son, Prince Paras, remained completely out of the public gaze. Although he now stood next in line to the throne, it had been decided to delay declaring him Crown Prince of Nepal, partly to calm popular hostility towards Paras, who had previously been blamed for causing two deaths in hit-and-run car accidents. The second of these incidents created uproar across the nation: the victim was the popular Nepali recording artist Praveen Gurung, but yet again Prince Paras was shielded by the Palace from any police charges or public enquiry into what had occurred. A public petition demanding that King Birendra take some action to discipline his wayward nephew had been signed by nearly half a million Nepalese, but nothing had been done about it. Prince Paras retained his royal titles and, despite his unruly reputation, he automatically became heir apparent once his father was crowned.

Not since the days of Crown Prince Surendra had a future King of Nepal aroused so much public anger. Paras's unpopularity rebounded on his father, making it harder for many Nepalis to accept King Gyanendra as their rightful monarch. The King was fully aware of his son's shortcomings but he could not exclude him from the royal succession: after the massacre in the palace there were no other princes of the blood royal left alive.

Some Nepalese argued that in a modern world it should be permissible for women to succeed to the throne, citing as examples the United Kingdom and the Netherlands. That would have opened the way for one of Princess Shruti's daughters to become the first Queen to reign over Nepal in her own right. But the Royal Constitution insists that there be a King; and in such a strongly patriarchal society as Nepal it might still be difficult to gain public acceptance of a female monarch. All of which makes Paras the only person capable of succeeding Gyanendra.

Prince Paras's reputation has improved slightly since the events of 1 June. His decisive action on that fateful night undoubtedly saved many lives, and for that he was won praise in some quarters. There has been no further wild behaviour. According to close friends of the family, his parents have kept him 'on a tight leash', restricting his outings from home to official duties. The gradual process of grooming him to be the next King of Nepal has begun. His first public duty was in late August 2001 when he attended a religious ceremony at Budhanilkantha, near the school which both he and the Dipendra had attended, where the statue of the Sleeping Vishnu that future kings must never look upon lies surrounded by flower-strewn waters. It was judged a success.

Palace officials also intimated that, after the traumatic experience he had gone through at Narayanhiti, Prince Paras had settled down to a quieter, more reflective life. He had taken to writing poetry, and was now more fully immersed in family life together with his wife Himani and their young daughter. The unspoken hope among traditionalists is that there would soon be a royal grandson. That, more than anything else, would confirm the future of Nepal's monarchy after the terrible blows it had suffered.

The new royal family made their first public appearance together during the Indrajatra festival, which normally marks the ending of the monsoon rains in September. But it was still raining when they came out on to a balcony, flanked by generals and foreign ambassadors, to watch as the living goddess of Kathmandu, the Royal Kumari, was dragged past in her gilded chariot. Later, the three-year-old girl was taken into Hanuman Dhoka Palace where, in a ceremony unchanged since King Prithvi Narayan's time, she placed a *tika* on the King's forehead as a sign of the goddess's blessing.

The next major religious festival, that of Badha Dasain, fell in October. By then all members of the royal family were regularly being seen in public, attending to their religious duties at temples throughout the Kathmandu Valley. This is a time when Nepalese families come together so that the elders can give their blessings to their children and grandchildren. Normally the King performs a similar ritual in front of Narayanhiti Palace, placing the vermilion *tika* on the foreheads of the thousands of his subjects waiting in line for his blessing. That year, however, it was deemed unfitting for King Gyanendra to officiate so soon after the tragedy that had befallen the royal house. For the first time in living memory no royal *tika* was bestowed.

The festival of Badha Dasain passed off peacefully enough. The ceasefire between government forces and the Maoists held, even though talks between them were going nowhere. Then, on 23 November 2001, the Maoists unilaterally declared an end to the ceasefire and launched a series of surprise attacks. The fighting was intense, raising the death-toll in the six-year conflict above two thousand. The Prime Minister requested that a State of Emergency be declared so that the Royal Nepal Army could be sent in against the guerrillas. King Gyanendra gave the royal assent, taking a critical step that his older brother had always avoided when he had been King of Nepal.

Initially the army's superior firepower, its use of helicopters and specially trained units, brought some spectacular successes. The main formations of Maoist insurgents were surrounded and hemmed into their mountain fastnesses. Provided that the army's morale does not crack under the strains of a civil war, it has sufficient forces to contain the situation militarily. But the conditions which allowed a full-scale Maoist insurgency to take hold in Nepal – the unreformed feudalism of its land-ownership, the corruption and short-sightedness of its ruling elite, the unremitting poverty and lack of development in rural areas – all these must change if the Maoists' call to armed struggle is to lose its attractions to those at the very bottom of the ladder.

Within the Palace there has been talk of a 'hearts and minds' campaign, of bringing tangible benefits to the most impoverished and alienated of royal subjects. This is not entirely altruistic. King Gyanendra has placed the survival of the monarchy in the hands of forces that are beyond his control. He needs ordinary Nepalis to protect the monarchy from the Maoists. If the Maoist insurgency is quashed and there are signs of real progress in Nepal, its monarchy will endure. If not, King Gyanendra's willingness to take up the challenge means that Nepal will not be a Kingdom for much longer. In its place there will be a new Republic of Nepal, probably a single-party communist state in which there will be no place even for a constitutional monarch. The possibility that monarchy might co-exist with such a communist regime, as Prince Sihanouk had shown was possible in Cambodia, has now evaporated. King Birendra had been careful to keep this option open. By ordering the Royal Nepal Army in against the Maoists, King Gyanendra has effectively closed that escape route.

Not since the time of Prithvi Narayan Shah have decisions by the monarch had such a profound impact on the shape and complexion of Nepal. His royal ancestors played out some extraordinary survival games, but they were about who would inherit the throne, or who would wield real power within the Kingdom of Nepal. The Shahs and Ranas may have resorted to internecine bloodletting in the manner of Shakespeare's Montagues and Capulets – indeed, when it came to treachery and intrigue, to surreptitious poisonings and trumped-up charges, the Nepalese royal family and nobility could at times make even the ruthlessness of the Borgias seem pale by comparison – yet, throughout those turbulent times, nobody in Nepal seriously questioned whether there should be a King or not. Only during the last decade of the twentieth century was the very existence of Nepal's monarchy seriously challenged.

By then, King Birendra had already surrendered his absolute powers to democratically elected politicians. He kept his side of the bargain, and did his utmost to behave like a thoroughly modern constitutional monarch. But elsewhere in Narayanhiti Palace, as the surviving royals are now revealing, the old habits of expecting unquestioning obedience to the royal command were not shed so readily. Most of the royal family, including Crown Prince Dipendra, had been accustomed to a world in which the Palace was the real centre of influence and the King exercised absolute power. It has been difficult for the Queen and others of the older generation to adjust to such a sudden change in their circumstances. Most other royal families have experienced gradual transition from wielding autocratic powers to the powerlessness and mainly ceremonial duties of a constitutional monarchy. In Nepal, the change came later than elsewhere, and was much more sudden.

When monarchies long accustomed to exercising absolute power sense that they are no longer in control, there is often a tendency to extreme and ultimately self-destructive action. The last of the Hapsburgs and Romanovs gladly gambled on joining a Great War that put at risk their vast multi-ethnic empires. The Nepalese monarchy abandoned its absolute powers without any real struggle, but found it hard to abandon the culture of absolutism that had supported the royal family for so long. It created a tension that proved fatal – the Crown Prince could only express his fury at this empty yet autocratic culture within the confines of his own family.

The royal family's failure to adapt to changed circumstances did not make a bloody showdown inevitable. The immediate cause of the palace massacre was the bitter conflict between Queen Aishwarya and the Crown Prince over whom he should marry. Additionally, there was a long tradition in the family of resorting to violence in order to settle what appeared to be insurmountable differences. But internal relationships between Shah family members had deteriorated during the 1990s, as each came to resent their own powerlessness and tried to compensate by being more stubborn or autocratic within the confines of the palace. A dysfunctional family already existed before the 'marriage question' became the focus of the problems of the royal dynasty. Old values, of filial obedience and arranged marriages came up against more modern ideas about marital relationships and personal fulfilment. Nepal's royal family tried to make the leap from its own ancient and autocratic traditions towards more contemporary values, but it manifestly fell far short.

*　　*　　*

In the aftermath of the palace massacre, many Nepalese lamented that 'this could only have happened in Kathmandu'. To them, the royal family's self-destruction was a symptom of a broader malaise affecting the entire nation. Rather than try to build the economy and disperse the benefits more equitably, elected politicians seemed eager only to fight over the diminishing pool of patronage and money available, just as the noble families of Gorkha had done two hundred years before. The same feudal habits of mind, of putting their own interests and those of their extended families before any concept of service to the state, still prevailed. The founding monarch, King Prithvi Narayan Shah, would have recognised these same tendencies among his generals and *bharadars*, and acted to contain them.

Most Nepalese are conscious of another echo from two hundred years ago. Crown Prince Dipendra fulfilled the dreadful prophecy of Gorakhnath. His father, King Birendra, who was of the tenth generation of Prithvi Narayan's heirs, also proved to be the last of the royal family's senior line to rule over Nepal. The monarchy may have survived its greatest crisis, but it has now passed to the cadet line in the person of King Gyanendra.

Although there is still a Shah king on the throne of Nepal, the massacre of the entire senior line of the royal family has left Nepalese bereft and confused. Some have sought solace in religion. The file of pilgrims climbing the stone-clad stairway up to the temple of Gorakhnath that stands beside the Shahs' ancestral palace is greater than in previous years. The deity's powers had been made plain to all in the graphic completion of the ancient prophecy. The pilgrims come to assuage the often wrathful god and seek his protection, so they make their offerings of rice cakes and flowers to the royal family's tutelary deity as the temple priest looks on with a benign expression. The priest's assistant busily stuffs a stone pipe known as a chillum full of freshly harvested marijuana mixed with a brown liquid, this being considered 'an aid to meditation'.

Once they have completed their offerings, the pilgrims wander around the empty palace from which the ancient Kings of Gorkha had ruled. They peer through the latticed window into the room where Prithvi Narayan Shah was born. A light still burns there, a reassuring symbol of continuity in a kingdom which has so recently lost a living link with its past.

Finally, before descending the stone stairway back to the town of Gorkha, some pilgrims look out northwards to the main Himalayan range. More often than not, the mountains are wreathed in mist; but a fortunate few were vouchsafed a brief glimpse of Annapurna or Ganesh Himal before they disappear once more behind the clouds.

Index